INDUCTIVE SCRUTINIES

FOCUS ON JOYCE

INDUCTIVE SCRUTINIES
FOCUS ON JOYCE

Fritz Senn

edited by Christine O'Neill

THE JOHNS HOPKINS UNIVERSITY PRESS
BALTIMORE, MARYLAND

First published in 1995
in the United States of America by

The Johns Hopkins University Press
2715 North Charles Street
Baltimore, Maryland 21218–4319

ISBN 0-8018-5214-5
LC 95-76276

A catalog record for this
book is available from
The British Library.

CONTENTS

EDITOR'S ACKNOWLEDGMENTS   VII
INTRODUCTORY SCRUTINIES: FOCUS ON SENN   IX

INSTEAD OF A PREFACE: THE CREED OF NAÏVETÉ   1
JOYCE THE VERB   7
JOYCEAN PROVECTIONS   35
IN QUEST OF A *NISUS FORMATIVUS JOYCEANUS*   59
ANAGNOSTIC PROBES   75
SEQUENTIAL CLOSE-UPS IN JOYCE'S *ULYSSES*   97
REMODELLING HOMER   111
PROTEAN INGLOSSABILITIES: 'TO NO END GATHERED'   133
'ALL KINDS OF WORDS CHANGING COLOUR':
    LEXICAL CLASHES IN 'EUMAEUS'   156
EUMAEAN TITBITS—AS SOMEONE SOMEWHERE SINGS   176
IN CLASSICAL IDIOM: *ANTHOLOGIA INTERTEXTUALIS*   197
BEYOND THE LEXICOGRAPHER'S REACH:
    LITERARY OVERDETERMINATION   216
LINGUISTIC DISSATISFACTION AT THE *WAKE*   226

INDEX   238
PASSAGE INDEX   244
FRITZ SENN'S WRITINGS SINCE 1985   248

EDITOR'S ACKNOWLEDGMENTS

Eleven years after the publication of *Joyce's Dislocutions: Essays of Reading as Translation* (John Paul Riquelme [ed.] [Baltimore and London: Johns Hopkins University Press 1984]) I approached Fritz Senn with the idea of publishing a new collection of his essays. The enthusiasm of The Lilliput Press for the project provided the necessary encouragement.

The essays, for the most part on *Ulysses*, have already been published with the exception of '"All Kinds of Words Changing Colour": Lexical Clashes in "Eumaeus"'. There are only a few minor changes, and no attempt has been made to avoid partial overlap for where the same passages are discussed, they are under scrutiny from different angles. I wish to thank the following for permission to reprint: Heyward Ehrlich, editor of *Light Rays: James Joyce and Modernism*, for 'Remodelling Homer'; Morris Beja of Ohio State University Press for 'Joyce the Verb'; Thomas F. Staley of the *Joyce Studies Annual* for 'In Quest of a *nisus formativus Joyceanus*'; Associated University Presses for 'Joycean Provections'; Robert Spoo of the *James Joyce Quarterly* for 'In Classical Idiom: *Anthologia intertextualis*'; Mary Snell-Hornby, editor of *Translation and Lexicography: Papers read at the EURALEX Colloquium 1987*, for 'Beyond the Lexicographer's Reach: Literary Overdetermination'; Christine van Boheemen for 'Linguistic Dissatisfaction at the *Wake*', 'Protean Inglossabilities: "To No End Gathered"', and 'Anagnostic Probes'.

The editorial work was carried out in Dublin and Zürich. I wish to thank Antony Farrell and Mari-aymone Djeribi of Lilliput for their support throughout, and the Friends of the Zürich James Joyce Foundation for a generous grant. I am grateful to Mary Power and Katie Wales for editorial advice, and to Ruth Frehner and Ursula Zeller of the Zürich James Joyce Foundation for reliable back-up. Tim O'Neill was essential for help and encouragement. My best thanks go to Fritz Senn for giving me the opportunity to undertake the project and helping me to see it through. This collection is a tribute to his dedication to Joyce and the Zürich James Joyce Foundation, now in its eleventh year.

CHRISTINE O'NEILL
Dublin, May 1995

INTRODUCTORY SCRUTINIES:
FOCUS ON SENN

The present volume collects some of Fritz Senn's major essays of the last ten years, mainly on *Ulysses*. They display anew his regard for Joyce's text in all its detail. The selection does not attempt a broad overview of Senn's writing nor is it organized around a single theme; rather it is meant to show his lifelong interest in the workings of language, its limitations, disruptive energies, its allusive potential within and beyond a single work, in particular his ongoing concern with the problems of annotation as well as the reader's pleasurable and active participation. His chosen playground is Joyce as something written, to be scrutinized with dedication. An extraordinary familiarity with the text underlies his response, and his imaginative and nimble explorations always start with and return to Joyce's word. Not that this excludes forays to non-Joycean areas; classical references are particularly frequent. His essays also convey a sense of a mind at work, developing, exemplifying. Senn probes with agility and argues and extrapolates sceptically. Not for him interpretative certainty or the monolithic argument drawn out to book-length. Hence a volume of inductive scrutinies.

In his introduction to Fritz Senn's *Joyce's Dislocutions: Essays on Reading as Translation* (1984), John Paul Riquelme, the editor, looks at Senn's particular advantage as a non-native speaker in reading and explicating Joyce. He stresses the fine awareness of linguistic irregularities and disruptions in a reader who takes nothing for granted. As the essays demonstrate, such a sensibility turns reading into an act of translation and criticism into a running commentary on the text. The view of Senn as foreign commentator helps one understand his critical preoccupations.

For the last decade Fritz Senn has been directing the Zürich James Joyce Foundation. This institute, the most comprehensive Joyce library in Europe, consists largely of his former private collection of work editions, translations, criticism, background material and realia. A favourite haunt of many Joyce scholars, it provides ideal research facilities and is a welcoming place where ideas are exchanged. At the regular workshops Senn's chairing is invariably unpolemical, stimulating and friendly.

As this collection coincides with the tenth anniversary of the Zürich James Joyce Foundation and with thirty-five years of Senn's published writings on Joyce, it seemed appropriate to invite Joyce scholars to comment on his status. The spectrum of views which follows should be of interest to novice and seasoned Joyceans alike. However, to present a balanced picture, I also asked Senn to talk about himself, and this interview, characteristically informal, concludes the introduction.

In a letter to some twenty-five Joyce scholars of varying age, nationality and critical inclination, I wrote of my endeavour to 'situate Fritz among other Joyceans concerning his particular interests, strengths and critical preoccupations, but also with regard to his limitations or, if you wish, blind spots', and asked for frank and descriptive rather than evaluative comment. I mentioned that Senn knew of the letter and condoned it. As it turned out, those who answered were pleased to have been asked for comment even if some felt daunted by the task. Despite my promptings I received no replies with strong negative criticism.

There is general agreement on the nature of his work. It is considered unique in Joyce criticism. This is to do both with the nature of his contributions and his personality. His feeling for Joyce is based on an affinity of temperaments, and some consider him the best reader Joyce ever had. He seems to read Joyce in the writer's own spirit. Without ever dominating the text by his intellect, Senn puts all his knowledge and critical ability at its service. He does not curtail Joyce's dynamics. His readings are invariably lively, clear and original, and even the most familiar passages still yield surprises under his scrutiny. The attention he brings to bear on textual detail is painstaking, and his interest in period trivia comes close to Joyce's own.

As for the nature of Senn's contributions, they are of particular value to readers interested in philology and stylistics. Ever alert to the strangeness and comedy of Joyce's language as well as to the experience of reading it, he responds with a text very much his own. His style is inimitable, incisive, witty and lucid, however complex the issues he discusses. Also, Senn is one of those rare scholars who do not need to keep citing theorists. This is partly because he is unusually independent in his thinking, so much so that often he can only express himself with the help of newly coined terms. Yet many Joyceans feel that Senn's ideas are in tune with some of the most important 'theoretical' writing of the last few decades, especially Derrida's. They see his writing parallel and, more so, anticipate currently fashionable theory. Some Joycean scholars think him unwilling to acknowledge, others unable to see, how much his approach to literature shares with the best examples of post-structuralism; one scholar put it that he 'obstinately denies affinity and understanding' (with or of Derrida). Senn's own view of his relation to theory finds expression in the interview and in the preface. Maybe this is the place to mention Senn's mischievous, quizzical personality and his sly and sometimes punishing sense of humour.

Fritz Senn is known to encourage and develop up-and-coming Joyceans. He shows great patience with them, but less so with renowned scholars. At the same time, he is unusually open to the ideas of anybody interested in Joyce.

Senn is thought by many to be a gifted teacher. He manages to make Joyce's works approachable and fresh without sacrificing their complexity and strange inventiveness. He considers questions more fruitful than answers. It is his familiarity with the texts that enables him to be continually surprised by them. However, he is least patient with dullness and scholars lacking textual knowledge or clarity.

Senn's classical knowledge is remarkable, likewise his extraordinary feeling for the connections between *Ulysses* and its Homeric precursor. Far from referring to the *Odyssey* as a simple grid for *Ulysses*, he never tires of searching into Joyce's unique translation and rewriting of Homer and exploring the interaction between the two texts. Joyce through Senn, and Senn through Joyce do agitate the *Odyssey*.

Several scholars referred to Senn as an authority on *Finnegans Wake*. He is considered a pioneer in its exegesis, and the enormous importance of *A Wake Newslitter* in the history of the work's reception is undisputed; Senn was co-founder and co-editor (he insists that Clive Hart did most of the work). For one thing, the *Newslitter* helped towards establishing reasonable and verifiable standards for interpretation. That he has detached himself from the *Wake* in latter years (see the last essay in this collection) seems almost completely ironical to some scholars, who feel it is only now that the consequences of his original endeavours are coming to fruition.

A few individual remarks from the thumbnail sketches, assembled without connection or comment, may add up to a impressionistic collage. His 'gadfly' presence at conferences has been mentioned, or how when struck by certain ideas he seizes on them with a 'tenacious fixation'. His insistence on looking at the text directly with the invariable result of seeing what was otherwise neglected marks him, according to one scholar, as 'singularly smart'. There was the pithy remark that everything he says or writes could be placed 'under the banner of common sense operating at expert level'. It was felt that Senn's recognition '*honoris causa*' from the University of Zürich was a 'tribute from all scholars', and that he is '*sui generis* and indispensable'. Lastly, many a Joycean would share in the wish that closed one letter: 'Long may he write as he does.'

Thanks are due to Derek Attridge, Morris Beja, Bernard Benstock, Christine van Boheemen, Vincent Deane, Michael Gillespie, Hugh Kenner, Terence Killeen, Margot Norris, Marilyn Reizbaum, Joe Schork, Jacques Aubert and Katie Wales for their frank and incisive observations.

INTERVIEW WITH FRITZ SENN, MAY 1994

How do you view your development as a Joycean over the past thirty-five years?

'Development' suggests a maturing process or an ascent towards some commendable peak. Come to think of it, by hindsight, I wonder if in the long run—and the run has been long—I developed sufficiently (I'm talking Joyce here). Somehow it seems I've been doing the same thing all over all along, with of course stupendous advances in sophistication and refinement that anyone could spot with a magnifying glass. Probably I should have changed more.

Overall, I have been trying to figure out, often in close-up— Joyce, after all, offered extended close-ups, *Ulysses* for one—just how language works, what it can achieve, and what it fails to put

across. So in some way I am a case of arrested development, and
my interests now resemble those of thirty years ago, with a few
illusions gone. It is not the worst kind of development to be
arrested in, but a limitation nevertheless.

I should hasten to add that my fellow Joyceans have never, as
far as I could make out, held this against me. In fact I have been
treated extremely well and graded all too leniently. On the whole,
we are a tolerant and appreciative lot, if anything too agreeable to
each other. Self-styled 'Joyce Wars' are an exception.

Of course, not to sound too modest, I also know that I have an
interest shared by few, and fewer in recent trends, that in language. Not Language. I could provide you with a handy rule of
thumb to find out who does not care about language.

And will you?
No.

*Could you say a few words about shaping influences, or the lack of
them?*
I've had an advantage early on. As an autodidact—I still sometimes flaunt an amateur status or, rather, I watch myself creeping
back into it in escalating disillusionment—I have not been conditioned by any academic school I know of.

Wrong, of course. As Gerty MacDowell or, for that matter Stephen
Dedalus, could teach us, we are all shaped by something, and most
of all by what we do not even perceive. But I mean since I was generally not on an academic payroll—just exceptionally as 'visiting
professor' in the US and, over the years, in association with the University of Zürich—I could take up what suited me. I picked what I
found congenial and was never obliged to string along with any
trend. Call this 'eclectic', it sounds better.

Are there critical activities you refrain from?
'Refrain' implies a policy or strategy. I simply avoid, like most animals, what I cannot cope with. I was never really trained in Joyce
criticism or disciplined to enlarge my skills outside a narrow
chosen field. So you'll never catch me criticizing Foucault's views
on Husserl in their bearing on Martha Clifford's male gaze within a
commodity culture (post-colonially en-gendered). In fact I ran
away from the language of German philosophy into the relative
safety of the *Wake*, which one is justified in not understanding,

and this after many years, and which even *not* understanding is fun. As you can observe now, the language of philosophy has been infiltrating big, via France and the US. So much for safety. Others, at any rate, are much more competent at metaphysics than I am, so I gave up on it. You see that a student nowadays cannot afford such defection. So I never have really kept abreast, certainly not to what is apotheosized as, say, '*Literaturwissenschaft*' in Germany. Scares me stiff. Distinct from my colleagues—perhaps I have no right to call them that after all—I am ill at ease in cryptic abstraction, and I am not, as everyone else seems to become, a critic of Culture. In fact I am not a critic, but at heart a commentator, a scholiast, a provider of footnotes. And a prequoter. (Somewhere I must have explained that term.)

Could all this be connected with possible blind spots?

Most spots are blind. If you want to know about me, as you seem to—sense of duty, no doubt—I am characterized, as far as introspection goes, but outsiders see it much better, by a few oddities that it took me a long time to become aware of. One, as said just before, is uneasiness with transcendencies. I am too dumb—try to find a euphemism—for all theory. Period. 'Theory' for me is everything that excludes an audience not elaborately trained in it. That explains some of my groanings and bleatings, even outbreaks of frustrated anger. It has led to continuous self-doubts. It's not that I 'disagree' with theories, I wish, rather, I knew what they are so that I could engage in arguments about them. As I say somewhere else, I have been waiting fairly long that something worth knowing from all these occupations would seep through. Irrespective of the value of theories, which is for others to judge, they have the lasting scorched-earth side-effect. Words, once innocent, cannot be used any longer. It happened to 'desire', 'gaze', 'space' and now even to 'other' as a noun. Every time we (still) have to use 'absence' or 'silence' a little bit of self-respect crumbles off.

'Cyclops' teaches us that we never see our own blinkers, so the second quirk took me much longer to put a finger on, as it seemed too natural to me. That is, when a topic is announced, say for a workshop or panel, I instinctively turn to the text and see what I can come up with that approaches relevance. Such *naïveté* I never questioned until it dawned on me gradually that, in decent academic procedure, a detour is required, some (often arcane) sanctioning by authority, even if the authorities adduced seem to be categorically denying any sort of authority. And then there is another peculiarity of which I am not even ashamed. Whenever I knocked out a footnote or an article I always took it for granted that—apart from adding to the store of perennial universal knowledge—my subjective enjoyment of the text should be passed on. The pleasure principle. I am surprised right now that this has to be said at all. New potential readers are helped, I believe, if they get a sense that Joyce may be worth reading, that it adds to their lives, though for the life of me I could not say what.

I always thought basics are more important than all superstructures above them. Maybe not, then let's say they are more basic. Basics for me meant learning to read—continuing present tense. Once you get some rudiments of that you may well graduate to metaphysics, and I am always a little nonplussed to find that rudiments actually can be skipped so cavalierly.

But then I also admit that what most of us, in the old text-oriented camp, are doing can be atrociously stolid and uninspiring.

Over several decades of Joyce criticism, what shifts of focus do you observe, and how do you relate to them?

Out of interest and necessity I did survey the scene early on, in my budding enthusiasm more than now. You know, there were times when we were actually looking forward to a new study of Joyce. And made sure to read it. When I set out—as a reader entirely, until James Atherton prodded me to do something on Zürich allusions in *FW*, which pushed me over the edge *into* the arena—I saw two main directions: one was traditional and in many ways 'positivistic', with the focus on biography, source studies, quotations, comparisons, influences, background: few Joyceans then were familiar with Dublin. And then there were the interpreters who offered, as often as not, symbolic readings, some inspiring, some mechanical. Myth had a big run, and all the more so because one didn't have to explain quite what it was nor how it worked, but it gave one's pronouncements vibrating universal scope. Irony came to be all the rage.

I soon drifted to the *Wake*. Some of us, belonging to the early explorers of what was largely uncharted, were trying to find meaning. We thought we knew what finding meaning was in those days. And we needed contact, especially me, who was dabbling along in complete isolation. There was a bunch of early *Wake* annotators, Adaline Glasheen, the most brilliant correspondent of them all, Atherton, Hodgart. Thornton Wilder travelled with a copy of *FW*, its margins brimful of minute pencil marks. One day I got a letter with some enquiries from a student in Cambridge by name of Clive Hart; another emerging student had finished a rare dissertation on *FW* and was surprised to get a letter from across the Atlantic: Bernard Benstock. So we soon developed an unofficial network, based on curiosity and capricious rapture, which no doubt later was infused by politicking and career strategies. One of the results are the Joyce Symposia that now, ironically, seem to have become the Establishment Olympics. If you knew how scared we were at our first attempt in 1967 in a Dublin that was at best indifferent, at its wittiest scathingly sarcastic.

Naturally the scene expanded, approaches diversified in all directions. At some point it was hard, and soon impossible, to keep track. Joyce scholars outside of the United States became less negligible. And correctives to the mainstream were needed, especially to those articles that seemed oblivious of fiction being fiction, confected, forgeries, verbal phantasms, affairs of permutated letters. Or 'Text'! That term has had such a career that it now has become advisable to look around for new metaphors. Change was overdue. Along came 'Structuralism', which surfaced, for me at any rate, in the person of Jacques Aubert in 1972. This may show the secluded life I had been leading. Officially Structuralism raised its disquieting head with a flurry of new droppable names at the fourth Joyce Symposium in Dublin in 1973. This was alongside the primeval feminist panel, inaugurated by Ruth Bauerle. Well, I for one never got the hang of the pioneering novelties, though, by one of fate's little tricks, I remember that a talk of mine at a *Ulysses* reunion in Tulsa 1972 was labelled a 'structuralist reading'. So perhaps our minds are, *naturaliter*, structuralist—or whatever comes along, for comparable suspicions have been levelled at me later on. As it turned out, and to show how behind the times some of us were, we found that in the middle of the stream all of this—in particular Lacan, whose teachings Aubert had perpetuated of his own accord in the early seventies—had been changed or relabelled Poststructuralism, in collusion, for all I can tell, with its sibling, Postmodernism. We entered a great phase of sign *posts*. Well, all of this has had a great impact on the Joycean scene, and after some efforts I even gave up trying to have it explained to me what the impact was. But of course all the exciting, new, overdue departures were where the action was, and certainly not in the perpetual recirculation that these theories tried to break away from.

You are without doubt a passionate Joycean; do you have allergies?

Passion, funny, that has sometimes been applied to me. I saw my preoccupation with Joyce more as a distraction, a survival technique. Yes, I do have allergies where I overreact. In the old times there were those dreary moralistic judgments. Professors of English seemed to look down from Olympian heights on the poor people in Joyce's Dublin and they were arrogantly sticking labels like 'paralysis' and 'simony' on characters that they found wanting, morally or spiritually. Critics judged life or human behaviour and I never quite figured out how they should be better qualified than others. In those days fertility and sterility were freely dished out at the drop of a symbol. Well, perhaps young Joyce proclaiming that well-touted 'moral history of my country' was taken up seriously. I resolved not to hold that one against the author. Some critics even spotted Christian miracles. To show my obtundity, I have never been able to see Buck Mulligan or Boylan as particulary wicked or despicable, and I always felt great affinity for Gerty MacDowell. To me Joyce's moral impact always appeared to be empathy with our shortcomings—*our* shortcomings, not just Farrington's or Eveline's, or, as I tried to put it, sympathy with varieties of human failure. The main books are epics of failure: we don't reach our goals and, above all: '*Nil humanum a me alienum puto.*' Wholly subjective, of course, such views, not to be proved, but then you asked.

Yes, and another overall allergy: the propensity of even battle-proved professionals to get up at a conference and to read—brilliantly or platitudinously, as the case may be—preformulated text from a typescript. The result is aptly called a 'paper', named after the most insignificant part of the whole production, the material on which thoughts become fixed. You know that I have been leading a losing fight against the recital of papers, and you can still annoy me very easily by inviting me to read one.

Do you sometimes feel your points have been missed?

To be sure. Our points are always missed. It's what Joyce writes about. So one should be immune. But it is sometimes odd to find oneself quoted, out of context naturally, or rather within a wholly distorting new one. Or else a statement long forgotten or something so trivial as hardly worthy of mention surfaces out of well-deserved oblivion. That's all in a day's work, I suppose, or the way of the word. But on occasion one is a bit piqued. I may find one of my views dug up as though I had framed it with an implied 'nothing but', the kind of formula I not only religiously avoid but go to great lengths to refute the very notion of. What stuck most dishearteningly is that I once in an essay on 'Nausicaa' steered pointedly clear of the once-common condemnations of Bloom's masturbation and briefly summarized them in order to take a more profitable turn—and then in a fine book on Joyce's sexuality I discover myself as a spokesman of precisely those censorious voices I had distanced myself from. Of course that showed I had not expressed myself as clearly as had been my purpose. Incidentally, you'd hardly imagine in how many ways a simple name like Senn (common in Switzerland) can be misspelled: Sin, Sen, Zen, Zimm, Senft, etc., all follow in the trail of M'Intosh, L. Boom and several others. 'Eumaeus', I find more and more, is true to life.

Have you any comment on the appearance for the third time of an edited collection of your essays?

If for the third time—or fourth, depending on what you include—someone else, in this case you, goes to the trouble of assembling scattered articles into one volume, then it is a safe bet that this triple-edited author will never 'write a book'. Psychoanalysis might look into this block and dredge up fascinating unsavoury diagnoses, probably fear of some sort. It's not that I have not toyed with the idea. Once I thought of investigating what Joyce does with time, '*NarraTime*' it would have been called, if it had ever got beyond an accumulation of electronic notes. Or I thought I would do something on the chapter relations in *Ulysses*. Well, to paraphrase L. Boom: 'Still an idea behind it. But nothing doing.' I just don't have that wide horizon, or the illusion that any impetus could profitably expand to book length without becoming both tedious and laboured and, somewhere along the way, plain wrong. Sour grapes, but then anything systematized to any great extent stumbles into the kind of dogmatism that Joyce's works seem to counteract, especially the *Wake* with its built-in scepticism. Therefore I am scrutinizing minutiae, but I try to extrapolate and to generalize tentatively and with visible signals of reservation. In my better moments I flatter myself, not for very long, that some incentive has been given.

*Could you elaborate on your preoccupation with processes, dynam-
isms, kinetics, urges, excesses, for which you have to invent your own
critical terms such as* provection, anagnosis, dislocution, allotropy?

It was just my interest. I didn't know that I was doing so until it
dawned on me and I felt—wrongly in part, no doubt—that many
others concentrated on what there *is* in Joyce's texts and did not
seem alerted to what *happens*. Our minds are skilled categorizing
things, and things are easier to pigeonhole than elusive processes,
such as, in extreme, *Finnegans Wake*. Joyce texts seemed alive, in
motion, verbs rather than nouns, kinetic in another sense than
what assistant-professor Dedalus had in mind in his fame- and
pompous lecture. Textual energies serve as antidotes to the inertia
of reification. That's why I was getting annoyed, and have publi-
cized, not always kindly, my impatience with static annotation
that tends to freeze the text and to stop further inquiry.

But then again, since Joyce brings many such truisms to unexpected light, I have hardly ever done anything that I did not also
think obvious. Everyone could have seen the same processes at
work. Some corrective commonplaces of years ago have become
mainstream clichéd pomposities. What once was necessary to
point out may have turned into new dogma. I do not know
whether I was amused or irritated when once I had used a talk
merely to illustrate that Joyceans, against all the evidence under
our eyes, can still be so certain about their own precious findings
without any trace of doubt. Two years later at another conference
it appeared, paradoxically, as though Uncertainty itself had
become infallible dogma, so much so that one participant referred
to 'that uncertainty we are all looking for'. As though we had to
make an effort to discover what is so conspicuous all the time.

So I see myself rather tritely on the old beaten, maybe outdated,
humanist track. Joyce never invented, but only illustrated anew,
the old Socratic *caveat*, 'Are you quite sure?' Some of us *still* are.
Quite sure. It took me years to experience fully the import of one
early aside in *Ulysses*, attributed to Haines: '— I don't know, I'm
sure.'

INSTEAD OF A PREFACE:
THE CREED OF NAÏVETÉ

The following letter arose from an article in the 'James Joyce Broad-sheet' which contained a reference to a stray letter to the editor I had composed. The persons involved do not matter, but it occurred to me that extracts from my statements of the time might clarify in advance what up-to-date readers will not find in the following probes, and why. Joyce was very good at circumscribing limitations: those of Eveline, James Duffy, Boylan, Gerty, Stephen, but also those of styles and modes—he seems to include, in particular, our rare haphazard insights. I think we should therefore state our own, right from the outset, our weak spots, the blinders we have.

(...) I would also like to clarify a few things that are on my mind. First of all I have no judgement on Deconstruction, or Theory, as such. I know it is there, it is important, is taken up, means a lot to many. I simply do not understand it, and even trying to do so may set me back for months of depressive paralysis and resignation. I have nothing to say on your subject in general. There are some very good friends whose work and minds I highly respect and who have been into these theories. So I deduce there must be something there that is of value. But it does not reach me. So I always ask just one thing: What then is it that *you* can do, with *your* approach/theory/ philosophy, that we fogeys cannot?—what questions, what answers, perhaps. And, please, demonstrate it to me *in concrete textual detail.* Now for reasons beyond me this is not to be done; the rules of the union do not seem to allow that. OK, then that has to be accepted. But, *when*, as I tried to make very clear in my letter, on rare occasions, they (the 'theorists') do stoop to a bit of text and when, very very rarely, it becomes clear what they mean, *then* (and only then) I always felt—at least until now—we could have achieved the same results or have reached similar conclusions in the traditional way. My remarks refer to these exceptional cases—are more or less in the conditional.

When the prophet descends to the market-place then he has to be judged *by* the market-place. Things may be different on Olympus; but there, though it gets crowded more and more, I do not belong.

My view is not that '*a* disseminative reading is not really different'—I do not know what disseminative readings *really* are nor what they disseminate. I wish I could see them *as* disseminative. But when something is applied to a bit of text then I can agree or disagree.

My concern is *lucidity*, nothing else. The one thing I require of book, talk, panel—to be able to follow. Perhaps lucidity is not compatible with certain approaches. But once you address a large audience, say at a Symposium carrying the label 'Joyce', a tacit assumption is that you want to put something across. I find the unwillingness of theorists to do this—on the level of the uninitiated—depressing. Now this may be my problem, up to a psychological point it is. At the same time, believe me, I would like to learn, to learn from them as well.

Of course there is the impression that 'they' (perhaps *all* theories) have relatively little (visible) interest in Joyce, they put the focus somewhere else. Nothing wrong with that; scholarship is open, must remain so, no holds barred, there must be a wide scope, new angles; and we all have a right to our own brand of curiosity. No-one should be forced to focus on Joyce. At our Joyce conferences, however, a minimum of such focus or interest seems to be implied by the name, and when current fashions take over a bit much, disproportionally much, then a feeling of waste becomes painful. Now for all I know, 'they' may have a great deal of interest in Joyce, and great insights too—and I am sure some of their enthusiasm is very genuine and exciting—but somehow the insights do not penetrate outside the hermetic circle. So I am still waiting.

However, there is a bias that you noted. My implication of a difference in interest is simply based on a notion that, if theorists have something of interest to say, to say on Joyce, then in the long run something of this would rub off, something would get around—so that it might even reach the likes of me, the obtuse, pedestrian, naïve simple-minded readers. It may happen tomorrow. It hasn't yet. But within decades of so much Joyce scholarship sailing under all those French (mainly) flags, don't you think a few results might be expected by those without the temple? Or, to put it differently, if 'By their fruits ye shall know them', as the chap said, is a valid rule, then some fruits should be forthcoming at some stage—fruits, mind you, not treatises on metadendrology, though this may be a fascinating subject in itself.

Perhaps it is an insult to expect something as commonplace as results from on high. Theories, I know, are not vending machines. This too would have to be accepted, but it would have to be announced first, and announced plainly and unmistakably. In the meantime, having heard and seen and watched from afar the mountains in protracted and much-published labour, we Philistines are still waiting for the mouse to emerge. Barking up, no doubt, the wrong mountain.

And again: I do not distinguish between simply those interested in Joyce's works and *the* 'voguish [etc.] Larridians', but *those* among them (as distinct from the Masters) who *are* in demonstrable fact voguish, epigonal, dilutive and flag-waving: I assume their legion gets on your nerves even more than mine. In fact I think that those concerned with theories should safeguard against the bandwagon syndrome. There are a few Joyceans I could name (and won't) by whose taking up a theory you know it has now been debased into a fashion. I also mean the name-droppers, the authoritarian quoters. The Joyce world is free to accommodate them (at any rate, they would be a nuisance at any period). And another thing you should be concerned about, I mean you as a *Fidei Defensor*: Why are (and here I am really inclined to generalize) all theorists, from inspired top to epigonal bottom of the barrel, such poor translators? Why do they not (want to?) communicate? At least some of them, by the law of probability, might be expected to try.

You will have noticed that none of my remarks refer to Critical Theory, Deconstruction, or any of the philosophies concerned. I am not qualified, I do not know about these things (most of my friends still think I am being coyly or facetiously modest when I confess that I am too dumb for theories). My remarks refer solely to the performances in Joycean contexts that I have witnessed. (I am not sure the Masters would always have been pleased with those performances.)

I realize full well that looking at a bit of text and trying to figure out what it may mean (which delimits my own narrow, philological garden), is not sufficient. We need to go beyond, widening our contexts and horizons, by all means. Some scholars, Joyceans, naturally want to aim higher. And we certainly depend—for new input—on those who are able to lift their noses from the close reading and who concern themselves with the Larger Issues. It's not that I am simply speaking up for the old-fashioned traditionalists (of which I am one by constitution), all those plodders who produce glosses, sources, influences, biographical, symbolic, or (Joyce help us!) moralizing readings, etc., etc. I know all about their tedium. Or rather, as I also tried to express in my letter, we get some very dull, uninspired scholars in all camps; the majority of us are just not very brilliant, no matter what we do.

You see now why I do not belong to the academic world and have always remained an amateur. I want to increase my knowledge, understanding, and pleasure in the text, works, language—and beyond that, inductively, into all areas: language, psychology, history, etc. all the way to Culture, Metaphysics, and perhaps even Life. Everything that helps me in this is (subjectively) good, everything that does not help me I cannot assimilate, it runs off my back. My complaint is restricted to our own gatherings. There it has happened a little bit too often that someone, instead of telling us something about Joyce, got up and proclaimed, in substance, some name in current use. I supposed for a considerable time it would be possible to say something about both areas, something that is *meaningful* in our own. Maybe this *has* happened, and you can tell me where it has.

You realize that according to my reiterations here it would be enough to produce *one* single insight, *one* single gloss, *one* single reading that is both new and clear, to make the general gist of my complaints null and void. Just a single one. The demand may be unfair. But then, and that would be OK too, it would have to be explained (as to a child) once and for all why theories (or a particular system) cannot be concerned with such trifling side issues.

Now in all of this, as I keep repeating, there is a large portion of subjective pathology. But I do compare experiences; I do talk to others, also young people, students. So I am not quite alone. It took me a long time to figure out a simple truth that does not apply to me alone, but, at least, to a scared minority. There are many reasons *for* theories: (wo)man is the theorizing animal, our curiosity—a metaphysical bent—new horizons, points of view, attitudes, exploration, our bases, ideologies have to be challenged, and all the rest. I know. But most current literary theories in their looming bulk also have *one* drawback, one that is wholly irrelevant to Research and Scholarship, but does have an impact nevertheless when they become obligatory or endemic: they increase human misery. And here I am not merely airing my own hang-ups, but thinking of students that have confessed to me how they feel when, apart from all the obscurity and challenges of Joyce's texts, they have to grapple with further obscure abstractions on top. I myself can get by, more or less, at least some of the time (I even get insincere compliments from the other camp), but many of those young and timid, lacking self-confidence, cannot. Perhaps the whole repetitive gist and appeal to you all up there is simply: For heaven's sake try to be clear and lucid on occasion—or even helpful. There is, after all, also a Little Chandler in Joyce's works, and a Bloom and a Molly.

February 1988

* * *

Such was that letter (now abbreviated and slightly modified) of years ago in which I now discover a faint trace of misplaced optimism. I have no intention of calling up an implied spectre of earlier, glorious times now gone—they never existed. Yet the old philological game, never too popular anyhow, has played itself out; it has certainly come to grief over *Finnegans Wake* (see the piece on Dissatisfaction). It has to make room for all the inspired Others who *have* won the day, those with wide outlooks and depth, scanning nothing less than the horizon of all Culture, and History.

On the other hand one may be forgiven for holding on to a conviction that Joyce is not such a limited writer that he can *only* be accessed through contemporary metaphysics. The approach taken throughout is of the Illegitimate Shortcut, of going (with all one's biases and preconceptions, wrong ideologies and what have you) straight to what appears on the page and trying to puzzle out, very provisionally, the mysterious dynamics of those signs, and to guess at meanings and how they come about. It looked like an interesting exercise in its day and may in fact never die out entirely.

JOYCE THE VERB

in the muddle was the sounddance (*FW* 378.29)

I begin with a few sample quotations. These are not for your applause or disagreement, but merely in order to probe and appreciate the semantic variety of the one recurrent word, 'Joyce':

Joyce was born in 1882—The Tenth International James Joyce Symposium—Joyce was conscious of his control of English and other languages—This book enters Joyce's life to reflect his complex, incessant joining of event and composition—From his late adolescence onward, James Joyce intended to be a writer—The sacred is at the heart of Joyce's writing experience—Joyce insists that man's will is free, that it can be exercised for good or evil, and that the state of the world's affairs will vary with the quality of leadership—What does Joyce assert or imply about guilt in *Ulysses*?—Joyce is disgusted by sexual impulses regarded as normal by most standards of behaviour—Joyce's mind was at all times engaged in the search for truth—When I first met Joyce in 1901 or 1902, he was beginning to emerge as a Dublin 'character'—Joyce was too scrupulous a writer to tolerate even minor flaws—Joyce spent his life playing parts, and his works swarm with shadow selves—Joyce's laughter is free and spontaneous—Joyce wrote not for literature, but for personal revenge—Jim Joyce devoted a whole big novel to the day on which I was seduced—Joyce is writing the book of himself.

There needn't be any contradiction at all, but meanings differ. It is equally true to say 'Joyce has been dead for forty-five years', as to claim 'Joyce is alive.' 'Joyce' does not equal 'Joyce': What is the statue of Joyce in the Fluntern cemetery of Zürich a statue of? Joyce Symposia, among other events, give partial answers.

The question will not be pursued here. It is the name, noun, *nomen*, 'Joyce', that interests us. It epiphanizes a bewildering diversity of meanings, semantic differences that we, the professional differentiators, do not always notice. The diversity at first sight would appear odd, for names, of all words, ought to distinguish persons; it is their function. They often fulfill it. Reading Joyce (you see, we use the name but don't mean the person), we might learn about the chanciness of easy identification by nominal labels. Insofar as names are for things, the distinctions work reasonably well. But even so, undoubtedly concrete objects like keys or bowls are not just objects. Keys can open or lock, they are for entering, for excluding, for taking along, for forgetting, for being handed over, for ruling or usurping. Bowls are for carrying (or 'bearing'), for holding aloft, for shaving, for mocking, they may play the role of chalices at times, and chalices, we have read, may contain wine, or be empty, even 'idle', can be broken—or not broken. Such objects, many at the beginning of *Ulysses*, are for actions, or acting.

Those privileged and, usually, capitalized nouns, however, that have no general referent, the names, serve to keep persons apart for convenient identification. Not unconditionally. You may remember Kitty O'Shea, the one that, Molly says, had a 'magnificent head of hair down to her waist tossing it back', and who lived 'in Grantham street' (*U* 18.478). This name then has different reverberations for a reader who (a) knows no Irish history at all, for one who (b) knows a little, and for one who (c) is an expert. It is the knowledge we bring to bear on the name that makes the difference. But even a historian well versed in late nineteenth-century Irish affairs will have to match Molly's acquaintance, at least for a fleeting instant, against the bad woman 'who brought Parnell low', and then decide against an attractive identification. A name translates into knowing, or not knowing. Walter W. Skeat, the English etymologist, makes one of his infrequent negative remarks in the entry on 'Name': this word and its Latin cousin *nomen* are 'not allied to "know".' The two word families are not related, but in practice they work together. The cognates of 'know', however, are allied to that one item in the much-quoted triad of strange words at the opening of 'The Sisters'—'*gnomon*' (*D* 9). And this gnomon merely sounds like, but has nothing to do with, Latin *nomen*, though it happens to be one; the similarity is deceptive and ominous.

The platitudinous pay-off of all this, predictably, is that in identifying we are *doing* something. All the meanings we concede, knowingly or not, to the term 'Joyce' imply some kind of activity. At one extreme the word does duty for a life lived in various cities in the course of almost sixty years; at the other possible ends of the scales it suggests writing, thinking, creating, developing, intending—you name it, and you name it appropriately by verbs. Such verbs also become our panels and lectures and animated disputes. Aware of such dynamisms, some of us have quite independently—when this could still be done with impunity and even self-respect—coined the verb *rejoyce* or *rejoycing*.

Even the adjective 'Joycean' predominantly means not some stable quality, but rather what Joyce actively provoked and what, conspiratorially, we now do in turn and with considerable energy. None of us may be able to define 'Joycean' adequately, but we vaguely sense that it connotes some heterogeneous, but characteristic hyperactivity: words seem to be charged, or else we readers charge the words, somehow, it seems, beyond the norm. Ask anyone in Dublin.

To simplify the foregoing, names, for all their accepted substantiality, soon dissolve into doings, into the verbs from which grammar distinguishes them, at least in Indo-European languages. If at this point you nod facile assent and find, rightly, that I am kicking outdated horses and dismiss notions long out of date—or that someone has already put all this into a system of trendy abstractions—then just look at most of our practical applications. Look at how we, commentators or critics, seem often at pains to re-reify all that elusive work in progress, to freeze it into solid theses, symbols, parallels, discourses, or even 'puns', things that we can categorize and administer.

Joyce might be the antidote. His works release the processes out of the nouns, nouns which are so much easier to handle than events or doings. The pioneering etymologists who drew up a set of language origins of common Indo-European ancestry, usually tabulated roots that tended to be verbs of action. Joyce seems to descend to such origins. The roots of the two cultures that he revived bear this out as well.

Dominenamine (*U* 6.595)

Once the God of the Old Testament had spoken light into being and approved of it, he went on and 'called the light Day' (Gen. 1:4). Genesis follows the birth of the world right away with the birth of the first noun. Somehow Joyce celebrated this pristine noun thus generated in his secondary creation; we in turn now also use 'Bloomsday'. God then, soon after, shaped a being that was called 'man'. His personal name emerges first in the midst of another naming process:

The Lord brought [the beasts of the field] unto Adam, to see what he would call them [and we find an almost Joycean sort of divine curiosity]: and whatsoever Adam called every living creature, that was the name thereof. (Gen. 2:19)

Calling ('quod vocavit', as the Vulgate has it) precedes the name ('ipsum est nomen eius'). And Adam, the first-named, started to give names to the animals around him; he also decided that the outgrowth of his rib shall

be called Woman, because she was taken out of man. (Gen. 2:23)

Adam is the object of naming and becomes its prolific active subject right away. Creator and first creature are both protonomastic, not only the first namers around, but also those who start with naming before almost anything else we find on the record. The names, of course, allow the record to be written. Conversely, the calling of names in the upward direction, towards the divinity, might be tabooed. Potent naming and ineffability go together. Naming is potent, and so is knowing or uttering a name. Adam's powerful prerogative is shared by writers of fiction.

The Hellenic version differs in conception and idiom, but the Greek epics, oldest witnesses, work the naming of some of their heroes into their tales. In the most famous digression in literature, Odysseus is named in what appears the most arbitrary and whimsical way, in almost Saussurean fashion, and yet the random signifier becomes potently ominous. Since grandfather Autolykos passing by at the birth happened to be 'odyssamenos', the child was called, 'eponymously', 'Odysseus'. The participle form 'odyssamenos' is either 'made angry' or else 'making angry' (reductive philologists, like their Joycean counterparts, may disagree); it suggests a man connected with wrath or odium, and it came to signify both a wrath inflicted and a wrath suffered.

So naming has been around from the beginning. Joyce, the Namer, is well within a tradition that allowed for metamorphotic scope. A central name 'Bloom' coincides with a common noun, offshoot of a verb, *bhlo* (cf. *florere*, blühen, etc.), but a noun for some live process, blossoming, growing, changing, withering, radiating, smelling, all astir with poetical echoes. When Miss Marion Tweedy adopts it by patriarchal custom through marriage, her rivals inevitably joke: 'youre looking blooming' (*U* 18.843). The verbal connection offers an appropriate flourish for the central onomastic cluster. Names, necessary social designations, arise out of, and turn again into, verbal energies, long before *Finnegans Wake*.

Joyce the Writer set off with almost no names, as suits lyrical poetry. *Chamber Music* can do, practically, without them. But not prose narrative; *Dubliners* has a wide range of appellative possibilities: full-fledged name (Ignatius Gallaher), last name only (Lenehan, Farrington), or first name alone (Maria, Lily), with or without a honorific (*Mr* James Duffy, *Mr* Duffy, but Corley), with a sprinkling of eponymous flourishes (Hoppy Holohan, Little Chandler). In all this diversity, the first three stories do not divulge what the protagonist narrator is (or the three narrators are) called. The technique of gnomonic elision or silence extends to names: one that is pointedly withheld seems to assume even more power than those known. But from now on there are names in abundance: a whole critical study can be devoted to them.[1] Some were taken from Joyce's own background, some appropriated abroad, from printed sources, or invented, many synthesized. Perhaps the most outstanding example of imaginative naming is 'Stephen Dedalus', in defiance of almost all realistic plausibility: it represents a soaring, mythical, high-water mark of portentous naming—its growing significance is thematized in *A Portrait*. But more and more, especially from *Ulysses* onwards, personal names are shown to be problematic. In the final work, they have lost their discriminative graphic edges, and identification becomes our readers' necessity and pastime more than an overt concern of the work. It would be difficult to talk about the *Wake* if we had no nominal handles for its profusion. But its nominal blurrings would not be accepted by immigration officers on our passports, and our computers too would be obstinately uncooperative.

So we might roughly sketch a curve rising from pristine, lyrical anonymity to mythological ostentation, and down again towards a terminal pseudonymous fuzziness. But such a simplification would obscure the innate perplexity in between, the inherent riddling nature of names. But throughout, I submit, the naming is at least as important as the individual names used. Joyce's methods are often genetic. Ironically, the first occurrence of 'name' in *Dubliners* is connected, not with something coming into being, but with the loss of the vital force. The reverberating term 'paralysis' is introduced as sounding strangely like the name of some maleficent and sinful being (*D* 9), attached to a mortal activity, an action which means the disablement *from* acting. Appropriately then, the priest's name is not communicated to us until it is read on his death notice, when paralysis has done its fascinatingly 'deadly work'.

Before any one person in *A Portrait* has been identified, the process of naming is put before us. The opening tale within a tale features a 'nicens little boy named baby tuckoo'—*named*. Named by others, from outside, imposed from above. It will happen to the main character soon '— O, Stephen will apologize', and whether guided by the precedent of Genesis or simply by empirical common sense, we take the name on trust ever after. Stephen hardly thinks about it until others remark on its strangeness. Once the naming of 'baby tuckoo' has taken place, incidentally, the fairy story is discontinued right away, as though it had now, the secret being out, lost all further interest.

When real names do take over, we are not always helped. One fully labelled 'Betty Byrne' is never heard of again. Soon we will come across a 'Michael Davitt', but few readers nowadays could tell, offhand, untutored, who he is; for all we know at first, it might be a member of the family. (If you disagree, you are simply substituting scholarly annotation for average knowledge.) One early conspicuous name, 'Dante', is flickeringly misleading. Most of us, semi-erudite, will have to discard the nominal association of an Italian poet who *will* be named, towards the end of the book. But the person called Dante early on will later translate itself unexplained into 'Mrs Riordan'. In life and in literature, we usually come to terms with such confusion. Joyce exploits the confusions inherent in naming. Coincidences and convergences will later facilitate the mechanistics of *Finnegans Wake*.

When Stephen's family name, commented on all along, is linked to its mythological origin and import, it translates into such actions as flying, soaring, falling, creating and, later on, estheticizing, or forging. Most of these active revelations follow close upon the mocking evocation of a Greek participle, *'Bous Stephanoumenos'*, in which Stephen's Christian, very Christian, name is made to derive not from crown, the object, but from a verb for crowning. The fourth chapter, where all this happens, moves from a static beginning of almost lifeless order and institutional clusters to an ecstasy of motion.

It would be idle to repeat how deceptively the first names come on in *Ulysses*, 'Buck' and 'Kinch'. Commentators who claim that 'Chrysostomos' in the earliest non-normative, one-word, sentence, 'is' the name of some specific saint disregard the inherent process of naming through characterization, a process which then may very well lead to *one* particular saint. Stephen silently bestows an appellation on the usurper[2] who towers over him, one that fittingly singles out his most prominent organ. In some way this is Stephen's tacit hellenized tit for Mulligan's loudly voiced tat, 'Kinch'. *Ulysses* starts naming procedures even before the absurdity of 'Dedalus' or the trippingness of 'Malachi Mulligan' are remarked upon.

One whole chapter is notably given over to the bafflement of naming. It begins with 'I', the polar opposite to individual verbal labels, a pronoun without a noun. Unique among words, its meaning changes with every speaker. As Stephen intimates in a passing 'I, I and I. I.' (*U* 9.212), the meaning may even change for any *one* person—through time; 'I am other I now.' 'Cyclops', whose governing saints are 'S. Anonymous and S. Eponymous and S. Pseudonymous and S. Paronymous and S. Synonymous', contains '*Adonai!*' in its terminal paragraph (*U* 12.1915), a word that looks and functions like a name but pointedly is not. It is in fact a substitute for one that is unspeakable and prohibited. 'Adonai' is making a nominal noise for a sacred onomastic absence.

One minor event in *Ulysses* is the devious misnaming of 'M'Intosh' by a collusion of oral, written, and printed communication. The mystery surrounding this figure is mainly due to its being given a name that we know to be chancy. If there had been no newspaper reference and if Bloom had wondered, at the end of his day, who the *man in the* macintosh was, very little print would be expended on him. It is our knowledge of his pseudonymity that provokes so much curiosity. As naming, however, the procedure is true to universal type. What we wear can turn into what we become known by (Robin Hood may be a case in point; his sister Little Red Riding certainly is).

The misnomering integrated into the texture of *Ulysses* is intimately tied up with fiction, a process of feigning (or the invention of 'figures'). As an obliging intermediary, Leopold Bloom assists in dissimulating the presence of M'Coy among the mourners (M'Coy is neither present nor mourning). Newspaper fictions get M'Coy as well as Stephen Dedalus, BA, into this second *Nekuyia*. In the midst of what looks like the least questionable list of mere names some fictions have intruded; we, in our superiority, translate the fictions into complicated actions and dysfunctions of information. We still don't know who 'M'Intosh' is (some readers have thought they do, others claim we never will; but knowing who he 'is' would mean substituting his wrong name by one that is considered circumstantially plausible—a change of labels), but we recognize 'M'Intosh' as a series of mishappenings. Joe Hynes's misunderstanding also shows the reporter's need for labels of that sort. As we do not know the civil service data of the person who tells us what goes on in Barney Kiernan's bar, we change this negative condition *into* a name and refer to him as 'The Nameless One', following a hint (*U* 15.1144). Namelessness is unsettling. So

that in *Finnegans Wake* we are striving for identification tags to attach
to the paronymous noncharacters, and we co-create Earwickers and
Porters, or pit Shems (in Hebrew *shem* intriguingly *means* name)
against Shauns even where these configurations of letters do not
occur, in the majority of cases, and we treat them as though they were
friends of the family we would recognize anywhere.

Naming confers power. The namer feels superior to the namee
(who is generally a helpless infant). Once a name is given, it tends to
stick. Only when we assume important positions, like Pope or King,
may we choose our own different names. Writers can do it too. They
can name themselves, or one of their figures, 'Stephen Daedalus' or
'Dedalus'. Or they can title a prose work about a day in Dublin
Ulysses, and we realize the potency of this when we consider what
difference it would make if someone discovered that Joyce's real
intention had been something like 'Henry Flower' or 'Love's Old
Sweet Song', 'Atonement', or 'The Rose from Gibraltar'.

if we look at it verbally

Naming is one of the many activities we find in Joyce's cosmos, but a
prominent one—of paradigmatic significance: an action through
words. My exemplification is simply a renewed demonstration of a
direction away from the stability of things or persons towards movement, change. Verbs, which here represent action, movement,
processes, are less tractable than nouns (nouns are ideal for catalogues or filing cards), less easy to pin down. Verbs have more flexi-
bility, or *flexion*. They extend beyond the immediate present, or
presence, into the past and the future; they are not restricted to what
is, but can imply variant attitudes towards factuality, what *might be*.
They have, in other words, *tenses, moods, aspects, voices*. At the present stage of ignorance it might be more profitable to phrase our
views of literature in general, and Joyce in exemplary particular, in
terms of inflexion and syntactic interaction than as an assembly of
themes, ideas, messages. Physics in the twentieth century developed
in a similar direction: things, bodies, mass, matter seemed to give
way to motion, energies, speeds—nouns into verbs. Contemporary
theories also tend towards verbal processes. I hope the simplistic
way of putting it here is seen for what it is, a corrective convenience
for illustration. As *Finnegans Wake* tries to spell out, 'perhaps there
is no true noun in active nature' (*FW* 523.10).

I am going to apply my figure of speech—taken from the *parts* of
speech—to the newly edited text of *Ulysses* on the occasion of its

first rebirth in a new dress, the paperback Blue Book of Errors Corrected. Some of the arguments of last year (1985) might have been controverted with more urbane understanding if the issues had not been treated as things, choices right or wrong, but had been seen as problems of the verbs that are implied. What the text of 1984 offered is not so much an object rectified in 5000 instances and made reliably stable—or else, in an opposing view, a product wholly misconceived and faultily executed. It is, if anything, rectification in visible progress. The process is spread over the entire synoptic array on the dynamic left-hand page, down to footnotes, into the back of the book with textual notes, a historical collation, and a discursive afterword. The constant scuttling it demands of its users is troublesome, but essential, work in progress. The left-hand page activates us.

One might say in metaphorical exaggeration that the left-hand page, the one with all the action, constitutes the verbs as against the deceptively stable nouns on the page that provides the final (not definite) results in undisturbed typography. By common, misleading, usage a text is called 'established'—the Munich text emphasizes establish*ing*. Those sinistrous verbs have changing forms, have tenses (the page is diachronic), moods, voices. All the nonalphabetic features, those elevated diacritical irritations, are functional imperatives: they tell us what to do, where to go[3]—to the drafts, fair copies, proof sheets, and all the rest. They also actively report what Joyce did.

It is for us to translate the left page, which by itself does not make immediate sense, and not because of the editors' instinctive nastiness. The pages on the left are 'genetic', they display *becoming*. Our own postcreative retracings match the author's creative bustling: an author who was indeed *auctor*, an 'increaser', and an excreaser. To bone-set, after the act, excrescences that extended over three cities and seven years is a task to tax the best prepared of experts, almost beyond the reach of prescriptive principles. That the synoptic, left-hand page and the internal explications offered in the edition require conjugations that happen to surpass my own mental capacities does not detract from the necessity for conjugation, Joycean conjugations.

What we face, inevitably, is not a text freed from error (though this in itself was a worthwhile goal which resulted in a great number of unquestioned improvements), but a refined documentation of what an error might be. The apparatus shows how errors came about. The text, in its hazardous growth, was in itself erring all along (the drafts show abortive attempts and wrong starts). It, *Ulysses*, in its laborious

progress from abandoned short story to no-longer novel, had its share
of vicissitudes or, to borrow some quotations, it,

travelled far—was fated to roam—many a way wound—was harried for years on end—
was driven far journeys—was made to stray—had a changeful course—*multum erravit.*

All these paraphrases refer, of course, to Odysseus, whose changeful course was due to force of circumstances *and* to his own nature.
The text of *Ulysses*, similarly, was redirected at various points, on
various pieces of paper.[4] It had to suffer countless injuries done to it
from outside, but it also, in the nature of its being, caused many of its
own predicaments. *Ulysses* was in need of re-editing, not only
because of the shortcomings of typists and printers, but because it is
as it is.

So it is now for us to sort out the highroads and the deviations and
to synopt. We know that some of our synoptions are chancy, many
wayward itineraries of long ago remain irretrievable. The new edition strives to leave out scribal sins—what inattentive or meddlesome copyists had committed or omitted by faulty conjugation,
departures that usually consist of words known to all men with the
possible exception of French typesetters in Dijon. What all this
implies, in practice, is that Joyce (here in the sense of someone writing, revising, adding, proof-reading), actively engaged in new creations, was passively overlooking thousands of wrong turns, or gaps.
Preoccupied with what lay still ahead, he was not undoing the doing
of fallible mediators. The Munich team stepped in and did the close
examination that Joyce was incapable of, had failed to carry out, and
so they incurred, as one might telegrammatically put it, the immense
debtorship of a thing done sixty years later.

From my given bias, I stress the verbal framework—Joyce actively
composing the end of *Ulysses*, passively overlooking numerous mis-
adventures of transmission. 'Passive authorization' is a conventional
technical contradiction of terms, the notion for a principle that is not
valid for the new edition of *Ulysses*. The principle defines Joyce's
oversights as failed actions, failures by inattention, which the
approval of a *bon à tirer* does not authorize. If Joyce *had* noticed the
errors, the assumption is, he *would* have interfered. You notice that
an edition of *Ulysses* can hardly remain in the indicative mood; conditional[5] or subjunctive aspects (what would have been, or should
have been) come into play.

The accomplicity long after the fact, which results in so many
improvements, worries me all the same. How are we to deal ratio-

nally with what, by definition, is not a rational decision, is outside the normal range of conscious volition? A new psychology that was coterminous with Joyce's development and coincided with some of his insights, diagnosed overlooking—forgetting, lapsing, erring (and all parapractic varieties)—no longer as neutral, accidental blanks among business as usual, but as negative *actions*, as significant *not* looking, *not* recalling—as twisted, deviant, aberrant *doings* outside of consciousness. Psychomorphoses of that kind are, furthermore, vitally part of Joyce's realistically erroneous cosmos of words; the verb *to err* is integrated into Joyce's works (and I still believe that its concurrence in the first word of *Finnegans Wake* is significant: 'riv-*err*-un'). What is the meaning of *that* other world, the one thought to be outside of what our minds know they know? How are we to deal with those verbs below the surface of reason and, perhaps, an author's conscious control?

Or, to put it differently, if so much care was not taken by Joyce, as evidenced by the much touted number of 5000 errors, would not this fact in its totality constitute a kind of vague cumulative volition? Authorization and will are related. 'Which will' ('We are getting mixed', *U* 9.794)? Who was it again that was troubled all day long about the correct voicing of—'*voglio*'—or is it perhaps '*vorrei*'? (auxiliary verbs are tricky and ubiquitous). I have no solution to offer for what the author's will may have been *when*. This was an author fretted, harried, optically handicapped, oblivious and, at that stage, not omniscient, certainly no longer scrupulous over minor flaws, an author who missed hundreds of commas that had been officiously introduced into the typescript of 'Eumaeus'. We all have overlooked commas in our petty time, nothing is easier. But can the wholesale sprinkling of them be missed? Does Joyce's noninterference mean Will, Impotence, Carelessness, or Passive Resignation? If Joyce— 'writing the mystery of himself' (*FW* 184.9), '*lisant au livre de lui-même*' (*U* 9.114), that is rereading the proofs of himself—so often forgot himself, which part of Joyce are we going to call up in his stead? I, for one, do not have the strong verbs to tackle such questions, and so commas will continue to haunt, subjunctively, the Eumaean prose for me.

My phrasings have been hovering, in subtle confusion, between activity and passivity in which author and transmitters shared. The text was made, begotten, augmented, changed, it suffered damage, neglect, was interfered with, but there is also a sense, much amplified in current vogues, in which Joyce's texts seemed to have a will of their own, appear to have written themselves, autogenetically. The synopsis of the new *Ulysses*, writes Hans Walter Gabler, using a reflexive form, displays 'a text as it constituted itself in the process of writing'.[6] The works, moreover, tend to comment *on* themselves in narcissistic self-preoccupation and internal reciprocality. Later texts also look back, retrospectively, on the earlier ones. We now discover more and more, and pontificate on, how *Ulysses* and *Finnegans Wake* are self-reflexive.

reluctant to use the passive voiced (*FW* 523.8)

Now verbs can be used either actively or passively in our languages (those that concern us here), and that seems to be all. But our Indo-European dialect once expressed a third, in-between, possibility, with separate forms. The Greek prototexture of a work entitled 'Ulysses' may permit a look into that language, a characteristic it had preserved from its ancestors. The verbal system included what was called a 'middle *diathesis*' (disposition), in Latin grammar the *genus 'medium'*, the so-called middle voice, partaking of the active *and* the passive. It was an old, original part of its inflected system (in fact the passive voice has been thought to derive from it). 'But learn from that ancient tongue to be middle' (*FW* 270.17).

Nowadays the main use of the middle voice is to bewilder the student of Greek and the translators, but it once expressed, very sensibly, a most common involvement of the subject beyond its own grammatical confinement within the sentence. Definitions speak of 'actions viewed as affecting the subject', which is a very general condition to which formal attention was paid long ago. The middle voice is an 'intermediate between active and passive', or a voice which 'normally expresses reflexive or reciprocal action.' Another traditional way describes its function as 'the voice of verb inflection in which the subject is represented as acting *on* or *for* itself.' By chance this may almost sound like, and remind us of, Stephen's Shakespeare: 'He acts and is acted on' (*U* 9.1021). A Greek writer might well have used one verbal form for this, and we would then wonder if the passive or the medial sense is dominant. The verb 'act', Stephen's choice, is a good paradigm: it shows that verbs too play roles, roles that were distinguished and highlighted in Greek. 'Epiphany', a favourite term of Joyce's youth, has much to do with the middle voice: '*epiphainesthai*', 'to manifest itself, appear, come into view'; it can also mean, of course, passively, 'to *be* manifested'. The Latin equivalents are the *Deponents*, verbs with passive forms but active function—

hybrids. Joyce acknowledged them. A defendant in court becomes a 'Deponent' (as a witness he would have to 'depone'):

the deponent... may have been (one is reluctant to use the passive voiced) may be been as much sinned against as sinning, for if we look at it verbally perhaps there is no true noun in active nature... (*FW* 523.7)

Anyone accused is likely to present himself not as an agent but as a passive victim; 'more sinned against than sinning' is a moral medial position between the voices that grammar keeps apart. A deponent verb is passive ('sinned against') in looks but active ('sinning') in intent. Another court-room situation also plays on the morality of the verb:

no longer will I follow you obliquelike through the inspired form of the third person singular and the moods and hesitensies of the deponent but address myself to you, with the empirative of my vendettative, provocative and out direct. (*FW* 187.2)

Grammatical terms reappear:

And egg she active or spoon she passive, all them fine clauses... never braught the participle of a present to a desponent hortatrixy, vindicatively... (*FW* 269.29)

The verb contained in 'hortatrixy' is a well-known paradigm for the deponent, *hortor* or *hortari*, passive in appearance, in the active sense of exhort or incite.

Being 'one of those mixed middlings' and volatile, unstable, formally not always distinguished from the passive, the middle voice tended to disappear as a separate category, though not as an inherent assignment in language. If we want to express medial participation in English, we usually choose a form in which the subject finds itself at either end of the inflected verb. My sentence did just that: 'the subject finds itself...' Characteristic is a bending (*flectere*) back (*re-*) upon the agent, so we call it 're-flexive'.

Stephen's theory can be rephrased in grammatical metaphor. One of its corner-stones is the report that Shakespeare the actor took the part of King Hamlet's ghost. A premise is that Shakespeare played, acted, himself in this role, and from this a whole algebra of equations is extrapolated. Of Shakespeare, named Will, the 'unremitting intellect is... Iago ceaselessly willing that the moor in him shall suffer' (*U* 9.1023). This is the activity and passivity of suffering.' Shakespeare's errors are 'volitional'; yet he is pained because he was 'overborne in a cornfield' (*U* 9.456) by Anne who 'hath a way' over others' will. So—always according to Stephen's self-projections—Shakespeare, partly driven, in varied reiteration wills himself into his writing.

Hamlet is, in Mallarmé's phrasing, '*lisant au livre de lui-même*, don't you know, *reading the book of himself.*' He does this, we are told, walking—in reflexive French: '*il se promène*' (*U* 9.114).

Stephen may vary his views in terms of scholastic actuality and possibility: 'He found in the world without as actual what was in his world within as possible', and he adduces a saying of Maeterlinck's '*If Socrates leave his house today he will find the sage seated on his doorstep*' (*U* 9.1041–3). The 'sage', reciprocally, is Socrates, the subject.

We walk through ourselves, meeting robbers, ghosts, giants, old men, young men, wives, widows, brothers-in-love, but always meeting ourselves. (*U* 9.1044–6)

The Shakespeare posited by Stephen is that of a compulsive and highly versatile auto-bio-grapher of enigmatic genius. Psychologically, the life acted and suffered and partly self-determined, can hardly help writing itself out into the plays. Autobiography is tautologically medial. So is a basic assumption of a writer's biography: the personality must be reflected, repeated, modified, conjugated, 'worked off', in the work. The consubstantiality of any writer's life and writings looks like a medial truism. Whitman's 'One's self I sing' could be seen as the traditional epic invocation translated into the middle voice and into English near-reflexivity.

In the following presentation I will deflect the middle voice (often using the Latin term *medium*) as an analogy or descriptive handle for Joycean features that are already well known, in what I hope will be mainly quick illustrative flashes.

What would grammar matter? (*D* 66)

'The Boarding House' may serve as a convenient sample. Consider dominant Mrs Mooney, who manipulates two lives with a firm hand, as almost exclusively expressed in the active voice, with purposeful active verbs. And isn't her voice active! She even does the speaking for others, her own last word is on behalf of Doran: 'Mr Doran wants to speak to you' (*D* 69). Mr Doran, in the role of victim (as he would see himself), is largely and momentously passive, in behaviour and in grammar: he is being sent for and being decided on; even his 'wants' are expressed *for* him: 'he was being had' (*D* 66). Polly Mooney, the strategic intermediary, conducts herself a good deal in the middle voice: 'She knew she was being watched... She would put an end to herself.' In her own little scene towards the end, 'she dried her eyes... refreshed her eyes... She looked at herself in the mirror.' She falls into a revery, withdraws into her own memories and visions. When her story is continued into *Ulysses*, the brief sketch of 'the sleepwalking bitch... the bumbailiff's daughter', retains its typical quasi-reflexive syntax even in hyperbole: 'without a stitch on her, exposing her person' (*U* 12.401).

Bob Doran finds fault with Polly's vulgar grammar: 'sometimes she said "I seen"' (*D* 66). What she means is, actively, I have seen, but her wording is passive, as though she were using a Latin deponent. Her 'being seen', of course, is literally an ingredient in the seduction (a scene mainly hidden from us). Seduction, as active strategy, passive entrapment, or some medial involvement, of the main persons, is one of the story's themes. Up to a point, the grammatical distribution works; if taken too far into a system, it would become as absurd and constrictive as all such attempts.

Stephanoumenos

We also find the detached artist-God in Stephen's esthetic proclamation on either side of the verb:

The artist, like the God of the creation, remains within or behind or beyond or above his handiwork... (*P* 215)

and no matter how refined out of existence, or indifferent, the pose expressive of such indifference is manifested by the type of verbal form which in Greek grammar is always instanced as typical middle voice (*louomai tous podas*: I wash my feet = myself): 'paring his fingernails' (*P* 215); which becomes, naturally, a reflexive form in French, '*en train de se limer les ongles*'.

The would-be artist who thinks like that is to declare, programmatically:

I will not serve that in which I no longer believe... and I will try to express myself in some mode of life or art as freely as I can and as wholly as I can. (*P* 224)

Our stress is on 'myself'. The triad of arms to be used in defense ends on 'cunning', and it is oddly fitting that the Greek prototype name Daidalos translates into 'cunning'. Dedalus using cunning (the skill of being *daidalos*) is a piece of philological reflexivity.

One of the classmates' appellations, '*Bous Stephanoumenos*', will be repeated and remembered in *Ulysses*, where it leads to another Greek participle of echoing ending and like form, '*Autontimoroumenos*' (*U* 9.939). The latter is close to the title of a play that Terence adapted from Menander. The title is conspicuously reflexive: it moves the self into the accusative case: *auton-*; the 'Self-Tormentor', as it is translated. The Greek participle written into *Ulysses* is in the middle voice. Tormenting and being tormented: so is Stephen. The verb *timoreo* (active) did not originally mean torment, but 'to help' and then 'to revenge'. In this collection we also see a change rung on the *Hamlet* theme. Prince Hamlet and Stephen do take revenge, but in part *on* themselves; an unvoiced middle participle brings this out.

Stephen's entry into *Ulysses* is revealing. He is first an object when Mulligan catches sight of him and goes into a mimetic routine of exorcism. Then the perspective changes:

Stephen Dedalus, displeased and sleepy, leaned his arms on the top of the staircase.

He leans part of himself (or, in reflexive French: '*il s'inclina*') onto the world outside. Soon after he will 'lean his palm against his brow' (*U* 1.100). In 'Eveline' such leaning had a strongly passive air, here it expresses a more in-between stage. Notice what Stephen is: 'displeased'. No doubt the overbearing Mulligan displeases him, perhaps also the raving Englishman in the tower; but the word mainly expresses an internal disposition. In translation such medial forms usually come out twofold: passive (as in '*contrarié*' or '*contrariato*'), or in partial self-inducement: '*malhumorado—misslaunig—med mishag*'. In *A Portrait* Stephen had been characterized twice as 'displeased'—one of his habitual moods. It is hard to imagine him pleased. The opening beat, 'displeased', is in the right medium. The epithet relates him to Telemachos, who was beset by afflictions from outside, and it also differentiates him from the Greek role and prepares the way, psychologically and grammatically, for *Autontimoroumenos*.

Psychogrammar

On a much grander scale, we may redescribe what has been Bloom's affliction. He suffers his wife's adultery, is being injured and victimized, yet he also co-determines this state of the affair, he connives and goes out of his way to make it possible. All of this is, in the characterization of the middle voice, action also 'for himself'. The hyperballistics of the Circean mode transform such attitudes into large stage action and passion. In a climactic scene Bloom watches and applauds Boylan's copulation with his wife through a keyhole in twisted enjoyment of cuckoldry, being 'bawd and cuckold' (*U* 9.1021). The situation leads right into the vision of Shakespeare's face in the mirror: the optical multiplicity involves Stephen and

Bloom and, in widening perspective, the creator of the scene and its voyeuristic readers. It is an interreflective node of voices and visions, a muddle of reciprocity.

Bloom's medial actions do not always, as we recall with divergent evaluations, conform to the stereotypes of sexism. It is on record that the male has predominantly been equated with active action, the female with passive submission. Something of this sexual grammar is mediated in an Ithacan passage,

the natural grammatical transition by inversion involving no alteration of sense of an aorist preterite proposition (parsed as masculine subject, monosyllabic onomatopoetic transitive verb with direct feminine object) from the active voice into its correlative aorist preterite proposition (parsed as feminine subject, auxiliary verb and quasimonosyllabic onomatopoetic past participle with complementary masculine agent) in the passive voice. (*U* 17.2217)

Into such a system, which Dublin society at the turn of the century would no doubt uphold, Joyce inserted a middle way which manifests itself first, mildly, in Bloom's sympathy, or compassion, for women: he can put himself in their position. This makes him an outsider, particularly in the male congregation in the maternity hospital. In a transitive sense, Bloom is not very active. Activity is the role of the Boylans and the Mulligans who in turn are not too sensitive and, on the whole, lack empathy. When critics, superior by self-appointment, judge Bloom a failure or decree, for instance, that throughout his day he takes the 'wrong choices' (not going home to assert a possessive masculinity), it is generally done within a transitive patriarchal framework.

Bloom, the reproach goes, is 'one of those mixed middlings... Lying up in the hotel... once a month with a headache like a totty with her courses' (*U* 12.1658). In 'Circe' such traits are externalized and Bloom is turned into yet another paradigm, 'a finished example of the new womanly man' (*U* 15.1798). This puts him midway between the 'manly man' of Gerty MacDowell's imagination, and how very soon after she views herself as a 'womanly woman' (*U* 13.210, 435). There is then, as Bloom asserts in one of his defense speeches, 'a medium in all things' (*U* 15.878). He is not explaining Greek grammar by a Latin term, but echoing Horace's familiar '*est modus in rebus*' ('there is a measure in all things'), and asking for moderation. But medium he is, all the same, also between male and female.

Circean androgyny enables the newly generated finished example to finish the example by giving birth to eight male children. It so happens that the number eight is also that of Molly Bloom's 'sentences' in her chapter, eight verbal units generated by the book's representative woman: there may be a numerical correspondence. Bloom's children are 'respectably dressed and wellconducted' (*U* 15.1824): both epithets are in the middle voice, in particular 'wellconducted': it can be construed as active or medio-passive.

Androgynous features animate *Finnegans Wake* and extend across genders or religions to appellations like:

In the name of Annah the Almaziful, the Everliving, the Bringer of Plurabilities, haloed be her eve, her singtime sung, her rill be run, unhemmed as it is uneven (*FW* 104.1)

in which august divinities are feminized and brought into line with Eve, or in which Moslem and Christian prayer become assimilated to the beginning of *Finnegans Wake* itself, with 'rill be run' echoing 'riverrun'. The equation of Annah, ALP, Eve, with Allah and the Lord looks like a cosmogenetic middle voice. All of this ties in with the observation that in Latin grammar verbs as well as nouns have *genus*, gender. Active, passive, and medium, are '*genera*'.

medial monologue

The interior monologue once seemed the most striking feature of *Ulysses*, the one that attracted most of the serious attention. It is a kind of speech not addressed to an outside object; the subject, as it were, is talking to and often about itself. In a very loose and yet coincidentally precise sense, Bloom, Stephen, and Molly become reflexive verbs. They mirror the outside world but also, and at times exclusively, their own selves, 'bend back' (re-flect) on themselves. In Homeric diction 'thinking' is often expressed by a person addressing his (her) heart, or breast, or mind: 'I think' is 'I said to myself'. By a definition that is almost grammatical and, again, tautological, everything thus expressed is 'subjective'. What is perceived is subjected to the perceiver's nature. One of the narrative advantages is the economy of such characterization that is two-directed: towards the world without *and* within: 'She understands all she wants to. Vindictive too. Cruel. Her nature. Curious mice never squeal. Seem to like it' (*U* 4.27). This tells us something about cats, and mice, but even more about Bloom (at a later stage we may find, moreover, that some of Bloom's attitude towards his wife is already caught in this observation). We can move, in other words, towards the thing said (thought) and towards the sayer (thinker). We generally recognize the reflector, can tell Bloom from Stephen or, by extrapolation, deduce the author himself who, biographically, is all to all, Bloom and Stephen and Molly and Lenehan. All the works are, truistically, *pièce de Joyce.*

The internal middle voice appears in a very brief flash on the first page: '*Chrysostomos*'. Insofar as it is a naming (see above), it characterizes the person named as well as the namer, indicates something about his erudition as well as his state of mind. The interior monologue's official initiation takes place fittingly at the moment when, looking at the mirror held out to him, Stephen begins internally to speak to himself: 'As he and others see me' (*U* 1.136). At this point perspective, pronouns, tenses, all have changed. The reflexion is optical, psychological and grammatical. The self seen in the mirror reflects back: 'Who chose this face for me? ... It asks me too': the face that is being addressed reciprocally asks back. Interestingly enough, Stephen sees himself when he 'bent forward'; bending forward is the mirror reflexion of bending (*flectere*) backward.

Gerty MacDowell, whose thoughts are presented more indirectly, also 'bent forward quickly', after 'being bent so far back' (*U* 13.742, 728); but her physical action is described more as leaning: 'she leaned back' we read several times (*U* 13.695, 715; 'ever so far', 717, 941), or she 'had to lean back' (744). We know that this enables her, medio-passively, to be seen in a particular way. Reciprocally, however, Bloom in his turn 'was leaning back', he 'coloured like a girl', also reciprocally (*U* 13.743). All these bendings and leanings are not connected with the thinking that goes on but with the chapter's activities which are more solitary (or 'ipsorelative') than other-directed (or 'aliorelative', as in *U* 17.1350).

Physically, the associations of the middle voice can be extended to masturbation. Whether through necessity or fastidiousness, the subject also becomes its own object. In 'Nausicaa', the arena for such economy or auto-reciprocity, Gerty and Bloom are not so much transitive verbs with each other as objects, at least not each other's direct objects, except visually. Something as erotic and tactile as 'the quick hot touch of his handsome lips' occurs only in Gerty's imagination (*U* 13.708). Bloom wets and stains himself. Even his watch has stopped. In Greek such intransitive stopping would be in the middle voice (*pauesthai* as against an active *pauein*, to stop): 'Funny my watch stopped at half past four' (*U* 13.846); the watch, clearly, ceased its activity, it 'stopped itself'; what Bloom considers 'funny' seems to be that whatever went on at home had some enigmatic influence and, actively, stopped it. In this view or superstition, the watch, like Bloom, acts and is acted on.

Both Gerty and Bloom reflect, often in reciprocal convergences. Nothing is passed across but looks, and 'a kind of language between them'. Gerty MacDowell, 'lost in thought' or 'wrapped in thought', as the medial phrases have it, acts, in terms of the grammatical descriptions indicated before, mainly 'on herself or for herself'. She is conscious of her effects on others, admiration that turns back on her. With the rest of humanity she shares the delight in the 'lovely reflection which the mirror gave back to her' (*U* 13.162). Her circumambient style shows her as the victim of forces that have shaped her. They range from society's conventions and imperatives to the injunctions of advertising and the illusions of compensatory literature. But she is also their subject and, in her own conditioned turn, now regenerates the same attitudes in cosmetic circularity. She reshapes life in the style that shaped her. Lest this sound too condescending, let me add that I believe such medial conditioning holds true for most of us in all cultural contexts. Stephen, for example, is similarly co-determined by the catholicism he projects in his very efforts of rejection. I can't answer for any of you, as for me, Gerty MacDowell '*c'est moi.*'

The chapter's events are set off against the 'voice of prayer' emanating from the nearby church, and the refrain of the litany, 'pray for us', is woven into the foreground. Prayer is a model for the middle voice; in practice it often amounts to wishing something for oneself: *ora pro nobis.* The Greek verb was naturally medial: *euchesthai*, both in Homer and in the New Testament. Bloom notes the repetition of 'Pray for us. And pray for us. And pray for us' and links it to his profession: 'Same thing with ads. Buy from us. And buy from us' (*U* 13.1122). Advertisements proclaim themselves; what Catesby's Cork Lino or Plumtree's Potted Meat spell out is, above all, 'Buy me!'

Middler the Holy Ghost

The economy of heaven, androgyny, and a masturbatory Everyman Immorality Play are combined with gusto by Bullocky Mulligan at the end of 'Scylla and Charybdis'. But we have never been far from the consubstantial intricacies that obsess Stephen. His silent creed looks like a travesty of a Divine middle voice:

He Who Himself begot middler the Holy Ghost and Himself sent Himself, Agenbuyer, between Himself and others... sitteth on the right hand of His Own Self... (*U* 9.493)

('on the right hand of His Own Self' has come true of the synoptic text of *Ulysses*). All of the middling has been transposed to patristic, Sabellian absurdity and incestuous economy. Unmistakable are the mocking reflexivity and the trailing, echoing Selves. 'Middler the Holy Ghost'—in a sweeping generalization one might yoke the third person of the Holy Trinity to my grammatical analogy in the conjugation of an all-powerful Verb. But in cosmogonic reticence I refrain from such comprehensive usurpation and merely indicate possible directions for research.

Even so, the heretical bending back on itself exaggerates ideas of creation. The world, as some of our myths have it, came into being by the emanating voice of a god, by his speaking. In the Greek transformation of Genesis (whose original Hebrew phrasing would demand separate, corrective attention) the Creator's voice was, inevitably, a middle one. The first word ever uttered is

Genetheto (medium imperative)

and it is followed (and *followed*, it would seem, in most languages) by the noun: *genetheto phos*, *fiat lux*, let there be light! The verb, preceding, brings the noun into existence. In a partial imitation Stephen begins one of his verbal creations (the one that recalls Joyce's first prose work and may also represent some of *Ulysses*) with an echo of Genesis: 'Dubliners... Let there be life' (*U* 7.922, 930).

The effect of the imperative expresses itself in a change of the verb form: '*kai egeneto phos: et facta est lux*—And there was light.' The verb used, '*genetheto-egeneto*', is the paradigmatic type of the medium, *genesthai*, the verb of becoming; it has no other voice (the Latin equivalent, *factum esse*, looks passive). This is not some odd coincidence, but the nature of the concept. Genesis, by definition and by essence, is medial becoming. The author of the world, it implies, also put himself into the oral work and participates in it. The naming processes immediately following have already been mentioned: words create the world, and within this new world, words have to be created to distinguish things and doings in genetic reciprocity.

In the rereading of the original account by Christianity—which of course projected itself into the reading—the aspect of becoming is circumstantiated. St John puts it like this: 'All things were made by him [the word, *logos*].' Again the passive English construction does duty for a medial '*panta di' autou egeneto*' (John 1.3). St John's memorable opening is as full as it must be of variations of *gignesthai* or *genesis* (in fact the first gospel begins as the book of *genesis*: 'Biblos geneseos Iesou Christou' (*Liber generationis Jesu Christi*, 'the book of the generation', Matt. 1.1). The term 'onlybegotten', which reverberated down patristic controversies and is taken up in *Ulysses*, belongs to the same

cluster, *mono-genes* (John 1.14, 18, 3.16, 18, etc.). 'Begetter' and
'begotten' are recalled by Stephen Dedalus. An approximation of the
consequential term *mono-genes* also appears in *Finnegans Wake*, with
just one letter changed that makes all the genetic difference—a Y for
an E—the last chapter personifies: 'if Monogynes his is or hers Dian-
der' (*FW* 613.33). This refers ostensibly to botanical generation
('monogynia' and 'diandria' are the first two classes in a sexual
system); genders are mixed, 'his or hers', and 'Monogynes' changes a
theological 'his', a divine male 'monogenes' to a female shape, *gyne*
(or *gune*), woman. The theological inversion is matched by one of the
usual Wakean constellations of one central male facing two girls: we
now find one woman, '*mono-gyne*' and two ('*di*') men ('*aner, andro-*').

Creating, begetting, giving birth, changing across categories make
up the economy of *Finnegans Wake*. There is no middle voice in
Hiberno-English, but countless muddled phrasings, like 'Creator he
has created for his creatured ones a creation' (*FW* 29.14). The sentence echoes and elaborates on its own subject, or its verb; again we
have reciprocity and mirroring self-perpetuation; or semantic masturbation. In 'understanding' such sentences we move forward and
backward: this is just what Latin *reciprocare* meant, going backward
(*re*) and forward (*pro*). So is the recirculatory technique of reading
the *Wake*, 'preprocession and proprecession' (*FW* 156.8), or a 'rotary
processus and its reestablishment of reciprocities' (*FW* 304 L3). This
essay too is an exercise in reciprocity.

At the opening of the learned, studious tenth chapter we seem to
be looking for our place:

we haply return... to befinding ourself

and we find ourselves (or in German, *befinden uns*) once more reflec-
tively on either side of the verb:

when old is said in one and maker mates with made. (*FW* 261.5)

The incestuous mating leads, in more echoing self-perpetuation
('having conned the cones...'), to the Seven Wonders of the World.
More narrowly, in the mythography of *Finnegans Wake*, the creator
sinned himself into the world by an original act of medial self-pollu-
tion, as James S. Atherton long ago pointed out. This creator is

the first old wugger of himself in the flesh. (*FW* 79.2)[8]

The 'old wugger' incarnates 'himself in the flesh'. The reflexive
duplication of 'wuggering'—offsetting the rather sterile act of buggery

implied—is similar to the *Wake*'s first clearly medial verb, the 'rocks' that 'exaggerated themselse' and went 'doublin their mumper' (*FW* 3.7). Part of the activity of exaggerating is directed towards others ('else'), part bends back on the subject ('themsel[ves]').

laughing-like to himself

I have wuggered myself into a hyper-emphasis of a grammatical ploy, what the Greek called the middle *diathesis*, the Romans the *genus medium*. The whole point could have been made, more briefly, by focusing on Joyce's first and last work. In 'The Sisters' a declining priest wants to reshape an impressionable boy in his own likeness; perhaps he obliquely tries to continue himself through the disciple. Professionally he listens to the confession of others, yet in the boy's dream and a reversal of roles, the priest seems to be confessing. In confession we say something to someone about ourselves; appropriately the Latin word for it is a deponent again, a medio-passive *confiteor* (the word is repeated in the partly auto-confessional *Portrait*: 78.9, 82.17, 143.31). *Confieri* (infinitive form) is derived from *fari* (to speak) of which it is a special, retroactive, variant. 'The Sisters' is a story in which the same boy later retells the events. Our last glimpse is of Father Flynn 'sitting up by himself in the dark of his confession-box, wide-awake and laughing-like softly to himself' (*D* 18). The distortive confession is repeated, as if for emphasis: 'Wide-awake and laughing-like to himself' towards the end, and we know that 'there was something wrong with him'.

Sitting, laughing to himself—that is one of Nora's reports of her husband composing *Finnegans Wake*, which has also been considered a twisted confession where much has gone wrong. It contains a 'convulsion box', a 'confisieur' and 'confussion' (*FW* 261.F3, 531.2, 353.25). It is a work that repeatedly speaks about itself, to itself, or tangentially admits that it is 'a letter selfpenned to one's other' (*FW* 489.33). This also ties in with the dream analogy of the *Wake* (which, to some of its commentators, who seem to know what a dream is, achieves axiomatic status). Most interpreters of dreams agree that whatever they contain, the dreamer is also voicing him/herself in intricate guises and that dreams are a tortuous kind of confession.

revoicings

With considerable metaphorical latitude I have been applying a grammatical analogy in free and easy dispersion. Analogy is what Joyce works with. On a small scale his Revoicings take the form of all those evocations of prior phrasings, often the most memorable ones of literature, sometimes the tritest of ready-made stereotypes. They may be formulas, clearly marked 'quotations', or the most evanescent of 'allusions'. There is a medial sense in them, insofar as only a portion of their semantic energies is directed toward external actuality. The rest bends back, or retroflects, on their origin or the fashion of their articulation. The ghosts of former texts are called up, called up for readers in proportion to their familiarity with them. Some attention then turns back on the source, literary or otherwise. In *Ulysses* the method is heralded by Buck Mulligan who exhibits, from the start, remarkable mimetic and recitative skills. One reason why some of our initial effort is required to figure out the external setting is that most of Mulligan's second- (perhaps golden-) mouthed pronouncements deflect our attention away from what referential direction they have. A ceremoniously intoned '*introibo ad altare Dei*' tells us less about what is really going on than about the history and proper context of the words quoted. A tension is set up between the two.

Quotations brought to bear upon 'reality' also detract from it. This is in the nature of the title 'Ulysses', or of an entire chapter like 'Oxen of the Sun', where indeed the literary parading so far has engaged most of our critical endeavours. Each Revoicing (which here subsumes all evocations of prior texts) contains a feature of the middle voice, standing midway between what is being pointed out and its own peculiar manner of pointing. Each quotation in part epiphanizes itself. '*Thalatta! Thalatta!*' (*U* 1.80) refers to the visible sea, but also to a speaker who flaunts classical knowledge: it looks forward to an object, and backwards towards a secondary quoter (Mulligan) and beyond to a primary author (Xenophon), and, from another angle, to one more adventurous journey with a return, analogous to the one of Odysseus. When Bloom enters his back garden in the morning and we read

No sound. Perhaps hanging clothes out to dry. The maid was in the garden. Fine morning. (*U* 4.472)

he is taking stock of what he sees and hears. But 'The maid was in the garden' does not belong to this order. At least to a majority of those initiated (having a nursery rhyme in their ears), this is not a comment on a maid's presence. The maid leads a mere fictional, evocative existence 'in the garden', she is in another grammatical mood, a subjunctive wish-fulfillment. The quotation—if recognized—displays itself as a medium. It refers back to a cultural the-

saurus and applies one of its items to an analogous occasion. If we do
not know the sentence as an echo we may misread the situation. 'The
maid was in the garden' means, if anything, its own opposite: a conspicuous, frustrating absence. The quotation fills the vacuum of 'No
sound.' It utters mainly its existence as language re-used.

In this allusive function, language still transitively refers to something outside: there is a possible transition to an actual situation. In
its self-expressive, autophanic, effects, however, it moves closer to
the middle voice. Semantic energies are divided as well as multi-
plied. Language itself, and by extension Literature, can be said to
have a middle voice, mediating between an external objective, and a
preening self-consciousness. Joyce, as usual, carries both functions—
referential potency and the retroflection of utterance—to extremes.

nominal shorthand

In my confession I have said nothing that might not have been
known before. Do not write this statement off as modesty—the same
claim could be made about *Finnegans Wake*. I just tried to use a
point of view (taken from classical languages) to subsume a variety of
Joycean features that might otherwise have little in common. The terminology chosen tried to do more justice to Joyce's kinetics than
what nominal stability might describe. There are, naturally, excellent
reasons for still resorting to the fixation that nouns tend to indicate.
Certain situations require classification or a provisional foothold. We
need reassuring support as we need the solidity of a verifiable city of
Dublin of 1904 to get our bearings and as a backdrop for the elusive
narrative processes in *Ulysses*. The format of Notes or Annotations,
of brief glosses, allows for little else. Nominal shorthand saves time
and space. The discursive articulation of verbal motion is laborious
and hardly ever completed: a Protean sense of not-quite-thereness
always remains.

As long as we know about the necessity for convenient simplification, the danger is minimal. Take the practical requirement for a concise commentary on *Finnegans Wake*. As an example we hold up for
inspection the first word in the text that is clearly not English:

by a commodius vicus of recirculation. (*FW* 3.2)

Annotations says—and must say, reductively—'Vico'. We have a
right to expect this sort of information, not to give it would be wrong.
But the abbreviated near-truth is less justified when we deal with
credulous novices. In a first learning process such premature label-

ling (nothing but the name 'Vico') is unhelpful or even impedimental. For 'vicus' (lower case) should be treated in its own right, or else brought back into the contextual currency (the English language) from which it sets itself off. In its *prima facie* inassimilability it acts as an imperative for transformation: translate me! (or else, it leads us to different environs). A Latin dictionary would offer several interconnected meanings: 'district of a town, village, neighbourhood, street, hamlet'. Out of this spectrum, 'street' or 'road' seems to fit best, for we are casting about for something to move in ('brings us back'). But even so, we have to discard—or hold in suspense—all the other possible meanings: this is already semantic work in progress. A diachronic view of language as growth through time (remember 'past Eve and Adam's') would assemble cognates like the English 'wick' (in the sense of hamlet, village, mostly in place names) and, in particular, the Greek *oikos* (house), and it would lead us back to an original root, deduced from existing words, which in this case would sound, of all things, like *weik*—very close to how we pronounce (*Finnegans*) *Wake*. Such a phonetic coincidence need not be belaboured as part of an intended meaning, but some readers might be intrigued that an early non-normative word can recirculate to an element of the book's title. What an etymological excursion into history reveals is that development, becoming, time, are involved. That oddity 'vicus' acts like a signpost and takes us elsewhere (and perhaps back to the context).

Going along the road of wakeful meanings, we will, in the course of further input, also arrive at Giambattista Vico, eighteenth-century Italian philosopher appreciated by Joyce. For the initiated the click may set in as early as 'recirculation'. At some stage and time, recognition *turns* 'vicus' *into* 'vico' as a plausible matching. Once this has occurred, supportive hindsight evidence then may become overwhelming (with the stress again on becoming): It was words of the type and ending like 'vic-*us*' that tended to turn into Italian words like 'vic-*o*' (though this one does not exist, Latin *commodus*, on the other hand, became *comodo*). We may recall that the philosopher of temporal patternings used Roman history and Latin etymologies to illustrate recurrencies and changes. *Finnegans Wake* anachronistically inverts the process. We can retranslate, by a similar leap across languages, 'riverrun' into a favourite Viconian term, *ricorso* (the flowing back, run, of a river, with the phoneme *ri-* as an external common link). Many additional roads can be travelled towards the particular goal. One is Vico road in Dalkey, obligingly incurvated, a parochial accident to be exploited by Joyce on further occasions. An instrumental preposition like '*by* a commodius vicus' would properly take the ablative case in Latin and change to 'vico'—but this would be our doing. 'Vico' in fact originates through our cooperation: the textual irritations prompt us into hermeneutic activity.

If you insist that, all right, many semantic manipulations may be necessary to construe an Italian name out of a Latin noun, but once that is done, on all recirculatory readings there will be an instant identification, and no further quibblings, then you simply neglect how much 'vicus' on all occasions also visibly protests against such violation. Wakean vital gestures towards dissociation are disregarded a trifle too complacently. 'Vicus', in other words, may well strive to collide with 'Vico', but with equal validity it aims to escape from the restriction. Neither turn should be ignored in our scope, nor the awareness that it is a matter of turning, of conversion. Vico, as a reductive name, is a valid and poor interpretation of 'vicus' (among other things simply because it leaves out 'us'), but it is an excellent verb to conjugate the *Wake*.

Nothing new has been said, nothing for which external sources, protographs, archetypes had to be called in, not even a smattering of little Latin and less Greek: other catalysts would have done just as well. Nothing has been put forward that might not have been noticed from immediate observation, unaided, by verbal communication with the text.

The most programmatically pertinent verb of them all may be *reading*. We know from experience it is both transitive and self-reflexive. What we gather, select, recognize, rearrange, construe, from the alphabetical configurations, we remake in our own likeness. It is no secret that some likenesses are more rewarding and conveyable than others, and, for better or worse, at a Symposium most likenesses are speaking—our vocal confessions—with a fair proportion of self-display. Leopold Bloom exemplifies one of the pitfalls when he hastily projects his own name into a word that for a few letters looks alike:

Bloo... Me? No.
Blood[9] of the Lamb. (*U* 8.8)

In his zeal and inclination—misreading the throwaway of himself—he has forestalled us all. It is to his credit that he corrects himself in time. We don't always. That is one reason why we depend on each other's self-pennings. And one reason why I have argued in favour of interaction, at our conferences, against long, monologous, medial, 'major' addresses, with all the tedium between active oral pontification and passive auditive suffering.

In the beginning, we have learned, was the joy. The enjoyment that makes life, perhaps, almost worth reading. It is a reading, also, of ourselves; but the selves may become a bit more aware, or refined, or sensitive, in the process, in all those processes that, when old is said in one, have gathered us here together and will continue to bring us back to Joyce—the Verb.

NOTES

1   Benstock, Shari and Bernard, *Who's He When He's at Home: A James Joyce Directory* (Urbana, Chicago, London: University of Illinois Press 1980).

2   'Usurper' (as in *U* 1.744) derives from a verb *usurpare*, one of whose meanings is 'to call names'.

3   One of the abbreviations used in the footnotes, *stet*, in the old code of the typesetters is an injunction, 'Let it stand!'

4   Such documents are called 'witnesses', not just passive products of writing or printing, but live persons actively making statements that have to hold up to cross-examination.

5   The conditional nature of the text that has been established is well in evidence in Richard Ellmann's wording: 'What Gabler aims at is an ideal text, such as Joyce would have constructed in ideal conditions.' 'Preface', *Ulysses: The Corrected Text*, Hans Walter Gabler and Wolfhard Steppe (eds) (New York: Random House 1986), x.

6   'Afterword', *Ulysses: The Corrected Text*, 649.

7   The verb 'to suffer', active in form, is medio-passive. 'Stephen suffered [Mulligan] to pull out and hold up on show by its corner a dirty crumpled handkerchief' (*U* 1.70). The transitivity is deceptive and reciprocal: something is done to Stephen and he suffers from it, he also suffers it. But there is self-involvement in the action. The Latin for suffering, *pati, patior*, is naturally a deponent; its derivatives are *passio* and our 'passive', the name for the *genus* which translated Greek '*pathetikos*', from *pathos* or a verb *paschein*, in whose system active and medio-passive forms intermingle.

8   Atherton, James S., *The Books at the Wake* (London: Faber & Faber 1959), 196.

9   Walter W. Skeat with some reservation ('doubtfully') mentions the root 'blow' for 'blood', which would connect it to 'bloom'. *An Etymological Dictionary of the English Language* (Oxford 1909).

JOYCEAN PROVECTIONS

Is there any thing whereof it may be said, See, this is new? (*Eccl.* 1:10)

The purpose of this presentation is not to say anything new but to subsume, under a specific focus, part of what we already know and to suggest how we might describe the graph of a recurrent, basic, Joycean motion and show some of its pervasive actualizations. This motion is, in short, an excessive bias, a tendency to overdo, to break out of norms, to go beyond.

Take the beginning of *A Portrait*. Whether we read it as a novel attempt at imitative form, as psychological realism, or whatever,

he had a hairy face—*O, the geen wothe botheth*—When you wet the bed first it is warm then it gets cold—*Pull out his eyes, Apologise*. (*P* 7–8)[1]

these passages, in their abrupt immediacy, without conventional exposition, are surrounded by the invisible broken shells of narrative norms and restrictions. It is a fair guess that *Stephen Hero* did not begin quite like that, and that some former version was changed in ways that must have appeared excessive at the time, that must have exceeded some convention. And so, at each turn of the development, something changed in degree and in kind. It is a long way from the early epiphanic sketches to the exuberance of *Finnegans Wake*. This exuberance or excess, an insistent drive out of—beyond—confines that had otherwise been largely taken for granted, will be looked into.

Joyce's own life-style was characterized by constant movement: Dublin—Trieste—Zürich—Paris are the best-known stations. Each

place involved numerous changes of address. Joyce did not stay put,
he kept moving, and not always out of external necessity. The restlessness is obvious. Literary prototypes like Daidalos or Odysseus
were on the move as well. In such cases the home life inevitably suffers, but restlessness also provides the stuff epics are made of. More
to the point is the way the works transformed themselves, none of
them repeating their predecessors; none of them, by the same token,
could have been predicted; each one is *sui generis*. We have no way
of guessing what Joyce might have written after *Finnegans Wake*. So
Joyce's dynamic development is well in evidence.

It is, by way of illustration, appropriate that Joyce's one central
prototype would be named 'Bloom'. Within that choice—which was
certainly overdetermined—*Bloom* is essentially something growing,
blossoming, budding to withering, with a whole range of possibilities
from an emigrant Virag to a Dongiovannish Henry Flower, *via* Don
Poldo de la Flora, Professor Blumenduft, or L. Boom as a typographical mischance; with arabesques-like *bloomers*; derivatives like
blooming and *booming* and further flourishes. It extends to the lush
language of flowers, which is shortened to the 'language of flow', or
else the 'language of flow', as in 'flowing' (*U* 11.298, both)—to name
just a few exfoliations.[2] We may appreciate these ramifications when
we consider that no such offshoots are derivable from the corresponding name, *Dedalus*.

enormous elaboration of the material

your Cork legs are running away with you. (*U* 7.730)

Early critics were outspoken about Joyce's enormities and excesses;
among a later generation, S.L. Goldberg was a very perceptive counsel for the prosecution: for him, Joyce was constantly overreaching
and had to fail in doing so (fail, of course, according to hidebound
norms, tacit or stated). According to Goldberg, it is a critical commonplace that Joyce 'laboured some things too much', time and
again, for example, 'lapsing into mere parody',[3] and little else, losing
a sense of sane proportion. In *The Classical Temper* the lapses are
detailed: what Joyce 'drifted towards'—and clearly shouldn't have—
are 'romantic infinities' and 'profundities'; 'infinities' suggest a sur-
plus and 'profundities' seem to be a mere appearance.[4]

What is wrong with *Ulysses* 'is obvious: [1] the enormous elaboration of the material, [2] the rather pretentious parade of literary
machinery, [3] the encumbering and mortifying boredom.'[5] Put more

concisely, *Ulysses* (and *Finnegans Wake*, for which Goldberg does not particularly care either) violates some middle-of-the-road (sane, life-enhancing) standard. Joyce, in short, went *too far*, did *too much* of many bad things, was '*e-normous*'—that is, went *outside* of some implied norm. The charge has often been repeated. If put neutrally, it is wholly justified.

If we focus not so much on the results but on the impetus behind them, one way of rephrasing all of the above is that Joyce, man and author, got carried away. The man got carried away when he went to court in wartime Zürich over a pair of trousers; when he appealed to the highest possible authorities; when he went campaigning for the tenor John Sullivan in Paris, when he persevered in a campaign against a Frankfurt newspaper that had erroneously inserted his name.

The author inevitably got carried away in his works. The addition of 'The Dead' changed scope, dimension, reverberation of *Dubliners,* a collection of stories that, even without it, was peculiar enough to frighten publishers in two countries—and changed the English Short Story. A slightly amorphous manuscript, *Stephen Hero*, was abandoned and reshaped into a novel of excessively imitative forms. Edward Garnett thought it, in a famous reader's report, frankly honest, 'unconventional', full of 'longueurs', without restraint or proportion, very much in need of pruning.[6] Joyce lost admirers all along the rocky way to the publication of *Ulysses*, and more so when he was engaged in his *Work in Progress*. The progress was a way fewer were prepared to go with him. Former friends and supporters, notably his brother Stanislaus, refused to be carried away when he was.

Being *carried away* determines a large part of Joyce. In writing, he seems to have been swept along by what he was doing, as though he were the victim of powerful impulses, which could be seen as an obsession, like making 'Anna Livia Plurabelle' more watery by fluvial accretions. But of course it was his own doing. 'Being carried away' looks like a passive description of a very active urge. As it seems in Bloom's musings on marital entanglements:

if he regarded her with affection, carried away by a wave of folly. (*U* 16.1387)

Careers, like Parnell's, can be ruined by such excess, whether it consists of acting or being acted on. The theme is one of the oldest in tragedy: Achilles or Othello succumb to some passion; hubris is one of the oldest dramatic forces; in another framework it becomes the subject of comedy, which exaggerates human traits. Naturally some

Joycean plots follow the familiar literary pattern, as in *Dubliners*:

Mrs Sinico in 'A Painful Case' gets carried away, twice, both times with painful results. An inanimate engine almost takes this—'carried away'—literally. Mr Duffy presents the alternative—of never being carried away—as a principle of life.

The hero of 'Araby' experiences a romantic passion that takes him on a frustrated quest.

In 'Counterparts', Farrington's 'felicitous moment' has dire consequences and precipitates the downhill chain reaction.

Mrs Kearney, in 'A Mother', is evidently going too far (her 'conduct was condemned on all hands' [*D* 149.10]).[7]

As against this, Eveline is not carried away, at least not by centrifugal forces or a spirit of adventure. But, in some mysterious way, Father Flynn once was.

Much in *Ulysses* hinges on Molly Bloom being carried away, and allowing herself to do so, in what has all the air of being exceptional behaviour. Her husband, in contrast, does not take conventionally expected action—does pointedly not go to the stereotype extremes of rage and revenge, or, to use the point of view adopted here, he engages in all sorts of excess deviations. Typically, as Joyce went along, being carried away becomes more and more an act—or passion—of literary form, of salient traits of narrative and technique, a mode of linguistic and stylistic existence.

The prose of the *Portrait*, especially passages of crisis or elation, tends to swell in successive waves, phases that become longer and more elaborate. The moments of rapture on the beach towards the end of chapter 4 are rendered in analogous exaltation. The 'fabulous artificer' in the form of 'a hawklike man' inspires soaring prose. It may set off in relative sobriety: 'His heart trembled'; a parallel clause is added, a slightly longer one: 'his breath came faster;' then, without pause, an expansive sentence puts inspiration into image and words: 'and a wild spirit passed over his limbs as though he were soaring sunward.' We then revert to an augmented variant of the beginning: 'His heart trembled in an ecstasy of fear and his soul was in flight.' In the next move the first motives become launching points for tumescent flourishes, in which both 'breath' (which is no longer Stephen's own) and 'spirit' are taken up and modified: 'His *soul* was *soaring* in an *air* beyond the world and the body he knew was purified in a *breath* and delivered of incertitude and made radiant and commingled with the element of the *spirit*.' This breathless expansion of 'his soul was in flight' has snowballed to thirty-five words, with many repetitions (here italicized for demonstration) and much elaboration. Another tumescent offshoot brings the paragraph to a soaring close: 'An *ecstasy* of *flight* made *radiant* his eyes and *wild his breath* and *tremulous* and *wild* and *radiant* his windswept *limbs*' (*P* 169). There is elation as well as dilation in the development from 'his limbs' to limbs that have become tremulous and wild and radiant as well as windswept. The ecstasy, a movement outside its origin, is not alone in what the words mean but in the intensified energy of their performance.

provection

But what do you call it? (*U* 7.1051)

It becomes necessary to label what we think we perceive. First, however, I will make it quite clear that the terms offered for convenience are emphatically *not* gasp terms, that is, they are to be understood without the respiratory indication of reverence, without that minimal pause and change of voice that accompanies a word being heaved onto an altar. This is not how I would like to be understood at all. The terms suggested here are without liturgical radiance and should be plainly descriptive and even helpful, maybe at some stage replaced by more efficient ones. For easier communication, carried-away-ness in all its deportment needs a terminological label. After some searching, and trying out verbal nouns like *ekstasis* (think of the last part of chapter 4 in *Portrait*), *transport*, *excess*, *effusion*, the term deemed optimal is that of the title, *provection*. The basic metaphor is Latin *pro-vehere*, a verb: 'go beyond limits set'; with a prefix *pro* to indicate a movement forward, and a stem *veh*(-ere)[8] (related to *veh*icles like '*wagon*' or '*wain*'): 'to convey or carry'. *Vehere* seems to be related to our word *way* as well as, fittingly, German *be-wegen*. The overall topic, of course, is movement. *Proveho* means 'I carry forward or proceed' (often to a particular degree, or stage of activity, feeling). It can mean 'advance' or 'promote' to a higher rank. In the passive or the middle voice (with passive form and active meaning) *provehor* includes 'being carried away'.

Virgil[9] used the verb in a rhetorical question. When quick action is called for, a speaker asks:

quid ultra provehor/et fando surgentis demoror Austros? (Why should I go on further [literally: be carried on] and by my speech delay the rising winds?) (*Aen.* 3.481)

Speech, the Romans knew, has a way of carrying us forward. We might even now see much of *Ulysses* as inverting traditional epic action; in Joyce's verbose novel action is partly supplanted by speech and the winds of rhetoric. In 'Aeolus' Professor MacHugh fittingly advises against provection:

We mustn't be led away by words, by sounds of words. We think of Rome. (*U* 7.485)

The chapter's mode is an inflated case in point. *Ulysses*—thus my digressive vignette—is very much based on verbal '*ultra provehi*'; the *Wake* seems to be its ultimate incarnation.

Exaggeration and Change

'*Mind C.K. does not pile it on*' is the advice passed on by the ghost of Paddy Dignam, in a text-generated spiritualist *séance*, to all those still on the wrong side of Maya (*U* 12.362). This is good advice at all times, and especially so within the episode which is one of salient exaggeration: 'Cyclops' does indeed pile it on, gigantically. The very interpolation in which the phrase occurs acts out the notion, jocularly thrown into the preceding talk, that someone has seen a ghost. The idea is not only magnified, but transformed—provected—into something else: the machinery and the vocabulary of *séances* are brought into play. At the same time the machinery of provection itself becomes manifest in textbook exemplification.

Provection is characterized by a forward motion in a given direction, by a marked increase (a tendency towards hyperbole); and by a change of direction, a departure, a deviation, derailment, whose exact point of origin may not be easy to determine.

The characteristics of provection are, in the first place: augmentation, intensification, hypertrophy, amplification, and then, secondly, some divergence, a turn, a change, some divarication, shunting (this diversion is naturally, again, in relation to some *implied norm* or *expectation*).

In other words, whatever new element will surface, there is going to be more of it, and it is going to become something—at least slightly—different. Progression slides into digression. Too much more makes a qualitative difference: 'Où le trop d'une qualité commence, la qualité finit et prend un autre nom.'[10] Hypertrophy results in a different turn, a change in kind. (Misusing a well-known Jakobsonian distinction, one might bring the contiguous forward movement close to metonymous augmentation and align the change in kind more to metaphor.)

In fact the graphic equivalent of provection is a vector, usually an iconic sign in the shape of an arrow, with a certain direction. The appropriate pictorial shape might be an arrow of increasing width, probably bent, or even bifurcated, to indicate the gathering of momentum and its deflection. Notice how Stephen's progress in *Portrait* might be diagrammed in terms of vectors: perhaps towards learning, or justice (in the first chapter); then towards sin (chapter 2); again in contrast, towards Christian purity and order (chapter 3); or (in chapter 4)[11] towards creation, flying and falling; and toward exile in the final chapter. Vectorial descriptions would of course vary with the observer, the graphic possibilities themselves, however, are evident: the novel *could* be charted.

Take an instance in *Ulysses*, as we find Stephen, early on and throughout, theologically—also psychologically—obsessed with paternal substances. 'Arius', he tells himself, was

warring his life long upon the consubstantiality of the Son with the Father. (*U* 1.657)

This, by the by, is already an exaggeration for emphasis; Arius, according to the documents, was hardly 'warring his life long' (but his name is derived from the heathen war-god, Ares). Whatever the origin of the phrase, it will soon be self-parodistically exaggerated in a protean change: the same idea, but more of it, and with a difference:

Warring his life long upon the contransmagnificandjewbangtantiality. (*U* 3.51)

A weight has been added to create the longest word so far in the whole book, a difficult one to articulate, an oddity and ostensible micro-provection. And, almost self-reflexively, a characterization is included: augmentation is signalled by 'magnificand'—something that is to be made bigger. The derailment finds expression in 'bang'— a highly effective, flagrant ingredient that is not part of the theological expectation.

Magnification and *bang* can serve as practical shorthand for Joycean developments and techniques. Mulligan, Ulyssean herald, foreshadows many provective techniques; as soon as he appears, he ceremoniously intones dislocated words from the Mass, and is noticeable for perpetual histrionic excess. Typically, he mimics Stephen's theorizing on Shakespeare. His exaggeration, moreover, precedes the original, we are given the mock echo several chapters before we hear the original sound.

He proves by algebra...

Proof and 'algebra' promise to be exact and demonstrable.

... that Hamlet's grandson is Shakespeare's grandfather...

The two *grands* magnify and they turn the proposition into something grotesque, absurd:

... that he himself is the ghost of his own father. (*U* 1.555)

One way of saying all this is that the Joycean text often deviates
almost instantly into parody, which is often more of the same, piled
up, with an additional twist. Correspondingly, Mulligan drifts from a
'snotgreen sea', based on Homeric patterns, right away to an augmented and diverted 'scrotumtightening sea'—an epithet no contemporary reader was prepared for—as well as from Swinburnian English into Homeric Greek ('*epi oinopa ponton*') and an Attic quotation
('*Thalatta! Thalatta!*' [*U* 1.78–80]). If we enter into the spirit of the
thing and, in our turn, Hellenize the book in which Mulligan wants
to 'Hellenise' the island (*U* 1.158), we are provecting it close toward
an ancient epic, and everything in the novel becomes—potentially—
something different, more grandiose and, at the same time, far
away.[12]

On a more subdued note, Bloom is introduced to us by his taste
preference,

Mr Leopold Bloom ate with relish... (*U* 4.1)

Then we are carried into an extended catalogue of five detailed
items, from 'thick giblet soup' to 'fried hencods' roes'. The third sentence offers more of the same, 'grilled mutton kidney' as a superlative choice; diversion then is provided, not by a bang, but a 'tang'
of—of all things—urine, urine affecting, mind you, Bloom's palate.
Somehow, the direction has taken an odd turn. Early readers had not
yet developed a taste for such a faintly scented gustatory provection.

Being carried away is signalled, for example, in what turns out to
be Mulligan's longest early speech in the first chapter, his What-is-
death? justification to Stephen. It moves from idiomatic depiction of
death as a medical experience to literary embroideries like 'sir Peter
Teazle', and on towards uneasily jocular hyperbole:

I don't whinge like some hired mute from Lalouette's. (*U* 1.213)

(There is, as we note in passing, an interesting touch in Mulligan
comporting himself like someone who is 'mute'.) The process of
escalation is signaled in a narrative comment (which implies Stephen's awareness of it as an observable process):

He had spoken himself into boldness. (*U* 1.216)

Mulligan has been carried away—has provected himself—*somewhere else*: into boldness. A similar escalation takes place when, at the end of 'Eumaeus', Stephen begins to sing 'an old German song' and then, moments later, is heard singing 'more boldly' (*U* 16.1812, 1883). These are common, everyday occurrences. They would hardly be worth pointing out if the whole novel did not speak itself—write itself—into a boldness that took decades to assimilate. *Bold* (as in 'bold hand') in *Ulysses* can cause a shock; in typography it is used for emphasis or an increase in volume. When we next come across 'boldness' it is in one of those inserts of 'Cyclops', where Bob Doran is made to say, in exaggerated, stylized courtesy:

But, should I have overstepped the limits of reserve let the sincerity of my feelings be the excuse for my boldness. (*U* 12.789)

Whether we call this parody or hyperbole, the form itself consists in overstepping limits of reserve, which in actuality might be due to sincerity of feelings, but in its verbal excess points to the opposite. The Cyclopean inserts (in one of which the passage occurs) are in themselves crassly provective. They pick up a trait in the conversation or action and take it to absurd lengths; within themselves they contain sub-inserts, at each point they are expandable into regressive side-spins.

Any vector analysis of a Joycean strand-entwining passage would be highly intricate, if it could ever be complete. For demonstration, only a few features are singled out in a Cyclopean interpolation, the one in which the not intrinsically alluring Dublin markets are upgraded into the romance of Irish legends:

A pleasant land it is in sooth of murmuring waters, fishful streams...

This leads to an elaboration of fishful streams: the epithet is implemented; specified fish are listed:

where sport the gurnard, the plaice, the roach, the halibut, the gibbed haddock, the grilse, the dab, the brill, the flounder, the pollock... (*U* 12.70)

At a certain point we may realize that, independent of the point of origin, fishiness has become its own goal and satisfaction. Most of the specimens listed are not to be found in Irish fishful streams and murmuring sweet waters at all, but in the open sea. In the Cyclopean spirit of incongruous enthusiasm, the list has written itself into unnoticed saltiness, or perhaps carelessness. Then, in yet another turn, the catalogue trails off into bathetic generality and awkward repetition, not at all in keeping with the initial note of picturesque stereotypes:

and other denizens of the aqueous kingdom too numerous to be enumerated. (*U* 12.70)

With a marked change of tone, enumeration itself imposes itself on the pattern. We have moved from water, streams, and murmurs to numbers. The expansive technique is not a modernist Joycean invention. In this case it was already used by one of Joyce's forerunners, Ovid, who in *Metamorphoses* has *his* giant Polyphemus make verbal and vapid love to the nymph Galatea in precisely such provective bursts of piled-up enumeration and self-perpetuation.[13] The practice is as old as the epic itself; Joyce found new ways of foregrounding it.

prolonged provocative (*U* 17.2243)

In the central chapters of *Ulysses* the provections of artifice are matched by carried-away-ness on the level of events. In 'Sirens', 'Cyclops', or 'Nausicaa', the protagonists can be carried away, each in his or her own fashion. Cyclopean narrow-mindedness, fanaticism, and prejudice make it all the more easy to escalate from mere words to arguments and the menace of actual ballistics. Typically, the Citizen is first seen 'having a great confab with himself', passes on to more and more haranguing and sermonizing, and ends up with 'Did I kill him or what?' and a 'volley of oaths' (*U* 12.119, 1901). In tumescent excess, fatuous words become an empty biscuit tin. The chapter's mode enlarges this intensification into a seismic catastrophe (or quasi-scientific dislocution of the power of Poseidon, the shaker of the earth).

But, more surprisingly, Bloom, apostrophized as 'prudent' in this episode, is extremely *in*cautious; is being carried away, too, forgets his usual social reserve, becomes argumentative—in fact a voluminous talker—and is, atypically, going out of his silent way to ask for trouble. He too ascends toward rhetorical climaxes with precipitate exits. We know why he is worked up and why his aggressions are displaced. This is the moment when a painful provection that his mind does not want to dwell upon is likely to take place in his home, too.

Getting worked up is natural, often of great human interest, and therefore a prime topic for all literature. There is nothing new in the various emotional climaxes that *Ulysses* still contains. Of concern here is that, once more, the emotion, in textual empathy, moves the style. The Hyperbolic Asides, the non-realistic insertions, act like a provective chorus that comments on what is going on, a further remove from the narrator's internal and already hyperbolic remarks. Overstatement and intensification are the order of the day. The chapter sets off with a harmless encounter that is magnified into a near accident—'he near drove his gear into my eye' (*U* 12.3)—and fittingly ends with the superlative human achievement of transfiguration, in accordance with classical and biblical precedent. One of the Latin meanings of *provehere* is to 'promote in rank': apotheosis is the highest conceivable promotion.

The instances given have already proved it almost impossible to separate mini-examples neatly from the larger issues. It may well be that the impulse from the microcosmic particle to the universal application is the most central of all provections that characterize the reading of Joyce. Synecdochically, we move from the discussion of small particles to more comprehensive entanglement.

'Ithaca' magnifies a scientific approach into a disorienting accumulation of facts and relations. In one instance an imaginary route leads from 'the cliffs of Moher', Irish and terrestrial, to 'the delta in the constellation of Cassiopeia' and into 'incalculable eons of peregrinations' (*U* 17.1974; 2019); meditations may lead into imaginary, absurd (and faulty) numbers. Or else we may find deviations from the deadpan, scientific diction into one that is incompatible; take Bloom's doings on entering his bed:

He kissed the plump mellow yellow smellow melons of her rump, on each plump *melonous* hemisphere, in their mellow *yellow* furrow, with obscure prolonged provocative melonsmellonous osculation. (*U* 17.2241)

Here a sudden burst of sensuality provects itself in a flutter of fruit and smells and physical impressions, *or else*—to change the angle of observation—a choreography of signifiers that clamour for attention. In this sensuous whirl, abstractions are momentarily suspended. We may experience *mellow* as touching *yellow* and generating *smellow* and squinting at *furrow*. Or we notice how *plump* kisses the distant word *rump* and *obscure* strives to mate with *osculation*. The sounds and shapes of words seem to match the bodily shapes and sensations.

All of this de-Ithacizes Ithaca for an inspired, digressive moment. Yet it also magnifies Ithacan contrastive symmetries and adds an ultra-Ithacan coinage like 'provocative melonsmellonous osculation' with a compound adjective posing as a scientific one. Language as an orchestration of acoustic, echoing and mating sounds, is what we might expect to find in a chapter like 'Sirens' (where, chances are, we would assimilate the melons to Greek *melos*).

There is no need to articulate—at this late hour in Joyce exegesis—how 'Sirens' is provected, how its raptures are put into sound effects. Music can serve as a welcome, though intermittent, anodyne to stave off perturbances. Father Cowley, Ben Dollard, Simon Dedalus are enraptured by music, 'a kind of drunkenness', Bloom muses, 'enthusiasts' (*U* 11.1192). Enthusiasm is a particularly inspired variety of being carried away, originally by intervention from above.

Stylistic correspondences to theme and subject matter are now taken for granted. But even sympathetic first readers had not yet been conditioned the same way. One staunch supporter in 1919 showed himself highly allergic to the chapter's then radically novel features: 'You have gone too far', he wrote; 'you have once again gone "down where the asparagus grows"'—a direction not desired. The writer who turned out metaphorical illustrations for what I call provection was Ezra Pound, who not only commented on the chapter, but imitated it:

The peri-o-perip-o-periodico-parapatetico-periodopathetico—I dont-off-the markgetical structure of yr. first or peremier para-petitec graph.[14]

He parodied the mode, singing the Sirens into absurdity, exaggerating Joyce's excesses. He provected the provections, and in the process was carried away himself. His vivid implication is not only that Joyce went too far—the wrong way—but that he deviated into the 'off-the markgetical'. 'Sirens', Pound remarked,

—will cause all but your most pig-o-peripatec-headed readers to think you have gone marteau-dingo-maboule—

We don't have to know what 'gone marteau-dingo-maboule' precisely calls up, but we recognize charges that were often to be levelled, in less imaginative wording, against the author. Joyce's answer was typical and curt in terms of being carried away, that there was no other way open to him, and of negative justification:

[it] is not capricious.[15]

What may look like excessive capering, in other words, may have its intricate justification. To show new angles of the noncapriciousness of Joyce's ways has now become a mainstream scholarly occupation. The tendency nowadays is to characterize the *Ulysses* chapters precisely in terms *of their provections*. Many of the entries in Joyce's schema, or schemas, consist in labels for their excessive programs. Carried away in my turn, I add to them in blissful contagion.

Circe

In a different sense, 'Circe' by its very nature is predisposed for provection. A change into animals, not just swine, by metaphorical convention, suggests the exaggeration of certain traits to the exclusion of others.[16] Psychologically, the chapter is codetermined by a seeming lack of conscious restraints. Lust, fear, wish-fulfillment are blatantly brought forward, magnified, staged with phantasmagoric bangs. In perspective, we are not confined by the circumferences of any one mind—or the sum total of the minds of the figures in it.

'Circe' is egressive: it frankly steps outside of limits that were, so far, still observed. In 'Circe', *Ulysses* is getting beyond, or beside, itself. Changes of voices and roles, as they abounded in the first chapter, where they were still restricted by everyday verisimilitude, have taken on a life of their own; what used to be Mulligan's conspicuous role adverbs at the beginning are now blown up into spectacular masquerades. By design the chapter is expansive and distortive (its opening already mentions *stretches* and—conversely—*stunted*). The design itself was further expanded and distorted. Joyce reported on its progress and setbacks: 'It gets wilder and worse and more involved.'[17] We can study its expansion and elaboration as almost step-by-step provection.

Michael Groden, in his study of the genesis of *Ulysses*, distinguishes three stages; the third one, a turning point for the whole book, was the ebullient 'Circe', whose continual excrescences affected the rest of the novel, including what had already been written. Revising 'Circe', Joyce once more changed gear, and decisively so.[18]

Typically, a scene that most readers would now consider central, the messianic scene, was a later addition. Groden reports that it 'results from Bloom's tendency to correct other people and to lecture them.'[19] Joyce inserted the whole extended scene after Zoe's request for 'a swaggerroot' and Bloom's lewd remark that 'the mouth can be better engaged than with a cylinder of rank weed' (*U* 15.1347). The mouth then instantly does become better engaged. The 'stump speech' that grows out of such a triviality will promote Bloom to imperial heights and again *de*mote him to carbonization. At the end the mouth will be magnified into 'six hundred voices', while, anticlimactically, Bloom becomes 'mute, shrunken' (*U* 15.1953). In reality, the whole, elongated episode takes up next to no time. It may be appropriate that the entire swaggering and rank arabesque sprouts from vegetable cues like 'swaggerroot' and 'rank weed'.

The medical testimony that is given at Bloom's trial features biological excesses, exaggerations: Bloom is 'bisexually abnormal'— 'born out of bedlock'—'there is unbridled lust... traces of elephantiasis' (*U* 15.1777). This 'womanly man' (*U* 15.1798) deviates into the other sex, with instant pregnancy and the birth of eight children, whose names in themselves form a minor provective list patterned on gold and silver. Of course, by the time we come upon these passages we have become used to the chapter's hallucinatory enormities and are no longer surprised. Homer's Kirke with her charms, I might add, was herself a great and magical provector, the only one, moreover, who managed to hold back Odysseus for a whole year.

We may turn to the whole chapter, the messianic scene, the notesheets, the galleys, or individual passages, or words, to find, at each level, minuscule or larger samples of what is here being exemplified. At this stage there is no reader of this essay—unless it has failed grievously—who could not, off the cuff, think of numerous further instances and applications.

vectorious readyeyes (*FW* 298.14)

As always, there is a certain pointlessness in applying some earlier, evolving principle to *Finnegans Wake,* and this is not just because of our abysmal ignorance about it, which turns each utterance into a scholarly imposture. But also because of its own, extreme, culminative nature. How to show provection in what is already provection *per se*? A work which looks, at first and most subsequent glances, to be based, manifestly, on excess, carried-away-ness, on exuberance, on effusion (*riverrun* sets it off); that sports its 'toomuchness, the fartoomanyness' (*FW* 122.36) throughout? Each single word seems made up of magnification and of bangs. Reading the *Wake* is mainly a matter of hermeneutic provection. Its phrases are (but we use other synonyms) multivective. Something like

Jungfraud's Messongebook (*FW* 460.20)

(even without any context) piles a manifest *Jung* on a latent *Freud* (and inverts their traditional causal sequence); it suggests a German virgin (*Jungfrau*) and, perhaps, a book of *messages*, or a book to be taken to Mass (German *Messe*)—in which case *virgin* would more likely become *the* Virgin. Psychoanalysis commented on virginity and on mariolatry. Old men (as the two analysts are generally envisaged and were so in times of *Work in Progress*) are pitted against young (*jung*) women (*Frau*). Old and young men and women have dreams (*songe*); Jung and Freud interpreted them—differently. And it may be all *fraud* and lies (*mensonge*); if so, the French ghost word introduces *men* and couples them with *dream*: when men and women and analysts get together, there may be messages or lies (and what about *song* and *songbook*?). All of these readings have been done many times over; my phrasings are old wine in appropriately labelled new bottles to show nothing more than that Wakean provection need not be proved in detail; on its very surface it has always intrigued us.

If anything, we might observe that provection can turn into revection. The vehicularity is spelled out, say, in a return from

Carry me along

on the last page, to

brings us... back

on the first. The text, at one point, displays an iconic

greater THaɴ or less ᴛʜaN

with diminishing and then increasing size of the letters; and follows it by

vectorious readyeyes (*FW* 298.14)

which is, geometrically, some vector radius, but no doubt also one of those numerous self-descriptive confessions. The ready eyes are also ours.

But then, what would we *not* find in *Finnegans Wake*? Looking at it with vectorious ready eyes, however, we might come up with a few specifically Wakean provections. One characteristic variant is its kaleidoscopic splurges—multiple displays of its verbal material. They may look, but are not, 'whorled without aimed' (*FW* 272.4). They are small-scale replicas of the whole, which reprocesses its themes and elements. Typical for such autodinetic (from *dine*, or *dinos*, 'whirl') runs is the one example, certainly representative:

Totalled in toldteld and teldtold in tittletell tattle. (*FW* 597.8)

This is vertiginous, tongue-twisting, same-anew-ness in phonemic permutation; or else self-generative variety; or elaborative dilation. A pattern is extended in apparent self-complacency. Here I merely rephrase, in the chosen terminology, what every reader can observe —duplication and reprocessing. We find a symmetry that is askew, with an increase towards the end: *toldteld* mirrors *teldtold*, but *totalled* is magnified into two words—with a change of syllabic elements: *tittletell tattle*.

Semantically there is also decrease from *Total*, or *all told*, to what is very small: *tittle*. Or else: the whole—*Totalled* (*total* plus *all*, and something big, *tall*, as well)—is split up into various *tellings*, past and present, tellings obviously not all reliable. So the *Wake*—again nothing new—is variably retelling what is has been saying; and I am again doing what the quote says, concentrating on the energies of the whole process—amplification and minuscule bangs.

Finnegans Wake often drifts into what I would call *par(a)echoes* of itself, which merely describes an acoustic feature of 'the same anew'. Our sentence tells us 'the same anew' and *does* it visibly and audibly. The Greeks actually did use the term *para-echo: parechema* was a succession of similar sounds, alliteration. *Finnegans Wake* tends to become parechetic. Parechetically, I am here making similar sounds for similar features.

The *Wake's* opening alerts us to the processes that will follow. When a bit of the story gets under way, we have a rearrival that has not yet occurred, and then—the second movement in the second paragraph—we come to a programmatic:

nor had topsawyer's rocks by the stream Oconee exaggerated themselse. (*FW* 1.6)

We begin with exaggeration, but in the original sense of piling up heaps (*agger*) of rocks, needed for building and civilization ('buildung upon buildung', we will soon hear). Something is piled on. Conveniently, *agger* derives from a vehicular action: *ad-gerere* (carry to). But already the implication is of *too much*, at least too much verbiage, of disproportional augmentation. What is heaped up, or exaggerated, is, *reciprocally*, *oneself*, and in the same sweep—*transitively* —something *else*. If we expect 'selves', we have been sidetracked into 'else'—again, increase and difference. Exaggerations change the nature of what they exaggerate. The reproduction called up is human and cultural but reminds us, epiphenomenally, of the textual autogenesis so typical for the book where the phrase occurs. This sentence takes us to another Dublin, beyond the Atlantic,

to Laurens County's gorgios

the country of topsawyers and different Finns. Relevant for the present purposes is that such a Dublin in Georgia may not be the same as the one many Irishmen left behind. Something changes in transit. We also come across a strong female (and riverine) element that has been absent from the first movement: the stream Oconee. It reinforces birth (as in *née*) and perhaps the place of birth (if *con* is taken to be French): the first letter, *O*—round and open and gaping—will acquire iconic significance later in the book. All the while, the text goes on, those rocks exaggerating themselse were also

doublin their mumper

Doubling a number all the time is one of oldest tricks of increases that exceed our imagination. In this case the reduplication is of not quite the same. Dublin becomes *doublin*, *number* turns into *mumper*. At certain times the variations matter more than the points of origin. Leaving Oedipal *mums* aside, as well as *member*, note that to *mump* can mean 'deceive, overreach, to beg'. A *mumper* is also an imposter, or a beggar. And in part, the most effective part, the word still remains opaque.

The rocks by the stream of Oconee in the next phrase—'thuartpeatrick'—transform themselves into the rock on which the Church was founded. That, too, from the humble beginnings to the establishment of a mighty Catholic church, was quite a provection. If, however, we draw *gorgios* into the orbit of stone and rock and Greek *Gorgo*, we get a metamorphosis of different, and grim, consequences (Greek *gorgos* means 'grim, terrible'). So we, affected readers, pile meanings upon meanings in extrapolative excess. After decades of *Wake* exegesis, our multivectorial urge has been well attested.

Countercurrents

My tautological ramifications must not obliterate the correlative counterprocesses. In true paradoxical confirmation, a devective reading should supplement the ones given here. As always, it would be possible to phrase all the foregoing descriptions in exactly the opposite way. The *Wake,* sure enough, exaggerates itself, but it also seems to return to a nearly simple, low key, fade out at its end, just as *Ulysses* regresses to the semblance of an earlier mode. In one way 'Penelope' is also the simplest one, the most homogeneous in the whole book.

It is 'Cyclops', with its blatant egressive insertions, that has been used as a showpiece. Naturally and truistically, it is also characterized by *devection*, *deflation*—by bathetic drops, anticlimaxes. In the end, the Citizen, waddling and 'puffing and blowing with the dropsy' (*U* 12.1785), is less of an athletic giant than the words expended on him might have indicated. But, of course, no reader ever trusted those descriptions of 'a broadshouldered deep-chested stronglimbed' hero (*U* 12.152) in the first place. We subtract what the exaggerating agencies pile on. Obviously, Bloom's vehicular elevation to heaven, an Elijah 'at an angle of fortyfive degrees', is at the same time a descent into the ludicrous. Before that, he rhetorically and emotionally stands up 'to it then with force like men' but collapses, all of a sudden, 'as limp as a wet rag' (*U* 12.1475–9), a movement that the subsequent chapter, 'Nausicaa', will magnify in its own curve of swelling and deflation; Joyce termed them 'tumescence—detumescence'.

In general we move from realistic events to more and more imaginative flights, move—a trait of *Ulysses*—from indicative modes, as things are, more and more toward *what if* or *imagine that*, which is to say, subjunctive ones, events doubly fictitious. The parallactic interpolations in 'Cyclops' tend to be conjunctival.

On the level of content, devection is a theme of *Dubliners*, the shorthand for which has conventionally been 'paralysis': reality lags behind expectation. Joyce's first prose sentence deprives someone of hope before we know who the someone is. In some essential sense, the stories trail off devectively. Goals are not reached; escapes not made; lives not changed; desires not satisfied; poetry remains unwritten.

If the implications of the title 'Ulysses' guided our expectations, then the drop from antique heroic exploits to domestic quotidian fumblings is felt to be, at first glance, a devective letdown. *Ulysses* was considered lacking in momentous events. Conventional heroism is not achieved; Bloom does not seem to jerk himself up to assume command and re-establish disrupted orders (though this is debatable, dependent on interpretation). When Stephen is ejected out of *Ulysses*—and out of the Joycean canon—into the wilderness behind Bloom's garden, nobody (except a few critics) knows if he is also provected into authorship and creativity; most of us doubt that he will be launched into a musical career managed by Leopold Bloom, man of many counsels, or into a liaison with Marion Bloom. We cannot tell how Molly will act next morning, only a few hours away— who will be master and who servant. In view of predominantly devective cues, it is remarkable that an interpretative and habitual bias leads us to provect meaning, often in 'symbolic' expansion.[20] Conversely, one commonplace view of Joyce's later works is that the paucity of events has been compensated by the well-known provective artifices.

Secondly, the provective exuberance is caught up by schematic devices, by repetitions, cross-references, by structural reinforcement, architectural bracketings. Repetitions, kaleidoscopic permutations—the sort of motives we like to tabulate—are cognitive supports in what might become a chaotic whirl (as early readers testified).

All of Joyce's works had a way of getting out of hand. It is characteristic of *Ulysses* that its episodes tend to get longer and more involved and more pointedly arabesquable. The later works often resemble a sentence under way, in which (as in 'Eumaeus') more and more subordination can be added. Against such increase in length and complexity, there are structural checks, coordinates. Once we can look at *A Portrait* or *Ulysses* panoramically, spread out in space before us, not as ways to traverse in time, they appear symmetrical, contrived, dovetailed, with balances that may even appear too neat, too carefully elaborated.

The schemas are such checks. With their fastenings, clamps, braces, correspondences, they make the supporting devices visible: they also reveal a groundplan, order, arrangement. A schema is essentially, originally, something that 'holds'. Joyce's schematic symmetries, however, are lopsided, conceptual, and abstractive. It may take an effort to discover them (which does not make them less functional). Schematically, 'Nestor' balances 'Ithaca'. There is positional symmetry; we have catechism, personal or impersonal; further analogies can be uncovered. 'Nestor' suggests a way to come to terms with the later episode, and vice versa. But the differences are overwhelming as well. There is considerable provective development from 'Nestor', the shortest chapter of the book, to 'Ithaca', the second longest, most fragmented one, expandable *ad libitum*. Spatial relationships help us to get our bearings and to make additional sense in retrospect.

Dynamic drives have to be balanced by static checks; we need both, and at certain times in our critical understanding we may have to give more prominence to one over the other. In a first phase of bewilderment readers needed a Stuart Gilbert tabulation to chart the chaos into the surety of order and schema. Once we have been systematizing too long, it becomes necessary to stress the counterforces.

Joyce's works came into being in a tension between luxuriating urges and a need for control. The dynamic drives had to be caught by systematization. But then, in the workshop, the material got out of schema again and had to be recaptured in a continuous process of (as the *Wake* has it)

a sot of a swigswag, systomy dystomy. (*FW* 597.21)

In motive paradox Joyce reintegrated what is in essence an egressive feature, one that pushes beyond confines. The graph might be seen as a vicious circle of emergent *patterns*, then a *pattern extension*, which leads to a *pattern eruption* (the recurrent two stages of provection as they have been reiterated here extensively), and finally the *repatterning of pattern eruption* in contradictory reintegration. This essay has naturally put its stress on *dys*tomy, the *ex*-cess, whatever transgresses the current system.

a winged form flying above the waves (P 169)

Both dynamic drives and the static checks are present in the myth of the artificer Daedalus, whose deeds were of excess. His mind took him to reaches not explored before. Out of exaggerated envy he killed a rival (who had outdone him in artistry). He fled to Crete, created the likeness of an animal to gratify the lust of a no doubt greatly provected queen. The resulting hybrid, Minotauros, was too much of a bull for comfort or prestige—something monstrous, a being *sui generis* (he occurs, rightly, in the *Ulysses* chapter of the most monstrous births, *U* 14.994). Daedalus built a maze that forced intruders to go forward and to deviate constantly. He was the first human to fly above nets. In contrast, his son's exuberance turned out to be disastrous; he aimed too high and fell too low. The family biography is one of overreaching, as myths always are. But Daedalus was also a structurer, contriver; the labyrinth was an engineering feat, carefully planned and laid out. The fabulous artificer was in artistic control of his material (he systematically arranged the feathers for his wings),[21] someone looking ahead. He cautioned his son to a middle course of sane restraint.

The other prevalent Greek myth was in one sense a lesson *against* unbridled provection. Odysseus of many resources and counsels kept a tight rein on his emotions, was in control, did—with a few consequential exceptions—*not* allow himself to be carried away. Nor, on the whole, does Bloom (except in the encounter with the Citizen). But the novel's exuberant modes carry him away, allow, for example, the urges of his psyche to take over. In contrast to the *Odyssey*—with its relatively even hexametrical flow and conventional diction—its Irish dislocation keeps changing the venue almost as an end in itself.[22]

Many stories set off with a deflection from an expected or prescribed course of events. The *Odyssey* is such a story. Odysseus wanted to return, but was deviated, geographically, at the fateful Cap of Malea (*Od.* 9.80), at times by divine interference, occasionally by the folly of his comrades, sometimes by his own nature—so an epic came into being. Stories worth telling are often based on provective disturbances. Once exposed to a series of adventures, Odysseus was prudent and purposeful, in other words, less at the mercy of distractive forces than most humans or one-track monsters, which gave him an advantage. Above all, he was able to use provection strategically in opportunist manipulation: by eloquence, strength, perseverance, disguise, equivocation, or the use of potent Greek wine—by what can be called his polytropy. But there *is* a restless strain in him (his final reconciliation with Poseidon is still far away and conditional). Later writers magnified the Faustian streak, an unsatisfiable curiosity and lust for adventure. Dante's Ulisse confesses that 'desire to gain experience of the world'

l'ardore... a divenir del mondo esperto. (*Inf.* 26, 97–8)

This Odysseus is provected past the straits of Gibraltar to flounder on the high seas. Leopold Bloom inherited some of that quality too.

exsogerraider! (*FW* 619.30)

Simplifications like all the above are permissible at the stage of initiation to introduce a notion like the provective urge. As we go on, we would have to acknowledge—without much surprise—the multivectorial nature of Joyce's work, especially and self-evidently *Finnegans Wake*. There are, naturally, several provectors at work at all times, in perpetual concert. It is up to us to recognize and to describe them as adequately as our perceptions let us.

Imagine a vectoral disentanglement of, say, 'The Dead'—in how many ways we might characterize the movements of increase/ decrease and the swervings. There is an increase of emotion, a concentration backward in time, then inward, away from the extensive world of surface without. There is a narrowing of scope, less and less action. (One action ardently anticipated does not take place.) The cast diminishes, with fewer and fewer people on the scene, and more and more isolation. There is also, at the end, a cosmic widening. The language escalates to supreme cadences—or else it degenerates into purplish kitsch. As readers, we take and bundle our vectoral choices and call them interpretation.

Separating and perhaps characterizing provective features may help to sharpen our observation and to articulate what we notice. It is arguable, for example, that the comparative neglect of Joyce's poetry or of his one play, *Exiles*, may be due, in part, to the lack of artistic provection in those works, which emphatically need not thereby make them less valuable. Provection does not automatically confer significance. But it has to be admitted that a certain provective conditioning seems to be a trademark of the Joycean reader who is likely to become spoiled, in the process, beyond retrieval.

For, of course, in the ultimate act that every reading is, *we* are the provectors, the exaggerators. We rise to the challenge. We get carried away, physically, from many parts of the world to attend a few days of conferential excess in Dublin, Trieste, Seville, Cesena, Leeds, Frankfurt, Philadelphia, Honolulu or Dubrovnik, in our characteristic elation or symposiasm. To fly, sail, drive, all the way from Amsterdam, Kuwait, New Zealand, or Zürich to distant Milwaukee is what the Romans originally meant by *provehi*. Our publications are prolific, immense in size, and some very odd in kind. In our lectures and essays and workshops or, in particular, *Wake* reading groups we exceed, we keep piling it on, we deviate, we go beyond the boundaries and sometimes have to be called back by Bloomian common sense. Joyceans are provectors *par excellence*—which does not always translate as 'by excellence'. On the whole, unlike the old Daedalian provector, we excel more by quantitative magnification than by inspired bangs.

January 1988

NOTES

1 James Joyce, *A Portrait of the Artist as a Young Man: Text, Criticism, and Notes*, Chester Anderson (ed.) (New York: Viking Press 1968). Hereafter cited as *P*.

2 *Ulysses*, Hans Walter Gabler (ed.) (New York and London: Garland 1986). Hereafter cited as *U*.

3 S.L. Goldberg, *James Joyce* (Edinburgh and London: Oliver and Boyd 1962), 95.

4 'And in the expression of that [classical] temper—despite the romantic infinities and 'profundities' towards which he drifted himself and, even more, those saddled upon him since—lies all that is most fundamental, free and vital in his work.' S.L. Goldberg, *The Classical Temper* (London: Chatto & Windus 1961), 314–5.

5 Ibid., 21–2.

6 'It is too discursive, formless, unrestrained, and ugly things, ugly words, are too

prominent; indeed at times they seem to be shoved in one's face, on purpose, unnecessarily... His pen and his thoughts seem to have run away with him sometimes.' The strictures are that there is too much, and that something got out of hand. Garnett's report is commonly available in The Viking Critical Library edition of *A Portrait of the Artist As a Young Man* (New York: Viking Press 1968), 319–20.

7 *Dubliners: Text, Criticism, and Notes*, Robert Scholes and A. Walton Litz (eds) (New York: Viking Press 1969). Hereafter cited as *D*.

8 Its Sanskrit relative *vah* obligingly begins a paragraph in part IV of *Finnegans Wake*: 'Vah!' (*FW* 594.1).

9 Quintilian gives examples of the verb's usage, as in *'audacia provecti'* ('carried away by daring', or 'emboldened'; *Institutio Oratoria* I, 3, 4); or when he writes: 'Grammar must know its own limits': *'Et grammatice... fines suos norit, praesertim tantum ab hac appellationis suae paupertate, intra quam primi illi constitere, provecta'* (especially as it has *encroached so far beyond the boundaries* to which its unpretentious name should restrict it and to which its early professors actually confined themselves, *Institutio Oratoria of Quintilian* II, 1, 4), H.E. Butler (trans.) (Cambridge: Harvard University Press, Loeb Classical Library 1979), I:206–7.

The term *provection*—still to be seen as provisional (occurring so to speak still on the synoptic, left-hand page, and not part of the clear-reading text)—also easily lends itself to convenient derivative forms (as they will be used), including antonyms (it would be possible to characterize S.L. Goldberg's views on Joyce descriptively as 'invective' ones).

10 Pierre Marivaux, *Réflexions, Journaux et Œuvres diverses* (Paris: Garnier 1916), 501.

11 The first section of chapter 4 clearly shows Stephen in excessive dedication to a laborious Christian life, but it also shows how the accumulated devotion gradually slides into something else (*P* 147–53).

12 Stuart Gilbert's charting of Homeric analogies and Buddhist-theosophist correspondences (*James Joyce's 'Ulysses'* 1930) has frequently been considered excessive.

13 The echoes and the literary manner are developed in 'Ovidian Roots of Gigantism in Joyce's *Ulysses*', *Journal of Modern Literature* XV:4 (Spring 1991), 561–77.

14 Letter of 10 June 1919. Forrest Read (ed.), *Pound/Joyce* (New York: New Directions 1967), 157ff.

15 Letter of 6 August 1919 to Harriet Shaw Weaver. Joyce, *Letters*, Stuart Gilbert (ed.) (New York: The Viking Press 1957 & 1966), I:129.

16 'The essence of the animal into man metamorphosis seems to be that man becomes an animal when he loses his many-sided human wholeness. One of his functions gets out of hand and usurps the powers belonging to the governing authority of his virtuous republic.' Frank Budgen, *James Joyce and the Making of Ulysses* (1934; 2nd edn, Bloomington: Indiana University Press 1960), 229.

17 *Letters of James Joyce*, 1:147.

18 Michael Groden, Ulysses *in Progress* (Princeton: Princeton University Press 1977), 166ff.

19 Ibid., 173.

20 From this point of view, *symbol* is considered nearly synonymous with provection: *symballein* also meant a move in a certain direction.

21 '*nam ponit in ordine pennas*' ('he lays feathers in order') (*Metamorphoses* 8, 189).
22 Both statements are valid and untrue: of course the *Odyssey* is also provectively
    diversified, and *Ulysses* is much more coherent than it once seemed.

IN QUEST OF A *NISUS FORMATIVUS JOYCEANUS*

caussa latet, vis est notissima.
The following is a naïve probe into genetic undercurrents, a probe that puts provisional labels on hypothetical germinal formations that are wholly inaccessible to us and from which we will remain excluded and which nevertheless may be posited. The terminological searches into what eludes us may conveniently start with the notes and drafts that Joyce left behind in such profusion. The earliest extant stages in the elaborate and convoluted genesis of his works, are extremely helpful and animating, and good use has been made of them. Even so, many remain frustrating, and the issues, at any rate, are problematic. There is not alone the question of ideas that do not seem to have been developed, turns not taken after all; do those notes that were not visibly advanced by Joyce still inform some of the texts, or are they dead ends among the 'infinite possibilities' that have been 'ousted' (as in *U* 2.51)? The psychology of note-taking would itself be a worthwhile subject. More directly disconcerting are entries in Joyce's notebooks that simply do not reveal very much. Often Joyce jotted down notable, *extra*-ordinary words (for example 'intussusception') or phrases like 'a much injured person' in one of the notesheets; the latter we find in a list labelled 'Eumaeus'. This Homeric type of compound, an English rendering of the epithet *poly-tlas*, fitted into the chapter which aims at epic diction—Bloom becomes like Odysseus: 'that muchinjured but on the whole even-tempered person' (*U* 16.1081). But against such fairly memorable entries, many others look flatly unspecific. The same notesheet also

contains 'despite its—all very fine—hold its own',[1] all of which may
have had reverberations for the author in his workshop but does not
induce momentous insights in us now. It would not be easy to determine the intended allocation of such nondescript entries.

Such notes do not open portals of discovery, and yet they may
have been meaningful for the author, who relied on finding a place
for what he came across. Joyce was a great fitter into context. But that
supposed context or aura or private association may not surface in
the notebooks at all. The context, presumably, was in the creator's
mind. Almost all was grist to Joyce's mill—but what was, in each
instance, the mill into which the grist could be accommodated with
such confidence? 'Hillary rillarry gibbous grist to our millery!' (*FW*
314.18).

the arc of his drive (FW 129.32)

Joyce's jottings make sense in relation to something that is not part of
them, but towards which they are directed, some—and here we
already lack a term, for all terms are self-fulfilling—design, matrix,
concept, blueprint, *gestalt*, configuration. Notebook items are peripheral fragments, pieces in some mosaic design. We do not know what
that shaping design is, our names for it are vague and groping, so that
we are left with metaphorical gesturings towards something dimly
felt or credulously conjectured. Joyce himself might not have been
able to articulate consciously what he had in mind, his letters to
Frank Budgen about some *Ulysses* chapters probably come closest.
The *schemas* are some of the best-known outward and visible signs
of what he may have had in mind at certain stages of conscious
artistry. It is typical that the schema itself changed. As indicated
before, the notes may have made a lot of sense in relation to some
creative nucleus, some mental image, let's call it *archemorph*: the
archemorphic center helped Joyce to define its peripheries; *we* have
only the peripheries and may feebly guess at the focal points. With
admirable imperfection, we try to get to the elusive core, the set of
programming rules (computer language has now contributed a new
type of analogies).

In describing Joyce's individual works, or their parts, we traditionally tend to list characteristics; their number is not limited, the task
never completed. To trace sources (psychological, biographical, literary, etc.) is rewarding and never quite satisfactory, it merely paves
the way from the question *where from* for the more important *what
for?* Some young women Joyce once knew in Dublin, the birdgirl on

the beach in *Portrait*, Marthe Fleischmann in Zürich, a young medical doctor Gertrud Kaempffer in Locarno, Joyce's 'own arousal by
his daughter's approaching puberty',[2] books 6–13 of the *Odyssey*, *The
Lamplighter* by Maria Cummins, novels, fashion magazines, etc.—all
of this still does not add up to the whatness, the feel, the peculiar
energy of 'Nausicaa'. Nor does Joyce's own sketchy itemization at a
certain period of composition, written in a certain mood, when he
called the episode 'namby-pamby jammy marmalady drawersy (alto
là!) style with effects of incense, mariolatry, masturbation, stewed
cockles, painter's palette, chit chat, circumlocution, etc. etc.'[3] The list
does not seem either a comprehensive inventory or essentially to get
to the chapter's throbbing design, or its palpable *quidditas*. Try to
imagine, just on the basis of Joyce's description, what the episode
might look like. What remains intriguing is that such a miscellany of
components could assume its individual, unmistakable shape and
idiomorphic coherence.

It would be worth knowing a subcurrent formula for the fusion of
such heterogeneous raw material. In the following, a range of tentative labels will be displayed in a basically futile attempt to come to
terms with a shaping drift that is supposed to be at the core of an
artistic process and which also infuses the works with their highly
individual parts. The terms, meant to be nothing but quick analogical
flashes, are often spatial, taken from architecture, like 'structure',
'mosaic'; they, however, tend to freeze the processes into static solidity. Chemistry or physics offer another set of analogies; those would
at least deal with processes. Suitable terms might be culled from
Joyce's works. One of the earliest to spring to mind is in the germinal
source of *A Portrait*, the unclassifiable 'A Portrait of the Artist' of
1904, which begins with a separation of those

who seek through some art, by some process of the mind as yet untabulated, to liberate
from the personalised lumps of matter that which is their individuating rhythm, the
first or formal relation of their parts. (*P* 257–8)

The phrase 'individuating rhythm' shows the young Joyce was
groping for a formula that combined something unique with a hidden
process. The word *rhythm* in itself would be appropriate; *rhythmos*
(from a root *SREU, to flow)[4] was used for measured motion, time,
proportion, symmetry, arrangement, disposition, form or shape of
thing; much of it went into 'rhythm of beauty' in Stephen's early theorizing: 'Rhythm... is the first formal esthetic relation of part to part
in an esthetic whole' (*P* 206). The Aquinian *consonantia* or harmony

is illustrated as 'balanced part against part', when 'you feel the rhythm of its structure' (*P* 212). The present day sense of 'rhythm', however, has narrowed to a very limited kind of motion or symmetry which does not seem to accommodate the integral disruptions and incongruities that are part of most Joycean idiomorphs. Joyce, through Stephen, returns to the term and offers two more alternatives in a famous passage that we feel suggestive of Ulyssean dynamics:

So that gesture, not music not odour, would be a universal language, the gift of tongues rendering visible not the lay sense but the first entelechy, the structural rhythm. (*U* 15.105)

Here the former 'rhythm of its structure' is elaborated, a phrase that aptly conflates a temporal notion with an architectural or Daedalian one. It becomes an alternative to an Aristotelian term Stephen had called up before, when it occurred to him that 'I am other I now': the molecular combinations that made up the debtor of a few months ago have changed. Yet something must remain immutable after all:

But I, entelechy, form of forms, am I by memory because under everchanging forms. (*U* 9.208)

Here *entelechy*, appended to 'I' and 'form of forms'—a definition of 'soul' (souls are difficult to pin down)—comes close to a formgiving cause and actualization, that which assures *Stephenitas* even when bodily molecules and cells have been replaced. Entelechy came to mean a vital force urging an organism towards self-fulfillment. The word is connected with *telos* (end, goal, completion, perfection), is 'that which has its end in itself.' When an ecstatic Stephen thinks of 'prophecy of the end he had been born to serve' (*P* 169), he imagines some actualization of a mythical Daedalian preordained destiny. *A Portrait* is based on some notion, that through all vicissitudes of growing and changing Stephen Dedalus at each separate stage is what he is. In this sense, each of Joyce's works, and distinct parts thereof, have their entelechy, are what they are and nothing else.

The most suitable metaphors, continuously resorted to by Joyce himself, are biological, relating to the growth of living organisms. In 'Oxen of the Sun' Joyce used embryonic growth and demonstratively linked it with literary development. Borrowing from biology, one might try out a term like idioplasm (part of protoplasm in a cell that is supposed to determine the character of the resulting organism);

this would mean something formed, moulded, *plasma*, in a particular shape, one of its own, *idio-*; the Greek adjective *idioplastos* meant something 'self-formed'. Joyce's justification of the book to Carlo Linati is built around a similar notion: 'Each adventure... should not only condition but even create its own technique.'[5] The 'adventures' of *Ulysses* are indeed idioplastic, but that of course is merely a way of describing anew what we have sensed all along. All metaphors not only fall short, they also distort and introduce their own traps.

There must be—'must' is purely speculative—some generative, formative urge or program that selects and arranges even the most unspecific items into the highly idiosyncratic shapes of Joyce's works, of which each one seems to have its unique tone, style, rhythm, vocabulary, perspective, and its own brand of excess. No one would possibly confuse an extract of the prose of 'After the Race' with that of the fourth chapter of *A Portrait* or with 'The Mookse and the Gripes'. 'Everything speaks in its own way' (*U* 7.177). One sentence can be different in tone from the next even within the same paragraph, as happens in the last section of 'Wandering Rocks'. Note the singularity of each vignette:

The viceroy was most cordially greeted on his way through the metropolis. ... Above the crossblind of the Ormond hotel, gold by bronze, Miss Kennedy's head by Miss Douce's head watched and admired. ... From Cahill's corner the reverend Hugh C. Love, M.A., made obeisance unperceived, mindful of lords deputies whose hands benignant had held of yore rich advowsons. ... In Lower Mount street a pedestrian in a brown macintosh, eating dry bread, passed swiftly and unscathed across the viceroy's path. (*U* 10.1182–272)

Each sentence has its own rhythmic shape, as though in mini-scale prediction of the stylistic variations yet to come in the second half of *Ulysses*; and yet they all fit into the overall register of the chapter and its last section.

No harmonious 'organic form' is presupposed; the resultant shapes may be, and inevitably are, full of conflicts, contradictions, incongruities, paradoxes, none more so than *Finnegans Wake*, and yet through all its deviations and heterotropies we recognize the *Wake* as something unique and distinct from everything else—including attempts to imitate or parody it. We recognize each chapter of *Ulysses* almost instinctively and (with the possible exception of the early Bloom episodes) can tell them apart with minimal effort. We may not agree with other readers' characterization, but we would at least understand even short-sighted descriptions as basically valid attempts, no matter how inadequate or subjective. Many of us find

the standard portraiture of 'Eumaeus', as one of predominant tiredness, a stereotype of critical misdirection, more harmful than instructive, but at least we can all see where nervous fatigue comes in and
that tiredness is responsible for at least part of the Eumaean contor-
tions.

Even in our disagreement, we presuppose some *germinal deep
structure*. This is true of all, or most, chapters of *Ulysses*, which in
essential ways defy pinpointing description: we all have different
perceptional priorities and there is always more to say. But it makes
sense to talk about them *as* chapters: this is one way to differentiate
Ulysses from previous 'novels'. Each chapter has its own tempera-
ment, its idiosyncrasies (a 'peculiar mixing together'). The analogy is
of a mixture, a blend, a sort of recipe, obviously much more than the
quantitative total of its impulsive assimilation, not a stable groundplan, but a flexible, demiurgic, adaptive propulsion. Something in
the nature of a *Platonic blur*: as prototypically determinative as one
of Plato's ideas, and yet again blurry enough to enable multiple
assimilations.

procreating function (*U* 14.31)

In search for some *chromosomic* germ, we have one biological chapter which makes a show of linking cellular growth with language and
style. 'Oxen of the Sun' is concerned with generative forces, biological and linguistic. In a maternity hospital, the mothers[6] themselves
are relegated into a distance, while we are distracted, in the foreground, by male voices in talk, and talk and actions in turn are transposed into literary set pieces, overt imitations, counterfeits, each one
co-determined by a style that is authorial (Swift, De Quincey, fathers
of English prose) or 'period' (Elizabethan, nineteenth-century scientific, etc.), according to a predominantly literary program. The chapter is in itself an illustrative series of singular, marked passages, stylistic sub-entelechies, each one a unique creation not unlike (at least
by intention) what cellular organisms are. The literary labels that we,
in the wake of the author's *ipse dixits*, attach to the various paragraphs are fairly pertinent, though never sufficient. The 'Gothic
novel style' does not account for everything in the respective passage
(*U* 14.1010–37), above all not for its many incongruities; by itself
'Gothic Novel' would not include passages in a mock-Synge idiom
('and I tramping Dublin this while back with my share of songs and
himself after me the like of a soulth or a bullawurrus'), an anachronistic quote from Meredith ('The sentimentalist is he who would

enjoy without incurring the immense debtorship for a thing done'), or an echo of something Haines said in the morning ('history is to blame'; *U* 14.1019, 1016, 1030), and certainly not a relatively recent word, 'Dope' (*U* 14.1024). The paragraph has a biostructural formula that is far more complex than the simple tag 'gothic'; its diversified coherence sets it off from everything else.

Now within the chapter, biological generative processes are a theme that is taken up from time to time in the rambling conversation which can easily insert scientific commonplaces or obsolete hypotheses. One of them is touched upon casually when 'the future determination of sex' becomes the flippant topic of the students' interests. Authorities are called up, among them a phrase of a German physiologist, Johann Friedrich Blumenbach, from whose views one term is quoted:

This would be tantamount to a cooperation (one of nature's favourite devices) between the *nisus formativus* of the nemasperm on the one hand and on the other a happily chosen position, *succubitus felix*, of the passive element. (*U* 14.1236–9)

The passage looks like the narrative extrapolation of a parodistic display of scrambled jargon from various sources. What the whole statement amounts to still has to await interpretation. The focus in this essay is exclusively on '*nisus formativus*' as a suggestive term that radiates beyond its immediate application.

We do find the name of the German physiologist in Joyce's notes for the chapter, among a list of entries scribbled upside down on a notesheet, crossed out in red, amid terms like 'superfetation, intussusception, gestation', etc., which are thematically related. This is 'Oxen of the Sun' 19 in Phillip Herring's transcription:

R<Blumenbach>411:19
R<night formations>[7]

Most probably the second entry, read as 'night formations', should be emended to 'nisus formativus'.[8] Our reference books have glossed *nisus formativus* as 'a directing morphogenic force peculiar to living bodies',[9] or simply and literally 'formative tendency'. It is lifted from Blumenbach's 1791 treatise, *Über den Bildungstrieb*, which became an influential book before Darwin's views of evolution redirected interest and controversies. Blumenbach argued against the views that there are 'preformed germs' ('*präformierte Keime*' [*sic*]). The crucial passage is Blumenbach's conviction [that]:

Dass keine präformirten Keime präexistiren: sondern dass in dem vorher rohen ungebildeten Zeugungsstoff der organisirten Körper, nachdem er zu seiner Reife und an

den Ort seiner Bestimmung gelangt ist, ein besonderer, dann lebenslang thätiger Trieb
rege wird, ihre bestimmte Gestalt anfangs anzunehmen, dann lebenslang zu erhalten,
und wenn sie ja etwa verstümmelt worden, wo möglich herzustellen.

Ein Trieb, der folglich zu den Lebenskräften gehört, der aber eben so deutlich von
den übrigen Arten der Lebenskraft der organisirten Körper (der Contractilität, Irritabil-
ität, Sensibilität etc.) als von den allgemeinen physischen Kräften der Körper über-
haupt, verschieden ist; der die erste wichtigste Kraft zu aller Zeugung, Ernährung, und
Reproduction zu seyn scheint, und den man um ihn von andern Lebenskräften zu
unterscheiden, mit dem Namen des *Bildungstriebes (nisus formativus)* bezeichnen
kan.[10]

No translation into English seems to exist; so the following paraphrase must do: The conviction is 'that no preformed germs pre-
exist, but that, in the previously raw and unshaped generative material of organic bodies, once it has achieved maturity and reached the
point of its destination, some special urge will become and remain
active during the lifetime, an urge to assume its destined shape, then
to retain it through life and, should it become maimed, to repair it.
An urge that therefore belongs to the vital forces, but which differs
from the other kinds of the vital force of organic bodies (contractibil-
ity, irritability, sensibility, etc.) as well as from the physical forces in
general; it seems to be the prime most important force for all generation, alimentation, and reproduction, and, to differentiate it from
other vital forces, it can be called *Bildungstrieb (nisus formativus)*.'

Blumenbach's term was well-known and much discussed, taken
up by Immanuel Kant and Goethe. In 'Oxen of the Sun' it appears
very peripherally and in a specific context of mock-scientific levity.
It allows itself to be sidetracked for a vital principle in Joyce's own
work, in particular the chapter in which it occurs, as though the
author had implanted yet one more self-descriptive signal. One marginal reason for the introduction of *nisus formativus* may be that its
originator's name has some outward affinity with Bloom: some nominal ancestor succeeded as a famous scientist (Blumenbach has been
called the founder of anthropology). The Latin *nisus* is appropriate in
itself: it derives from a deponent verb *nitor, niti* (lean against, support oneself against something, strive, exert oneself, strain): *nisus* is a
pressing, straining, an effort, but in particular as the pressing called
for in childbirth, it could also mean the pains of childbirth. In this
sense it contributes yet one more indirect obstetric tinge to the chapter. The Latin noun became an English scientific term for a striving.[11]

In Blumenbach's original German label (and title of his treatise),
the word *Bildung* is worth a short digression. The noun derives from
verbs which in Old High German meant 'to give shape and essence'

or 'to form or imitate a shape'; it could be applied to God the creator, reflexively it refers to natural forms; today *bilden* still means 'to form, fashion', more narrowly to shape, educate, train a mind. In some such sense 'Oxen' is indeed one of *bilden* and *Bildung* (formation, creation, development, education, the generation of forms). It concerns itself with biological shaping and with the development of prose and with artificial formation. If you were to recognize all the stylistic semblances that Joyce confects, you would be said to have *Bildung* (education, breeding, culture, often a wide-ranging knowledge in the humanistic tradition).

No wonder Joyce used the word at the beginning of *Finnegans Wake*, when that work is just shaping itself in our minds. Bygmester Finnegan, arch-constructor, we read

piled buildung supra buildung pon the banks for the livers by the Soangso. (*FW* 4.28)

This is the master-builder, as well as the instigator of civilization: *Bildung*, formation and everything cultural we have come to remember, the whole tradition. Without *Bildung* we cannot call up Adam or Bygmester Solness or the emperor Caligula, or any quotation; *Bildung* often consists of a command of knowledge and languages. A charge levelled against *Finnegans Wake* is that it depends so much on *Bildung*, which at worst is a store of cluttering surface information. The word includes *Bild*, picture or image, sometimes also used in the negative sense of idol, or else a mental image; imagination in German is 'Ein*bild*ung'; what we need to form mental images out of the hints in the text. Blumenbach's generative striving may add a biological dimension. The *mot juste* (almost the ideal one to impress Wakean principles on German readers) includes *dung* as a gratuitous and appropriate counterpart of civilization, or one of its results, but also biologically a recycling of nourishment.

The point of all the digressive endeavours is simply that '*nisus formativus*' can be abused and deflected from its primary context as a convenient focusing device for Joyce's works. The *Portrait*—commonly seen in the tradition of '*Bildungs*roman'—displays stages in the protracted formation of a character. In Stephen's self-conscious and ecstatic phrase, this can be seen as a dark mysterious purpose somehow written into his destiny: 'the end he had been born to serve and had been following through the mists of childhood and boyhood...' (*P* 169).

and all down the form (*U* 12.241)

'Oxen' is a series of idioplasmic fabrications, each one shaped by its peculiar *nisus*. That is true of all chapters, and sometimes we can watch the author grope for a shape not yet found. 'Cyclops' is a case in point and will serve as an illustration. We first see Joyce unsure of his way. According to the evidence of the early surviving drafts, he seems to have tried out a parodistic manner, narrating in implied inverted commas, in borrowed voices, in the manner of Irish legends in contemporary translations. This was the opening:

In ~~green Erin of the west~~ {*Inisfail the fair} there lies a land, the land of holy Michan. There rises a watchtower...[12]

The wording was salvaged for what was to become one of the first interpolations (*U* 12.68f) that disrupt the main narrative. The elevated manner would have included the action itself, as can be gathered from the introduction of Bloom that follows immediately:

O'Bloom went by {on} {*Who comes} through Inn's quay ward, the parish of saint Michan. ~~He moved {*ing} {the son of Rudolph,}~~ {It is O'Bloom, the son of Rudolph [the son of Leopold Peter, son of Peter Rudolph] he of the ~~intrepid~~ heart, impervious to all fear} a noble hero, eastward towards Pill Lane, among the squatted {stench of} fish gills...[13]

Bloom's genealogy has been Hibernicized right from the start. The many deletions and substitutions, however, show Joyce fumbling and tentative. It looks as though the first probatory concept was primarily a mock-heroic style with occasional bathetic drops to city and market disillusion; this would have been interspersed with passages of gutsy dialogue, and, as in the earlier chapter, plain narrative and interior monologue:

Bloom went by Mary's Lane and saw the sordid row of old clothes' shops... Like culprits. Be taken to the prison... They want to be? ... Girl in a window watching... Hard times those were in Holles street when...[14]

With such a precept the chapter might well have found its morphogenetic formula. But somewhere along the way, unrecorded for us, Joyce must have changed direction towards an external narrator's oral report, which turns Bloom into an object seen or commented upon only from the outside. Such reformation then enabled the chapter to proceed sure-footed, with many additions and modifications that were adapted with supreme ease. 'Cyclops' had become what it was to be, and with the opening beat,

I was just passing the time of day with old Troy of the D.M.P. (*U* 12.1), the pace and tone are set, we sense the speaker, his biases, attitudes. The parodic insertions could be fitted in as intermittent counterpoints. The *nisus* was obstetric once more: a character was born through a voice, idiomatic, recognizable without nominal identification. Other elements would fall into line almost effortlessly, as Frank Budgen remarked:

The words he wrote were far advanced in his mind before they found shape on paper... He was a great believer in luck. What he needed would come to him. That which he collected would prove useful in its time and place... I have seen him collect in the space of a few hours the oddest assortment of material: a parody on the *House that Jack Built*, the name and action of a poison, the method of caning boys on training ships, the wobbly cessation of a tired unfinished sentence... No one knew how all this material was given place in the completed pattern of his work... several foggy shapes of letters which, however, were sufficient to give him his bearings.[15]

Budgen himself, to his surprise, could serve as a model for the sailor Murphy in 'Eumaeus', part of a fictional character.[16]

nisus characteristicus

Characters are what they are and not otherwise. This is mere tautology, what is implied in the word. Joyce helped to question the mere notion of character, but undoubtedly he also created many characters that are unique and recognizable, imaginative verbal semblances to whom readers as a matter of fact do relate (remember spirited debates about Molly Bloom as though she were a person, to be admired or condemned?), or with whom they can identify. Eveline is not Molly and not E.M. and not Bertha nor Anna Livia—even if it should be proved that some of them have umbilical connections with, say, Nora Barnacle. Sources for Leopold Bloom, ingredients that went into his substance, are partly known (Mr Hunter, Mayer, etc.). They are of limited help and cannot account for Bloom's wide appeal and his firm anchorage within a twentieth-century pantheon. Once something like Bloomicity, however flexible and adaptive, was in the author's mind, diverse traits from whatever source could be discovered and integrated, because of some early cellular program that made only certain features assimilable.

Character has become an extremely problematic concept; Joyce among others has shown how it can dissolve, his works may display an assault upon characters. Even so there is a sense in which readers empirically may feel—illusion themselves that they feel, sense—the characters as characters and not merely textual configurations. In the pragmatic task of translation we may feel that a certain character would not speak in a certain way. When some additional dialogue has to be confected for a script, as in John Huston's 'The Dead', some of it may not sound true to type or true to story. No, Stephen would not sing, even drunk, as he does in the Joseph Strick version of *Ulysses* in answer to Buck Mulligan: 'stick it up your arse.'[17] How do we know this? We know it because of our own subjective internalization of traits we picked up in reading, on the basis of some supposed internal entelechy. No matter how distorted our subjective internalizations are, Joyce's characters have a lifelike appearance. We think we can discern Bloomness even in the most outrageous distortive presentations of some later chapters. It is some such imaginative incarnation that makes it possible for Leopold Bloom, whose existence is entirely textual, to have a plaque attached to his birth house in Clanbrassil street, Dublin (which some neighbours determined to be the wrong address), and to have the door of his residence enshrined in a Dublin pub on Duke street.

Character was something, long ago, like a sign or mark engraven. Whatever theoretical stand we take on 'character' in fiction, whether we consider it outdated, assaulted, disintegrating, or highly problematical, Joyce was an expert at putting marks on his figures or figments, 'signatures of all things' that we too can read. Some internal whatness, at any rate, seems to epiphanize when, for example, we have a short passage devoted to Master Patrick Aloysius Dignam in 'Wandering Rocks' (*U* 10.1121–74). All his thoughts seem to be shaped by an individuating rhythm, unlike that of anyone else. It is tempting to find a formula for what makes it so uncannily effective; it is not just the repetition of 'blooming' (four times), but a kind of temperamental tune that we intuit much better than we could accurately describe. Or take one short parenthetical sigh of pensive Miss Douce after Boylan's hasty departure:

(why did he go so quick when I?) (*U* 11.463)

The words are the most ordinary, yet the alignment characterizes someone of whom we have read very little (and most of it in a musical kind of refraction) and seems the most concise, poignant expression of disappointment. Typically, claims like these could hardly be proved, at least not yet; all we can do is to appeal to a subjective chord that seems to have been touched.

Blazes Boylan looms large in *Ulysses*, but mainly as a set of memories, rumor, indirect and questionable characterization; he appears in just two chapters and only speaks a few short sentences:

—Put these in first, will you?—That'll do, game ball.—Can you send them by tram? Now?—O, yes... Ten minutes.—Send it at once, will you... It's for an invalid.—What's the damage?—This for me?—May I say a word to your telephone, missy? ('Wandering Rocks' *U* 10.302–36)

—I heard you were round—What's your cry? Glass of bitter? Glass of bitter, please, and a sloegin for me. Wire in yet?—Why don't you grow?—Here's fortune—Fortune—I plunged a bit... Not on my own, you know. Fancy of a friend of mine.—What time is that? Four?—I'm off—Come on to blazes... ('Sirens' *U* 11.345–430)

A few more than one hundred words suffice to show him as dandyish, easy-going, self-assured, shallow, goal-directed, competent, in charge of the situation.[18] Even without their descriptive stage adverbials ('gallantly'—'roguishly'—'with impatience'), we can infer the tone, the hurry, the aplomb, perhaps the 'Fascination' ('That keeps him alive', Bloom thinks grudgingly, *U* 6.202). Boylan knows the right words to pick for the occasion, he is to the point, he gets results immediately. It would be a challenge to analyse[19] his speech acts, commands or questions that serve as commands; features like the brevity of Hugh Boylan's sayings would not be enough. The point here is simply that a quintessential Boylan voice has been set before us in a few words; that we (we? who is we?) cannot imagine Bloom or Little Chandler, nor for that matter James Joyce himself, saying something like 'What's your cry?'[20] Each hue, the *Wake* tells us, has 'a differing cry' (*FW* 215.17).

nisus criticus

Naturally some formative bias, often unreflected, motivates everyone of us exegetes. The tendentious workings of our mind help to give shape to what we think we interpret. In this way Bloom has his opinion about poetry: 'I wouldn't be surprised if it was that kind of food you see produces the like waves of the brain the poetical...' (*U* 8.544); the view is not so much a vital contribution to poetics as it is expressive of Bloom (as well as 'Lestrygonians' alimentary striving). Similarly, though with more sophistication, Stephen Dedalus imposes specific formative patterns on Shakespeare's works and reveals as much about the critic Stephen as he may about the playwright, who in this light appears compelled by a traumatic *nisus* that Stephen wants to use as a key: 'some goad of the flesh driving him into a new passion' (*U* 9.462). Everyone, so the Library chapter seems to indicate, tends to reshape Shakespeare in his own likeness: so does Stephen in the foreground, so would the poet AE, or the Quaker librarian with his idealistic *Bildung*, Oscar Wilde, the Baconians,

Catholics ('Your dean of studies holds he was a holy Roman', *U* 9.763), the Irish ('Has no-one made him out to be an Irishman? Judge Barton, I believe, is searching for some clues', *U* 9.519). We are all straining ourselves in a certain way (Latin *nitor*), formatively reading the books of ourselves.

So each reader has his or her own *nisus* to grind, and our critical tendencies take over, ineluctably. We can all predict what kind of contribution to expect from a critic whose work is familiar to us. Joycean readers, not surprisingly, can be particularly formative and fertile. In extreme cases, the interaction of textual and lectoral proclivities—whether we call it connivance, collusion, synergism, concurrence, cooperation, conspiracy—produces the odd results of the *nisus hyperformativus lunaticus peripheralis*, from which few of us are totally immune.

If then characters, like individual works, chapters, paragraphs, have been formed according to some latent genetic *nisus* that enables us to distinguish its individual hues and cries, it is also worth considering that not very much has been achieved by the labelling process, except that a finger has been pointed at something truistically conjectured. The first one to recognize this was Friedrich Blumenbach himself, who instantly followed his hypothesis with a reminder that the word *Bildungstrieb* merely serves to designate a force, whose effects can be empirically recognized, but whose causes are still hidden.[21] Naming something does not explain it, it may help focussing on it.

Trying to investigate the internal dynamics of texts (not to be confused with Texts) and to describe what we think we perceive accurately and in some depth remains an ancillary task. A certain kind of conventional interpretation may be considered valuable in so far as it comes close to the hidden deep structure that has been labelled here, following Joyce's lead, *nisus formativus*. The present Comparative Literature Symposium[22] has been put under the heading of 'Modernism: Precursors and Inheritors'. A tacit assumption seems to be the live and invisible presence of some idiosyncratic shape-giving *nisus modernicus*, even if we may never be able to determine what its striving is and how it operates under so many diverse guises. Inevitably, some venturesome spirits have gone on to engage in a quest for an even more elusive *nisus formativus postmodernicus*, one of whose guiding principles may well be to deny the existence of any such consistent undercurrent.

NOTES

1   'Eumaeus' 2 in *Joyce's* Ulysses *Notesheets in the British Museum*, Phillip F. Herring (ed.) (Charlottesville: University Press of Virginia 1972), 376–7. 'Intussusception' is found in 'Oxen of the Sun' 19, 257; 'despite' does occur in the chapter twice, but the notesheet hardly throws any light on such a common word.

2   Brenda Maddox, *'Nora': A Biography of Nora Joyce* (London: Hamish Hamilton 1988), 229.

3   3 January 1920, *Letters*, I, 135.

4   Etymologies given here are from the most likely of Joyce's sources, Walter W. Skeat's *Etymological Dictionary of the English Language* (Oxford: OUP 1881, rpt 1958).

5   Letter to Carlo Linati, 21 December 1920, (*Letters*, I, 147).

6   Parenthetically, it is little wonder that Stephen Dedalus behaves with unusual verbal extroversion (which seems to manifest itself through all narrative refractions). All day long, he has been obsessively concerned with his own dead mother: now he finds himself in a stronghold of maternity, where dead mothers may never be more than a labour scream away. So he is ill at ease and tries to combat internal discomfort with more alcohol and increased verbal production.

7   Phillip F. Herring (ed.), *Joyce's Notes and Early Drafts for* Ulysses: *Selections from the Buffalo Collection* (Charlottesville: University Press of Virginia 1977), 257. The carets (< >) indicate items that Joyce copied and crossed out in red ('R').

8   The word 'night?/nisus?' as it is squeezed into the margin of a big notesheet (*JJA* 21:40), looks very much like the shape in Joyce's addition of 'nisus formativus' in the Rosenbach manuscript (*Ulysses: A Facsimile of the Manuscript*, Clive Driver [ed.] [New York: Octagon, and Philadelphia: The Philip H. and A.S.W. Rosenbach Foundation 1925]), Vol. II, 'Oxen of the Sun', 40.

9   Weldon Thornton, *Allusions in* Ulysses (Chapel Hill, NC: University of North Carolina Press 1968), 345.

10   Joh. Fr. Blumenbach, *Über den Bildungstrieb* (Göttingen bey Johann Christian Dieterich 1791), 31–2.

11   The *Oxford English Dictionary* entry for *Nisus* is instructive: '*Nisus*. [L. noun of action f. *niti* to strive, endeavour.] Effort, endeavour, impulse. **1699** *Phil. Trans.* XXI. 177 This condition of motion being chang'd, there is a lesser Nisus. **1741** Monro *Anat. Nerves* (ed. 3) 34 This *Nisus* of the Mind to free the Body. **1752** Hume *Ess. & Treat.* (1809) II. 476 No animal can put external bodies in motion without the sentiment of a nisus or endeavour. 1851 Sir F. Palgrave *Norm. & Eng.* I. 39 Species and their varieties seem to have been produced by an inward nisus. **1899** *Allbutt's Syst. Med.* VIII. 248 When the nisus of web-spinning dominates the spider, when the nisus of nest-building dominates the bird.'

12   *JJA* 13:85. The graphic presentation of Joyce's correction follows Phillip F. Herring's useful transcription in his *Joyce's Notes and Early Drafts for* Ulysses, 154.

13   Herring, 152.

14   Ibid., 154.

15   Frank Budgen, *James Joyce and the Making of* Ulysses (London: OUP 1972), 175–8; Budgen's memory seems to relate to 'Oxen' and 'Eumaeus' and their formative biases.

16   Budgen, 252.

17   James Joyce, *Ulysses: The Original Film Soundtrack* of the Walter Reade Jr/Joseph

Strick Production (New York: Caedmon Records n.d.), TRS 328–B.

18   Any reader disagreeing with this characterization (which of course is in need of modification) implies by disagreement that that characterization is possible.

19   It may be meaningful to contrast Boylan's curt 'I'm off' with Bloom's indirect, hesitant, justificatory, unfinished 'Well, I must be' in need of complementation: 'Are you off?' (*U* 11.1126); though such pedantic observations touch only on the fringes and prove once more how difficult it is to get to the core.

20   In defining the 'lyrical form', Stephen in his theory called it 'a rhythmical cry' (*P* 214). Somehow we can distinguish characters by their rhythmical, individuating cries. Stephen's and Boylan's cries need not be links ever intended by the author, of course, but even cries can be distinctive marks, as when Molly Bloom remembers Rudy at birth: 'the first cry was enough for me' (*U* 18.1308).

21   'Hoffentlich ist für die mehresten Leser die Erinnerung sehr überflüsig, dass *das Wort* Bildungstrieb, so gut, wie die Worte Attraction, Schwere etc. zu nichts mehr und nichts weniger dienen soll, als eine Kraft zu bezeichnen, deren constante Wirkung aus der Erfahrung anerkannt worden, deren Ursache, aber so gut wie die Ursache der genannten, noch so allgemein anerkannten Naturkräfte, für uns *qualitas occulta* ist. Es gilt von allen diesen Kräften was Ovid sagt:—*caussa latet, vis est notissima.'* (*Der Bildungstrieb*, 31–4)

22   The present views were first given from notes at the 3rd Annual Comparative Literature Symposium at the University of Tulsa, 24 and 25 March 1988.

ANAGNOSTIC PROBES

This essay is one of several attempts to present and characterize instances of postponed clarification: later passages throwing light on earlier ones. This is nothing new in fiction (in life too we often understand long afterwards, or too late). Joyce seems to have given the disruption of smooth sequences more functional prominence; it becomes an essential, restless animation of the reading process as a halting temporal progression with inevitable glances backward that reinterpret what was apprehended before, in perpetual retroactive resemantification. Enlightenment trails behind. We *also* read from right to left. *Finnegans Wake* changed *Dubliners* and—in a loose, sweeping way—all preceding literature into the bargain. At least the eyes of the beholders have changed. In the following observations the focus will be on the impact that, microscopically, subsequent words, phrases, passages may have on those that precede them.

girdling

An attentive reader might well be slightly puzzled over the second sentence in *Ulysses* :

A yellow dressinggown, ungirdled, was sustained gently behind him on the mild morning air. (*U* 1.2)[1]

where the movement comes to a halt with the highlighted attribute 'ungirdled', framed between pauses in a moment of static observation. What is it that Mulligan's dressinggown is not? Does the word suggest that, against unstated expectation, there is no 'girdle' in sight, or else that the one Mulligan has he wears loose, untied? Dictionaries will not decide this.

But what is a 'girdle' in the first place? A term that obviously belongs to the elevated, ceremonious, churchly diction of the opening paragraph. No further real girdles will turn up in *Ulysses*, unless in imagination or in parodistic passages.[2] The seemingly unwarranted negation has lured annotators to the word, but with a tendency towards instant symbolism:

ungirdled—an inversion of priestly chastity.[3]

This gives an ecclesiastical meaning to what has not been determined yet, even on the simplest of all possible levels: whether 'ungirdled' implies an absence of a girdle/belt or its not being fastened. Is the prefix 'un' privative, as in 'unattired', or does it connote a reversal, as in 'unfolded' or 'undone'? Questions of this kind, easily disregarded by critics in search of higher and more general truths, have to be faced squarely by translators. We can check whether they take 'ungirdled' to be something not present or something not done. Their views differ. Some think there is no girdle around: in French we find 'sans ceinture', in Swedish 'utan knuden', in modern Greek 'cheris zone'. The Dutch version is 'zonder ceintuur'. Others claim the girdle is there, but not fastened, as in German: 'mit offenem Gürtel', Norwegian 'Uomgjordet', or in Hungarian 'oldott övvel' (with loosened belt). Translators are, collectively, of two minds; the Danish one even changed sides in the course of revisions from an earlier 'snorløs' (beltless) to a mere loosening: 'Uomgjordet'.[4] The point is not that we inherently cannot know the meaning of 'ungirdled' (some native speakers may never entertain any doubt to begin with), or that there is some designed ambiguity, but that uncertainty is on record.

The sacerdotal symbolism of 'ungirdled', if not immediately evident, will be borne out only a little later, when Buck Mulligan intones his chant from the Mass, and even more so when Stephen Dedalus internally remarks on Mulligan's 'shaking gurgling face' and his

light untonsured hair (*U* 1.15)

It is Stephen with his preoccupations who notices that Mulligan's priestly parody does not extend, after all, to his hair: there is no tonsure. 'Untonsured' is doubly negative, it makes a point of the absence of a shaven crown, of hair that is not there. It also reinforces a liturgical portent in 'ungirdled'. The parallel, negative, uncommon, participles form a pair. So the annotators had a point, but were perhaps just a little hasty in forcing a priestly resonance on unsuspecting readers *before* Buck Mulligan had a chance to display his persistent mimicry. The annotators are right after all; they are right *after* all. A later 'untonsured' affects a previous 'ungirdled'. We might now conclude, by analogy, that just as untonsured means 'no tonsure', 'ungirdled'[5] might reinforce 'no girdle' and dispel lingering lexical doubt?

As it happens, semantic resolution will come in the same chapter when Mulligan, reverting to his ceremonial play-acting,

stood up, gravely ungirdled and disrobed himself of his gown, saying resignedly:
—Mulligan is stripped of his garments. (*U* 1.508)

Here the identical shape operates as an active verb that clearly presupposes a girdle in order to become unfastened. We now know for sure that Mulligan was wearing a belt or girdle all along, but that he first wore it untied (and must have fastened it in the meantime). We can *now* claim that the several beltless translations in existence are, on the basis of intratextual consistency, in need of correction. The participle, epithet, 'ungirdled' can be tied—fastened—buckled to the subsequent past tense 'ungirdled' and clarified by it.

What at first may not have been evident now has become so by circumstantial completion. Earlier understanding can be revised and modified, always supposing that the former occurrence is remembered and recognized (some translators evidently did not make the connection between the two related passages). Understanding proceeds in time. Meaning accrues, changes, with the progress of the reading. So a question becomes not only what something means, but *how* and *when* it may mean what, and HOW meaning comes about.

At times, as in jokes, we may deliberately be led astray. There may be an unforeseen twist. One of Lenehan's facile quips, referring to the prospective father of a newborn child, is that a Jewish parent is

Expecting every moment will be...

If we have not heard it before we will be surprised, though not necessarily amused, by the sequel:

... will be his next. (*U* 12.1649)

Expectation, truistically, is connected with the next moment that may or may not fulfill it. Joyce supplies us with many next (or future) moments of semantic momentum, or, etymologically, Latin *momentum*—motion, alteration, impulse. Some hindsight impulses are worth passing attention.

circumdation

We normally understand in the light of what went before. Memory enables us to make sense of odd collocations. As English teachers, stylists, purists, we might not accept an expression that tells us that a woman 'smiled *tinily*'.[6] The immediate context, however, justifies the unusual adverb:

A tiny yawn opened the mouth of the wife of the gentleman with the glasses. She raised her small gloved fist, yawned ever so gently, tiptapping her small gloved fist on her opening mouth and smiled tinily, sweetly. (*U* 10.125)

This shows a simple progression from a 'tiny yawn' to 'smiled tinily'. The manner of smiling appears to be a stifled yawn transformed and brought about by the same mechanics, such as those impassively reported in 'Wandering Rocks'. We see that what 'tinily' does, above all, is to link the resultant smile with its analogous origin (in a similar transition Davy Byrne had 'smiledyawnednodded all in one', *U* 8.969). We read from left to right, most of the time. But it was C.G. Jung who once observed that *Ulysses* could be read from anywhere in either direction.

We know what he had in mind and how he exaggerated, but at times the reversal is literally true. 'Metempsychosis' follows 'Met him what?' (*U* 4.336), but also explains it from behind, inverting the accustomed order. All reading is in part backwards, and in some cases more pointedly so. Poetry and prose in the classical languages do not make immediate sense at each turn; much has to be held in mental storage until semantic circuits are closed. In the sequential release of information, English has to be more orderly and explicit than highly inflected Latin. Joyce switches to Latin right after the first paragraph of *Ulysses*, but it is the relatively straightforward syntax of the Old Testament rendered into the Vulgate and used in the Mass: '*Introibo ad altare Dei.*' This reads almost like its vernacular equivalent: 'I will go unto...' Except that our Latin reader or audience would have to wait, minimally, for the last syllable of the first word, the terminal 'o' of 'introibo', to know who will be going.

When Stephen Dedalus obsessively remembers the death of his mother, he conjures up, visually: 'Her eye on me to strike me down', and then, audibly, Latin words from a Prayer for the Dying, words that have become a haunting, excruciating memory. Imagine you want to know what those words actually say as you hear them one by one. For purposes of demonstration we will break up the verbal sequence into slow-motion semantification—which cannot pretend to simulate in any way the serial processes of listening or reading. How much could we 'understand' at each singular step forward?

'*Liliata*' (*U* 1.276): a participle, in its nature the result of some process. Something undetermined as yet has been 'lilied': made into a lily(?), made to resemble a lily (?), provided, perhaps decorated, with lilies? The verbal derivative of a noun for a flower is dangling without any semantic anchorage. The sentence ironically begins with a word that suggests the end of a process.

'*rutilantium*' (glowing red): another participle, this time present tense and active voice, unrelated to the preceding one. There is no immediate connection between something 'lilied' ('*liliata*' is feminine singular—*or else* neuter plural) and an unidentified genitive plural participle, perhaps a contrast in colour: something white juxtaposed to something reddish.

'*te*': neither participle meaningfully coheres with the pronoun 'te' (you, accusative). The three disparate words add up to a cluster of contingencies. No plot, or pattern, or syntactical shape is discernible. Indeterminate (as yet) activities precede identities.

Comprehension is brought about by the next three steps, one by one, backwards.

'*confessorum*': this supplies 'confessors' in a plural genitive that we now can join to '*rutilantium*'—confessors are shining with some ruddy light. The light effects have run ahead of their source.

The next moment offers '*turma*' (*U* 1.277): a crowd, which reveals the delayed subject and a theme, to which '*liliata*' can be attached. This crowd is, perhaps, of lily-white appearance, or else each with a lily in hand, or perhaps emblematically purified. Grammatically it may be the subject or else have some ablative function.

Up to that point it remains obscure what a whitish group of reddish confessors does, until '*circumdet*' finally relieves a suspended 'te' from indeterminacy: the crowd may, or should, '*surround you*'. It also says what kind of sentence the whole construction is. In exaggeration, it is the very last vowel that gives the tone of the whole away. The final syllable, the conjunctive 'e' in '-det', indicates a wish, a petition, a prayer, and not a statement of fact.

Sense leaps out at the last possible moment. It is oddly fitting that, with the delayed verb '*circumdet*', meaning is in fact rounded off, 'circumdated': previous data link up. A semantic circuit is closed.[7] With the syntactical matrix in mind, we can now navigate the continuation with far less perplexity, right from the start: '*iubilantium te virginum chorus excipiat.*' Transient obscurity has given way to light.

The translations of the Latin prayer available to Joyceans[8] are not quite in agreement about the first word, '*Liliata*': it is considered to mean 'lilied' in the sense of decorated with lilies, or perhaps provided with lilies, and also more metaphorically: 'bright *as* lilies'. More intriguing is the inherent untranslatability of the dynamics. Modern European languages like English must rearrange the process and forgo the suspenseful choreography of delayed matchings in favour of instant, step by step, pre-orientation. We inevitably begin with an optative signal like 'May...' and are directed, right away, towards an appeal, with an identifying subject following soon after. This is a wholly different cognitive development, without the puzzles or mysteries that seem indicative of the many that are yet to follow in this book. Orderly, streamlined translations of '*Liliata rutilantium*' are as adequate to the motion of the sentence as a plot summary would be to the actual explorative experience of reading *Ulysses*.

Novices learning how to read *Ulysses* make laborious headway not unlike students spelling out a Latin period—a complex tissue of anticipations and delays, with pauses and retrogressive reassurances or revisions. Some of the most disturbing, modernist, features of *Ulysses* were routine in classical languages. In the first chapter we will figure out, not in the conventional, expositional order, but by circumstantial links, the setting on top of a historical tower, somewhere near Dublin, at a certain time. The last two chapters, 'Ithaca' and 'Penelope', put much of what we had taken for granted into a different light. Adjustment takes patience and circumspection, many retracings in an Odyssean progression of trial and error—unless such indigenous processes are short-circuited by outside information or tutorial interference. So the spelling out of '*Liliata rutilantium*' seems typical and representative, except that the resolutions do not tend to be as neatly satisfactory as in Latin grammar. As often as not we may still be waiting for the final, redeeming, '*circumdet*' that makes everything fall into line.

she could see from where she was

What we learn may change what we thought we knew before, even when we did not feel in need of explanations. '*If youth but knew*', Mr Deasy quotes sententiously to Stephen Dedalus in an entirely unrelated context (*U* 2.238), but as a matter of fact we never know *now* what we may come to see differently only a few insights later. Joyce's works tend to make such truisms poignantly appreciable.

Nothing appears puzzling in the first part of 'Nausicaa'. What we read is, moreover, and this is unusual in the chapters that came before, presented in a conventional manner, with a handy exposition and plenty of descriptive asides. It is easy to visualize the scene, the strand, and to know the time, evening. Girlfriends, we read, 'were seated' on the rocks (*U* 13.9). Not sitting, but 'seated'—a suitably elevated, dignified style for the sort of dignified poses that are on view. Of the three girls, one, Edy Boardman is soon witnessed with little Tommy behind the pushcar, so she must have left her position; another, Cissy Caffrey, seems to move about a great deal with the twins; at one time she walks over to a gentleman opposite. One moment 'she jumped up... and ran down the slope'; and she ran, we learn from the internal, unflattering, comment of Gerty MacDowell,

with long gandery strides it was a wonder she didn't rip up her skirt at the side... to show off and just because she was a good runner she ran like that so that he could see all the end of her petticoat running and her skinny shanks... It would have served her just right if she had tripped up over something... (*U* 13.474–85)

The observations are a bit less than friendly. When all the others leave, Gerty still remains behind:

If they could run like rossies she could sit so she said she could see from where she was. (*U* 13.688)

Much of this we take in as a tinge of jealousy and perhaps natural rivalry for attention. Gerty adamantly stays behind to watch, at which stage she is also conscious of being watched. It is only later, when Leopold Bloom eyes Gerty as she walks away, precariously, in a carefully delayed exit, with a limp that is no longer to be concealed in a becoming posture—it is only then that we learn of an additional reason for Gerty's resolution to remain on her rock, 'seated' indeed, leaning back, at her immobile best. She was right in a way we could not then guess: the others, they *can* run like rossies, but not she. She attempts to elevate her stasis into a superior attitude. The pose she lets herself be caught in for half a chapter is an optimal one. We can now see, *from where we are*, what we could not possibly notice when we were limited to a point of view that refracted her own selective mind and what it chose not to admit.

Once we are conscious of her handicap, what she does and does not do makes more pertinent, pathetic, sense and invites more understanding and empathy. With the hindsight of later readings, we can even review the sentence that introduced her in a previous chapter:

Passing by Roger Greene's office and Dollard's big red printinghouse Gerty MacDowell, carrying the Catesby's cork lino letters for her father who was laid up, knew by the
style it was the lord and lady lieutenant but she couldn't see what Her Excellency had
on because the tram and Spring's big yellow furniture van had to stop in front of her
on account of its being the lord lieutenant. (*U* 10.1205)

We now know that this early vignette does not show Gerty at her
most attractive; impeded motion is matched by impeded vision. We
may reinterpret the passage as a halting one, and can now give it a
corresponding rhythm and turn the prose into one that drags its feet,
in a possible imitation of the walk, 'with a certain quiet dignity characteristic of her but with care and very slowly' (*U* 13.769). Whether
such an intensification is justified or not, it could not even be
attempted without the postponed knowledge that this woman's locomotion is seriously impaired. Having witnessed Gerty MacDowell's
lameness, we will never recapture that pristine, innocent perspective
of before. That 'one shortcoming', the limp, is going to stay as a part
of all further readings. We cannot read the same chapter twice.

invalidation

In one of the sections of 'Wandering Rocks' we find Hugh Boylan
supervising a blond shopgirl filling a wicker basket with fat pears
and shamefaced peaches on top of a 'bottle swathed in pink tissue
paper and a small jar'. He wants it all sent immediately to an address
he scribbles down while he adds a discretionary explication:

—Send it at once, will you? he said. It's for an invalid. (*U* 10.322)

At that stage, most readers may guess at the identity of the supposed invalid and only wonder, perhaps, about the particular kind of
subterfuge.

The shopgirl's wholly unexciting response to this is worth a short
digression:

—Yes sir, I will, sir. (*U* 10.323)

Nothing remarkable; pure, though maybe flustered, politeness; but
potentially no longer so for readers who have the end of *Ulysses* with
Molly Bloom's closing 'I said yes I will Yes' in mind. They may
impose belated significance on the coincidental echo. For what it is
worth, a shopgirl now says to Boylan, or nearly so, what Molly
Tweedy said to Bloom sixteen years ago in a different context. The
end of the book enables us to pause, midway, at a commonplace
phrase.

Boylan erects a little smokescreen of an invalid or, as some translators slightly magnify it, a sick person.[9] We hardly worry over such a
trifle. Parallactic confirmation of Boylan's gifts will come later. On
the Blooms' kitchen dresser we again find the wicker basket with one
remaining pear (and learn it is a 'jersey' pear) and, again very specifically:

a halfempty bottle of William Gilbey and Co's white invalid port, half disrobed of its
swathe of coralpink tissue paper. (*U* 17.306)

'Ithaca' keeps minute track of concrete details. We discover what it
is that Boylan sent ahead to pave the conqueror's way—a bottle of
port (Lenehan, referring to his own, very minor and external con-
quest of Molly, thought of her as 'well primed with a good load of
Delahunt's port under her bellyband' (*U* 10.557). More specifically,
the bottle contained 'invalid port', and it seems clear now that this
word triggered off the evasive misrepresentation 'for an invalid'. This
gain of postponed comprehension is minimal; a tiny source has been
disrobed, an earlier scene becomes more ordinarily real. The brand
name, perhaps even remembered off the actual label, gave Boylan the
idea: what would be more natural and less original than invalid port
being sent to an invalid? One might even imagine a voice inflection
like 'It *is* for an invalid.' All of this looks quite in keeping with the
nature of 'Wandering Rocks'—transferences on the surface. At the
time, no matter how closely we scrutinized the scene in the fruit
shop, we would never have guessed such a trifle.

Such hindsight elucidation only works if we match a later occurrence with a prior one. An act of recognition is required which may
or may not take place. It often doesn't, given the wealth of details to
pay attention to.[10] Uninformed by external nudges, we may never
connect Bloom's 'I was (just) going to throw it away' (*U* 5.534 and
537) with the outcome of the Gold Cup race—but officious commentators usually take care that we do.

For easy reference what is common to all the above processes shall
be denoted by means of a Greek verb which simply means to recognize: *ana-gigno-sk-ein* (to know again). The noun suggested for
retroactive modification is *anagnosis* (recognition). The term is similar to the two Aristotle used in his *Poetics*: 'anagnorismos' or 'anag-
norisis', for very specific revelations or discoveries. The Greeks, with
fine insight, extended the meaning of the verb *anagignoskein* to the
analogous cognitive activity of reading. By common sense, reading
depends on knowing again what we come across, on *recognition*. We

are less likely to lose sight of this platitude in a book like *Ulysses*, where non-recognition often frustrates us. Making our way through a later chapter like 'Circe' is largely a matter of recalling earlier events, phrases, motives. The episode is, vitally, an elaborate orgy of anagnostic distortions and permutations. 'Circe' depends on its own past.

Anagnosis, by definition, is always secondary—*re*-cognition. Reading the Gerty MacDowell parts again allows us to see them readjusted. When Mulligan ungirdles himself we can project back and verify that he did have a girdle, by anagnosis. We do not always understand at once. Joyce instructs us to wait. Bloom remembers a night in the box of the Gaiety theatre with Molly, when he 'Told her what Spinoza says in that book of poor papa's. Hypnotized, listening... She bent' (*U* 11.1058). Even though we cannot make out whether she was hypnotized by his talk or perhaps listening to the music before or after, she appeared attentive. Her own point of view will set this right: 'and him the other side of me talking about Spinoza and his soul thats dead... I smiled the best I could all in a swamp leaning forward as if I was interested having to sit it out then' (*U* 18.1114). Not Spinoza, but menstruation was on her mind, and ever after, with this now in *our* minds, we may find Bloom's 'What do they think when they hear music?' or 'Nature woman half a look' (*U* 11.1049 and 1061) obliquely expanded.

The most elaborate passage sorely in need of elucidation is the verbal jumble at the beginning of 'Sirens'. 'Understanding' these pages (called 'Overture', 'Prelude', or 'tuning up') pragmatically consists in discovering the parts later on in the chapter from which the opening fragments look extracted. Conventional order is inverted. 'Bronze by gold heard the hoofirons' (*U* 11.1) makes sense since we have already come across bronze and gold and can identify them as Miss Kennedy and Miss Douce (*U* 10.962). Otherwise we would be at a loss: 'bronze' does not normally 'hear'. The second item, however, 'Imperthnthn thnthnthn' (*U* 11.2) remains cryptic until we find an insolent bootsboy who turns a haughty voice saying 'your impertinent insolence' into a mocking variation 'Imperthnthn thnthnthn' (*U* 11.99). Ever after, we are likely to think that 'Imperthnthn thnthnthn' actually *means* 'impertinent insolence', but it only does so in proleptic and unwarranted foresight. In this way the 'Overture' is being read backwards. The technique could be termed, by misappropriation, one of functional 'afterclang' (*U* 11.767).

protean postcreation

Where Joyce differs anagnostically from most other writers is in the vitality of these retroprocesses, in the postponed modification. Seasoned Joyceans may, in fact, forget how much of what they know is tacitly and rightfully projected onto the pages. We all know that Stephen on Sandymount beach is writing a poem. Or do we? What we are given is a muddle of associations:

He comes, pale vampire, through storm his eyes, his bat sails bloodying the sea, mouth to her mouth's kiss. (*U* 3.397)

Then a new paragraph says:

Here. Put a pin in that chap, will you? My tablets. Mouth to her kiss. No. Must be two of em. Glue em well. Mouth to her mouth's kiss.

His lips lipped and mouthed fleshless lips of air: mouth to her moomb.[11] Oomb, allwombing tomb. His mouth moulded issuing breath, unspeeched... Paper... Old Deasy's letter... Turning his back to the sun he bent over far to a table of rock and scribbled words. That's twice I forgot to take slips from the library counter. (*U* 3.399)

We realize that Stephen, after experimenting with sounds and enunciation, *scribbles words*—words, presumably that grow out of what he turns over in his mind. The passage is sketchy; we see nothing of the writing nor do we, at this moment, read the composer's thoughts (as we usually do in a stream of consciousness chapter). No reader could tell what exactly the words are that Stephen records, except that 'mouth' and 'kiss' are are probably featured. Revelation has to await a scene in the newspaper office of 'Aeolus' when a bit of paper torn off elicits comment. It is then that we read, this time in Stephen's mind, but arranged as though they were laid out on paper, four neat lines of verse:

> On swift sail flaming
> From storm and south
> He comes, pale vampire,
> Mouth to my mouth. (*U* 7.522)

So this seems to be what was taken down on the beach in moments of narrative inattendance. The processes that went into the making of a short stanza can now be reconstructed, in part. We can *now* tell—or at least tell with some assurance—what it is that was thought *then*.

We could never have inferred from 'Proteus' that *He comes, pale vampire*, was taken over unchanged. Surprisingly, what was *twice* '*mouth to her mouth's kiss*', and the variant '*Mouth to her kiss*', has become 'Mouth to my mouth'.[12] The female element has evaporated completely, three *hers* have been replaced by *my*. There is, in other words, more Stephen and less woman. Similarly, 'kiss' has disappeared in the final version, and all that experimenting with oomb-womb sounds went for nothing.

We can also potentially recognize an addition unsuspected before, most likely the unconscious recall of Douglas Hyde's English translation of an Irish poem from the *Lovesongs of Connaught*, which ends in 'His mouth to my mouth' to rhyme with 'south'. Both the borrowings and the differences from Douglas Hyde's metric pattern and wording are now more evident. We also see what has fallen by the wayside: sails are not 'bloodying', but 'flaming' (this was lifted from 'the sun's flaming sword', *U* 3.392). Other elements like 'swift' and 'south' have been added.[13]

The finished product throws retrospective light on the process of its finishing, but not too much. We cannot tell, of course, whether the version given in typographical arrangement (suitable for a chapter dealing with printing and newspapers) is what Stephen wrote down on the beach. For all we know, he could have transformed the four lines several times over in Protean perpetuation. We only know that selective and compositional changes were being made in between.

Without the later passage, the earlier one would remain highly opaque. This is especially so if we compare it to its analogue in *A Portrait*, Stephen's elaborate, and elaborately recorded, composition of the villanelle. What is of interest here is not alone that a later occurrence anagnostically elucidates its counterpart, but that it may prompt us to modify our views of Joyce's technical procedure. A chapter like 'Proteus', almost entirely given over to the interior monologue, might suggest *an almost unbroken stream* of perception and associations. We might easily think that—in a kind of psycho-transcript, or a translation of thought into words—we are consistently told what goes on. We later find out what mental processes (composing even four simple lines is a highly complex web of interactions) were silently elided, outside of our range. The processes of selection, matching and structuring were much more intricate than a sentence that directed us to the writer's shadow—'His shadow lay over the rocks as he bent, ending' (*U* 3.408)—would have indicated. Hindsight discloses a major narrative omission.

In retrospect we become more knowledgeable and at the same time perhaps more skeptical. More accreted knowledge implies an

increased sense of what further may elude us. Elusiveness itself
becomes part of the meaning.

on the boil

We cannot be aware of what we do not know. Many passages do not
seem to require clarification at all. In the first bedroom scene of the
Blooms, few of the trivia we witness raise questions. Molly's imperative 'Poldy!' hastens Bloom up to her bedside. 'Who are the letters
for?' she asks.

—A letter for me from Milly, he said carefully, and a card to you. And a letter for you.
(*U* 4.250)

On a first exposure we can hardly notice how carefully, indeed,
Bloom contrives his answer. On a return reading the studied casualness of his enumeration is striking. He first mentions his own letter,
then Milly's card. 'And a letter for you' sounds like an afterthought;
it is, however, we now realize, what he knows Molly wants to know
above all. The letter, picked up on the hallfloor, with its address 'Mrs
Marion Bloom' in a 'Bold hand', has already made 'his quickened
heart [slow] at once' (*U* 4.244). It made him lose his composure. His
plain answer is a careful act of dramatic retardation.

Having deposited Molly's mail on the twill bedspread, he might
well leave, his duties done, but he lingers behind and asks 'Do you
want the blind up?' and, unbidden, proceeds to let more light into
the room. A deviously appropriate word, 'blind': all during the day
Bloom will shut any thought of the man who sent that letter to his
wife out of his mind. Moreover, in the course of the novel, 'blind'
will acquire a sense of Odyssean subterfuge. With 'The courthouse is
a blind' (*U* 12.1550), Lenehan suggests that Bloom's words are a pre-
text.[14] It is easy to overemphasize such subsidiary connotations. What
makes them possible is a memory of their future.

When we know what the consequences of Molly's letter are, we
appreciate her impatience better than we did on our first encounter,
and understand why she hurries Bloom out of the room so she can
read its contents: 'Hurry up with that tea, she said. I'm parched.' He
answers: 'The kettle is boiling' (*U* 4.263). As he reaches the kitchen
soon after, with Molly's 'Scald the teapot' still in his ear, he finds the
pot 'On the boil, sure enough' (*U* 4.270).

Domestic routine, all of this, sure enough. For readers alerted to
the nature of the rival who will bring the programme and generally
manage Mrs Marion Bloom's impending concert tour, and familiar

with Bloom censuring perturbing thoughts, the doubling of 'boiling' and 'on the boil' is less of a harmless repetition. Mind you, at this point the name Boylan has not yet surfaced; but Bloom knows, as his reactions indicate, who sent the letter. Anagnostic substitution enables us to interpret a haunting non-presence. For this we do not depend on later alignments like Lenehan's 'I'm Boylan with impatience', or its near-resumption 'I'm off, said Boylan with impatience' (*U* 10.486; 11.426), but the two resounding occurrences infuse the morning's 'boil(ing)' even more. In other words, we understand much of *Ulysses* by what is not yet there on the page.

As he fiddled with the blind, Bloom's 'backward eye saw her glance at the letter and tuck it under her pillow' (*U* 4.256). His 'backward eye' can be taken out of context and interpreted as a tacit reading instruction. Backward glances allow us to interpret what we do not understand, and to reinterpret what we think we did. Backward eyes are the subject of this essay.

pointing to the title (*U* 7.516)

Titles, in their annunciatory nature, are proleptic. They direct, anticipate, raise expectations. They are *prognostic*. True to promise, *Dubliners* is in fact about Dubliners, there *is* a mother in 'A Mother'. In the first story we may wonder, afterwards, why Father Flynn's sisters should be singled out for mention in the title, if in fact they are; but the sisters, though perhaps off centre, at least are there. On the other hand, 'Counterparts' is more tricky—what does it project? The title 'A Painful Case' turns out to be a phrase lifted from a newspaper, though it then radiates beyond its immediate context to include Mr James Duffy himself. We can hardly foretell, at the outset, what 'Araby' is going to be about.

The announcement 'Grace' might promise various things, none of them too clearly (possibly a name like Eveline). The subsequent tale will define it; in the course of our reading we will narrow it down, theologically, to a gift of God, against which we can measure the various more secular occurrences of the word. We understand the title *after* the reading. 'Grace' becomes a handle to talk about the story, the story explains the title, the title in turn gives incongruous weight to a merely prepositional 'By grace of these two articles of clothing' (*D* 154). By anagnosis—*and* prognosis—title and story interact. 'A Little Cloud' is a different case, with, apparently, no anagnostic epiphany to emerge from textual insights. So far no interpreter has revealed by a plausible elucidation what exactly the Old Testament echo achieves. What it does is to help create unrest.

The headlines Joyce added to the seventh chapter of *Ulysses* at a late stage also serve, in journalistic fashion, to anticipate, summarize, whet the appetite. Headlines prepare for something. Interestingly enough, the 'Aeolus' episode also includes the opposite direction: Stephen puts a 'vision' into words, spontaneously, it appears. He makes up a story that ends abruptly and is then asked to supply a title for it. Three revisionary names are then suggested—afterwards— as alternatives (*U* 7.1057). So in a temporal sense it is not true that Stephen *tells* 'The Parable of the Plums'—what he has told *becomes* a 'Parable' or a 'Pisgah Sight' by annexion. The appended labels in turn open dimensions the tale itself might otherwise not have had. Similarly (though not by authorial hindsight) a fictive Dublin day changes some of its constrictions by being named 'Ulysses'.

Aeolian headlines prepare for what is to follow, often in conventional proclamation, 'RETURN OF BLOOM', but more and more also in phrases 'HELLO THERE, CENTRAL!', held in suspense of which the import has to be determined retrospectively. A certain type of newspaper thrives on distortive anticipation. Occasionally, an event is featured only in the headlines, not in the subsequent text. There is nothing in the last section of the chapter that would bear out the titular promise of 'ANNE WIMBLES, FLO WANGLES' (*U* 7.1070). It will turn out that this information, if anything, already *is* the story, displaced and perverted from the body of the text, where all we read is 'Tickled the old ones too', an item that was already taken care of by 'DIGITS PROVE TOO TITILLATING'. The wimbling[15] and wangling is self-sufficient and paves the way for an anagnostic blank.

Aeolian headlines become progressively more titillating and self-perpetuating. A sentence like 'ITHACANS VOW PEN IS CHAMP' (*U* 7.1034), takes part in two contexts. The immediate one is the environment of the excessive headline itself which includes such pointers as 'SOPHIST—SPARTANS—HELEN' as well as 'PROBOSCIS'. A Hellenic flavour may help to pinpoint 'PEN'. The Greeks, discordantly, never abbreviated their names in such a crass manner; 'PEN' remains indeterminate. In the major context of the chapter, such a word has already figured rhetorically in an earlier headline: 'THE CROZIER AND THE PEN' (*U* 7.62), as well as in metaphorical dialogue ('that was a pen', *U* 7.630); a member of the staff was seen with a real 'pen behind his ear' (*U* 7.34). None of these potential meanings are valid of course, nor does 'CHAMP' refer, as it did earlier in *Ulysses*, to horses. The excessive headline owes its origin to a wholly tangential remark: Stephen is compared to Antisthenes, the sophist, who is credited with 'a book in which he took away the palm of beauty from Argive Helen and handed it to poor Penelope' (*U* 7.1038). It is this aspect which has suffered inflation into the heading—inflated as well as dislocuted, changed. The beauty contest has been transferred to a splurge of parochial pride. 'PEN IS CHAMP', an anachronistic jumble, can be understood, once more, in hindsight. 'Penelope' postdefines 'PEN', without, however, entirely deleting a hovering surface sense of a dominating writing pen, which still functions thematically in a chapter that pits oral skills against written or printed ones.

From another angle or by Homeric conditioning, 'ITHACANS VOW PEN IS CHAMP' could be read as a paraphrase from the *Odyssey*, where one of the suitors, speaking for all the others (all Ithacans) vows to poor Penelope: 'You excel all women in comeliness and stature' (*Od.* 18:248-9).

By their privileged positions, titles and headlines demonstrate the interaction of before and after even better than other parts. Everything we find in *Ulysses* may still, potentially, contribute to the significance of its powerful title.

coming events cast their shadows before (*U* 8.526)

Often a shadow precedes the event, an echo its origin, a distortion its prototype, a rumour its reality. We hear the mass in parody before we attend one and absorb fragments of the real thing. Stephen's opinions on *Hamlet* are first offered in Mulligan's mock exaggeration ('He proves by algebra that Hamlet's grandson is Shakespeare's grandfather...', *U* 1.555). They have to wait several chapters to be unfolded in a less facetious and more extensive form. An important key term in *Ulysses* is introduced by, literally, nothing, by sound not recorded, a blank in the text that we would not even perceive if it were not followed by a request for completion: 'Met him what? he asked' (*U* 4.336). Right afterwards the word becomes visible and is spelled out, defined and implemented—'Metempsychosis?' (*U* 4.339). We hear of Bloom's potato long before we can guess why he should take it on a tour in his pocket.

In the third chapter Stephen calls up his 'consubstantial father's voice' (*U* 3.62) as it comments on the in-laws, the Goulding faction: 'The drunken little costdrawer' (*U* 3.66), and then again, Crissie, 'Papa's little bedpal. Lump of love' (*U* 3.88). Uncle Richie Goulding himself is partial to superlatives: 'The grandest number, Stephen, in the whole opera' (*U* 3.100). This happens in an environment of thematic change, the voices heard may be unreliably transformed by memory or by imagination. When later on we hear a live Simon Dedalus say 'the drunken little costdrawer and Crissie, papa's little lump of dung' (*U* 6.52), or when Richie Goulding rhapsodies to Bloom: 'Grandest number in the whole opera' (*U* 11.828), we realize that the pre-echoes were substantially true. The first part of *Ulysses,* at any rate, offers parallactic confirmation and a texture of realistic coherence.

A minor character, Tom Kernan (known to readers of 'Grace'), first turns up as a subject for thought or conversation. His favourite expressions, on Ben Dollard's singing of *The Croppy Boy*, are imitated by Martin Cunningham 'draw[ing] him out... pompously':

—*Immense... His singing of that simple ballad, Martin, is the most trenchant rendering I ever heard in the whole course of my experience.*
—*Trenchant*, Mr Power said laughing. He's dead nuts on that. And the *retrospective arrangement.* (*U* 6.146)

This prospective characterization will be validated, the parody justified. When Tom Kernan appears in person he lives up to this mimicry: 'When you look back on it all now in a kind of retrospective arrangement' (*U* 10.783) he thinks; and 'Ben Dollard does sing that ballad touchingly. Masterly rendition' (*U* 10.791); and again: 'Most trenchant rendition of that ballad' (*U* 11.1148). Report this time has been proven right. Kernan's cherished phrase, 'the retrospective arrangement', is a key term for the techniques that are examined in this sketchy survey; it illustrates acts of 'anagnosis'. Most examples presented are retrospective arrangements.

True to type, Tom Kernan will in fact propose 'The Croppy Boy' to be sung in the Ormond bar (*U* 11.991), its masterly rendition will be set forth in refracted quotation. As readers we can retrospectively appreciate that, with its teary emphasis on the death of Irish rebels, the ballad fitted very well into 'Hades' where it was first brought to casual notice as not much more than an attempt to keep a conversation going.

terminal (un)certainties
A later occurrence, as has been abundantly reiterated, may throw light on, or modify, an earlier passage, or reveal a surprising turn. When the documents in Bloom's second drawer prove his financial basis (including £900 government stock, *U* 17.1864) to be reasonably secure, all his little economies during the day take on another aspect,

and he becomes a bit of an Odysseus laden with treasures. When, on the other hand, we hear that 'it was Bloom who gave the ideas for Sinn Fein to Griffith' (*U* 12.1574), this entirely new angle need not turn him into a political schemer or grey eminence or clandestine agent, for the rumour is unlikely to be based on fact; and yet one wonders to what accidental fire this particular smoke may be due. The role projected on Bloom in this instance is potentially adequate and, for all its practical unlikelihood, helps to characterize him and displays how the others view him with suspicion as someone not to be categorized, a dark horse.

Postponed information, if reliable, often clarifies very little; it does not of course automatically, in an ultimate epiphanic flash, put everything into place or remove all doubt. Not all of us would agree with the following conclusion on 'How Joyce Ends':

'Two Gallants' was written so that the story's central idea—that Corley and Lenehan have conspired to defraud a servant girl out of a gold sovereign to finance an evening in the pubs—eludes the reader until the final line, when Corley displays the coin.[16]

One assumption is that 'Two Gallants' has a 'central idea', another that it is manifested through the coin in Corley's palm, the last thing we read. Consequentially we recognize, so the argument seems to go, that Corley and Lenehan have been hatching a plot, with malice aforethought, and with success. So we can reinterpret the whole story and see how Lenehan, with whom we are detained most of the time, was in the know all along (but we were not). We are finally assured that 'a gold coin eliminates any ambiguity about their motives', and 'that the story is another indictment of the Irishman's preference for clambering over a woman to get a bottle of stout' (Herring, p. 96 and 51). All of this may well be part of the story's meaning and the characters' motivation, but it does invest a final disclosure with inordinate anagnostic trust in wholesale disambiguation. Perhaps Joycean motives—and that is something the stories might also reveal—are a trifle more intricate. Anagnosis is not a finite process.

Not everything will resolve itself in hindsight. Hermeneutic gains induce new turbulences. Postponed clarification may never take place, often simply for lack of further evidence. Most of us, for instance, assumed from Bloom's memory of his father-in-law:

At Plevna that was (*U* 4.63)

that Major Tweedy took part in the battle of that name and fondly used to reminisce about it. Molly remembers 'Groves and father talking about Rorkes drift and Plevna and sir Garnet Wolseley and Gordon at Khartoum' (*U* 18.690). Several scholars have documented that no British troops took part in that battle of Plevna in Bulgaria (December 1877). It seems assured that a major of the Royal Fusiliers, or a drum major or sergeant major for that matter, could not possibly have first-hand knowledge of it. What does this mean for us? Was Joyce careless or sloppy; was Brian Tweedy dishonest or bragging to his own family; or is he 'the product of such fantastically loose historical manipulation that at no point can he be taken seriously' (Herring, p. 135)? Or should we perhaps give up the *prima facie* notion that he did claim, on several recorded occasions, to have participated at Plevna? After all he might have been retailing something picked up from army talk, or out of Hozier's *History of the Russo-Turkish War*[17] that he appropriated from the Garrison Library of Gibraltar. There do not seem to be anagnostic pointers for plausible reconstruction of this sort, and so we might have to reserve judgment.

ten pages of notes (*U* 1.366)

Anagnostic insights are a matter of temporal disposition. Postponed revelation or modification entails a very practical, didactic dilemma for those who provide outside information in the form of annotation, commentary, glosses, or in the classroom. Assuming that not every reader nowadays knows of the Ascot Gold Cup in 1904 (in fact it takes some time for us to find out that the date of Bloomsday *is* 1904—when do we really first know?), of the battle of Plevna, 'The Croppy Boy', the Latin of the Church, Irish history, Dublin topography, etc.. What sort of data should be given out *when*? Annotators tend to anticipate, to pre-identify, to shortcut the explorative processes of reading that have here been likened to the parsing of a Latin sentence. For the benefit of instant enlightenment, commentators officiously put '*circumdet*' before '*Liliata*', an orderly horse before the nebulous cart, since this is also what is expected of them.

On the first page of *A Portrait* we come across two names, 'The brush with the maroon velvet back was for Michael Davitt and the brush with the green velvet back was for Parnell' (*P* 7); and as readers of the late twentieth century we may have to rely on commentary. But of course Stephen himself does not yet know who these people are; he will learn later. That is, among much else, what the *Portrait* is about, learning. The reader is still to hear a lot about Parnell in scenes to come, but practically nothing new will be added regarding Michael Davitt, a far less known historical figure. So a note has to be supplied, and supplied right on the spot, at the first mention of the name. Premature information can hardly be avoided, yet it goes against the developmental grain of the transformative novel which, after all, begins with 'ignotas' in its epigraph. External Annotation replaces inherent Ignotation and must do so, unfortunately, often far too soon.

As the funeral carriage gets under way in the sixth chapter of *Ulysses*,

The wheels rattled rolling over the cobbled causeway and the crazy glasses shook rattling in the doorframes. (*U* 6.30)

Our guiding commentaries hastily inform us that this refers to a song, 'The Pauper's Drive' whose refrain is 'Rattle his bones over the stones.' Is this sufficient, pertinent, or convincing? It is likely to become more so as we rattle along and, pages later, come upon

Rattle his bones. Over the stones. Only a pauper. Nobody owns. (*U* 6.333)

These are the actual words of the song, echoing in Bloom's mind to the rhythm of the carriage. From there on the song accompanies Bloom for a short while, and of course it is now possible to say that, perhaps, the previous rattling (without either bones or stones) already alluded to a song few of us would ever know or recognize without its subsequent direct quotation. At best, the early rattle is a vague adumbration, an echo before the sound is turned on. The untimely note makes sense on the premise that Annotation must translate a sequential progression into spatially available simultaneous knowledge.

When, in the first chapter, Mulligan talks to an acquaintance who tells him that he 'got a card from Bannon. Says he found a sweet young thing down there. Photo girl he calls her' (*U* 1.684), our *Annotations* inform us, helpfully, that 'Alec Bannon is an associate of Mulligan's circle and has met Milly Bloom down in Westmeath' (Gifford, 15–6). That this Bannon is called Alec will surface in the fourteenth chapter, and readers who make the connection themselves will be mildly thrilled by subsidiary recognition. Who 'Milly Bloom' is, even the most ideal reader simply cannot know at this stage. There is, in the first chapter, no Milly Bloom. Certainly, in some way, the Blooms in *Ulysses* may be said to grow out of this sweet young photo girl, but her precipitate exposure also counteracts something as insignificant as the dynamic spirit of the whole work. It is as useful as telling the reader of a detective novel in the first scene what the gardener has got hidden in his pocket.

Quite apart from depriving novice readers of the oldest literary pleasures of suspense and surprise, such anticipation implies that a first chapter is not really first, but coequal with all the others. This state of panoramic synopsis and readerly omniscience may be a distant goal. It is an aim of annotation to spare its readers trouble and save them time, but this time is then also removed from the reader's engagement with Joyce's works, the time of incubation, exploration, discovery, qualification, and renewed questioning and probing. All that this peroration wants to do is to balance the tutorial intervention and the prognostic remedies (that are often pragmatically necessary) against the ingrained anagnostic enjoyment of progressive reading as well as the frustrations of failed anagnosis.

NOTES

1　Former editions of *Ulysses* used to read: '*by* the mild morning air.'

2　Stephen Dedalus: 'marybeads jabber on their girdles' (*U* 3.388); in a Cyclopean interpolation we find 'a girdle of plaited straw and rushes' (*U* 12.169). 'From his girdle hung' (12.173); in one of the transformations of the fourteenth chapter: 'a point shift and petticoat with a tippet and girdle' (*U* 14.600).

3　Don Gifford and Robert J. Seidman, *Notes for Joyce: An Annotation of James Joyce's* Ulysses (New York: Dutton 1974), 6.

4　'En gul, snorløs slaabrok...' in *Ulysses*, Mogens Boisen (trans.) (Copenhagen: Martins Forlag 1949), 7, was changed, lexically and syntactically, to 'Uomgjordet bares en gul slåbrok...' in a revised edition of 1970 (19).

5　Perhaps another absent word is conjured up, the Latin, also priestly, prototype of 'ungirdled'—'*discinctus*', 'ungirt', with the same meaning of 'having no belt', or having one that is slackened. Fittingly it could also mean easy-going or profligate, the type of figure Mulligan is. Horace refers to a '*nepos discinctus*' (*Epod.* I, 34)—a loose, feckless, spendthrift (literally 'nephew': Mulligan is a nephew). Ovid confessed *in propria* or as a literary *persona*, '*discinctaque in otia natus*'—that he was 'born in careless leisure' (*Amores* I, 9, 41). A modern version has: 'born to leisure *en deshabillé*' (Ovid, *The Erotic Poems*, Peter Green [trans.] [Harmondsworth: Penguin Books 1982], 102).

6　Translations tend to iron out the irregularity, or paraphrase: 'elle... eut un petit rire de rien du tout'.

7　This mimetic 'circumdation' sounds a bit like *Finnegans Wake* in action: 'long the' and 'riverrun' could be illustrated by a term like circumscription. A meaningful sentence is patched together by surrounding, encompassing, beginning and end.

8　'May the lilied throng of radiant Confessors encompass thee; may the choir of rejoicing Virgins welcome thee', Weldon Thornton, *Allusions in* Ulysses: *An Annotated Word List* (Chapel Hill: University of North Carolina Press 1968), 17–8; 'May the glittering throng of confessors, bright as lilies, gather about you. May the glorious choir of virgins receive you' (Gifford, 10).

9　'C'est pour une personne malade—Het is voor een zieke—É per un infermo—Es ist für einen Kranken.' These last two translations overdo the pretence by making the recipient of the basket a male, which, given the name and address, is somewhat improbable.

10   Not all translators remember, when they come across 'invalid port', that this ties up with a casual remark hundreds of pages before.

11   Pre-Gabler editions of *Ulysses* said: 'womb'.

12   Ironically, Deasy's letter, the part not usurped by Stephen, also contains 'mouth'. Ireland's agricultural threat and Stephen's fictional conceit seem to chime when, just after we read '*Mouth to my mouth*', Professor MacHugh puts his foot in: 'Foot and mouth?' (*U* 7.527)

13   Retrospective comparison can point to a minor thematic permutation: What in 'Proteus' was 'the sun's *flaming* sword—*sails* bloodying the sea—the *southing* sun' (*U* 3.391; 397 and 442, italics added), has been realigned into: '*sail flaming... south* ' (*U* 7.522).

14   Molly Bloom will also think of 'some blind excuse' (*U* 18.695).

15   If indeed, as Stuart Gilbert claims (with an alleged nudge from the author), 'WIMBLES' is a *hapax legomenon* (*James Joyce's* Ulysses [New York: Vintage 1955], 198), the situation becomes even more tantalizing. A *hapax legomenon* is a lexical unit that occurs only once and has to be defined from that one context alone. Only wimbling Anne could know then what it is that she is doing.

16   Phillip F. Herring, *Joyce's Uncertainty Principle* (Princeton: Princeton UP 1987), 196.

17   This book, we learn, contained: 'The name of a decisive battle (forgotten), frequently remembered by a decisive officer, major Brian Cooper Tweedy (remembered)' (*U* 17.1419). The contrastive array of remembering, forgetting, and decisiveness is far from clear. It might mean that Bloom does not remember (though he did earlier on) the name of the battle, but that major Tweedy often did since he played a decisive part *in it*. Or else the adjective indicates no more than that Tweedy was a decisive officer with regard to professional aptitude. Ironically, it is factual meaning that is not decisive.

SEQUENTIAL CLOSE-UPS IN
JOYCE'S *ULYSSES*

Ti proton toi epeita, to d'hystation katalexo?
(What then shall I tell you first, what last? *Od.* 9.14)

Events take place in a certain sequence, just as words are arranged in a sentence. In any narrative the sequence of words and that of corresponding events are sometimes congruent, but often are not. Every writer can make us conscious of such platitudes, but James Joyce does it more than most, even in his earliest prose. In 'Ivy Day in the Committee Room',

Mr O'Connor tore a strip off the card and, lighting it, lit his cigarette.[1]

The sentence presents three steps (tearing—lighting, first strip—then cigarette) in the order of the events. But storytelling need not conform to reality in this way; different sequences can be imagined. Another narrative disposition might very well arrange the actions according to other than temporal priorities. 'On hearing the guard's whistle,' we read in another story, the driver of an engine, who reports at an inquest (where accuracy is essential), 'set the train in motion and a second or two afterwards brought it to rest in response to loud cries' ('A Painful Case', *D* 114f.). The loud cries that caused the sudden halt must have come before the driver stopped the train—the rearrangement is due to emphasis on the driver's responsibilities and actions; it is also, as part of the many choices available to a writer, wholly conventional and hardly noticeable.

The beginning of 'Ivy Day',

Old Jack raked the cinders together with a piece of cardboard and spread them judiciously over the whitening dome of coals. When the dome was thinly covered his face
lapsed into darkness but, as he set himself to fan the fire again, his crouching shadow
ascended the opposite wall and his face slowly re-emerged into light. It was an old
man's face, very bony and hairy. (*D* 118)

has a strongly cinematographic flavour—in the literal sense of
describing (*graph-*) movement (*cinemato-*) as it occurs, as well as in
the more technical sense of the medium that evolved when Joyce was
writing *Dubliners*. We are not too far from a film script: a camera, as
it were, is moving from raking to spreading, from cinders to cardboard to a whitening dome of coals; a face moves into and out of
darkness and is given detailed attention when it becomes visible
again. But even a camera might have directed our attention quite differently, might have highlighted the piece of cardboard before revealing the agent; or the dome of coals or the fire might have been chosen
as an initial focus. Old Jack raking the cinders together with a piece
of cardboard is part of all that we might perceive simultaneously, but
which, in the narrative, has to be taken apart according to some plausible order of precedence. We can imagine all manner of alternative
sequences that would appear perfectly true to some hypothetical
reality.

Such descriptions of commonplace events become increasingly
conspicuous in Joyce's prose, as though he had become aware of the
inherently problematical nature of complex multiple occurrences,
effects, synaesthetic perceptions etc., once they are verbalized into
one of several possible linear arrangements of words: 'a stride at a
time... the *Nacheinander*' (*U* 3.11).[2] In conversation with Frank Budgen, Joyce remarked upon 'the perfect order of words in the
sentence'[3] he was trying to find. The following remarks will subject a
few word orders from *Ulysses* to elaborate commentary. In slow-
motion reading it will trace a gradual development from close
sequential adherence at the beginning of the novel towards its sus-
pension in favour of more intricate devices later on.

hold up on show

The morning chapters of *Ulysses* seem to note events in the strict
order of their occurrence, or rather in the probable order of the main
character's perceptions, which we share. At times this results in a
slightly unidiomatic jar, an odd ring, phrasings that may go against
the grain of English syntax. In the first chapter Buck Mulligan, in
search of something to wipe his razor with, puts a commandeering

hand into the pocket of an already disgruntled Stephen Dedalus:

Stephen suffered him to pull out and hold up on show by its corner a dirty crumpled handkerchief. (*U* 1.70)

Against English usage, the object 'handkerchief' is at an uncommon remove (eleven words) from its governing verbs. Other languages can accommodate such (possibly gratuitous) postponement less easily. Translations are excellent testing grounds: departures from the original arrangement can pinpoint some of its oddity. The team of French translators, for example, came up with a different order of events—one which Joyce could also have chosen:

Stephen le laissa tirer un mouchoir malpropre et chiffonné que Mulligan exhiba en le tenant par un coin.[4]

The object of the display is identified right away and we move with the sentence from Stephen to 'corner' for mainly grammatical reasons, as the verb *tirer* seems to cry for its immediate object. The re-alignment necessitates the explicit naming of the agent, Mulligan, in the relative clause, who thereby gets more of the limelight than in the original, where it is the action that is prominent. In this different 'film script' we see the handkerchief before we see the processes to which it is submitted, the static noun precedes the active verbs. Joyce's original sentence, in contrast, is a slow revelation, a protracted, almost cruelly elongated, close-up of what an observer on the spot might have noticed, but mainly of what Stephen might have felt. The sentence, a psychograph, does not name, but re-enacts, and draws out his embarrassment and mortification.

The lexical contents of Joyce's sentence translate—more or less—even in a variant retelling, but its whole syntactical motion is normally not conveyed in another language without a break or punctuation. An Italian version follows the order fairly well, but like most other translations it has to revert to a subordinate clause with a conjunction, thereby causing a syntactical shift and a change of tone:

Stephen tollerò che tirasse fuori e tenesse in mostra per un angolo un fazzoletto sporco e gualcito.[5]

The separation of a subordinate clause from the main clause breaks the sentence into two distinct movements. Romance languages tend to put the noun before its adjectives, so that the handkerchief is perceived before its properties, in contrast to the original, which impinges first with a sense of dirt and crumpledness (compare the analogous opening of the book: 'Stately, plump Buck Mulligan came from the stairhead'). Hans Wollschläger's German version follows the Italian pattern, but it lets the handkerchief out of the bag prematurely and thus works against the histrionic delay:

Stephen litt es, daß er ihm das schmutzige zerknüllte Taschentuch herauszog und es hoch an einem Zipfel zur Schau hielt.[6]

The earlier German translation of 1929, like the French one, had recourse to a relative clause:

Stephan liess ihn ruhig ein schmutziges, zerknülltes Taschentuch aus der Tasche ziehen, das er jetzt an einem Zipfel in die Höhe hielt.[7]

This retelling pointedly splits the action up into two successive phases: the extraction of the handkerchief, and then, secondly, some antics done to it that are appended as in an afterthought. All translations considered here make their scenarios less perceptional or psychological. Joyce's strained word order works by serial progression: we notice a corner, dirt and crumpledness—all accidentals—before we recognize the handkerchief itself. The protracted slow motion (the sentence almost automatically forces on us a slow reading pace) thus does more than scrupulously depict the act in motion: the sentence describes the curve of an affliction and humiliation; it brings out, almost painfully, Mulligan's dumb-show action and malicious ostentation and Stephen's helpless submission. We might read it also as Stephen's mental endeavour to postpone the recognition of the dirty handkerchief to the last possible moment. Reluctance is built into the arrangement: 'suffered' stresses inaction, passivity, helplessness, pain. The opening beat alone, 'Stephen suffered him', has its independent validity. We may be reminded of the treatment that Telemachos is awarded by merciless suitors—the *Odyssey* begins with much explicit suffering.

So far the sentence has been commented upon as though its main effect were to capture an actual perception in its psychorealistic impact. But the sustained curve also draws attention to itself as a verbal artefact, it parades its own machinery. We seem to appreciate—evaluate—see, and almost taste each single word (also compare the 'new art colour for our Irish poets: snotgreen' [*U* 1.73] that Mulligan enunciates right afterwards). What is stressed and placed right at the peak of the sentence is 'hold up on show', an action indicative of Mulligan's histrionics. The phrase thus foregrounded comes etymologically close to that well-known, discarded term of Stephen's pristine esthetics, *epiphany* (hold up: *epi*; on show: *phainein)* in its simple original sense. Mulligan acts out a showing forth. Holding up a dirty handkerchief in pointed dumb-show is 'a sudden spiritual manifestation... in the vulgarity... of gesture' (as defined in *Stephen Hero*).[8] The wording of Mulligan's act epiphanizes Stephen's condition while the syntax holds its own anomalous arrangement up on show.

Such interpretative extensions away from the realistic plot may set too much fussy store by the mere alignment of verbal units.*Ulysses*, however, has a way of carrying its motives and devices to excess. In one of the parodistic interpolations that disrupt the action of the twelfth chapter (homerically termed 'Cyclops'), another handkerchief turns into a prominent exhibit. The first-person narrator first works it in very casually: 'Joe, says he, taking out his handkerchief to swab himself dry' (*U* 12.1434). Only a few lines later, a long insertion is devoted to this no doubt very ordinary piece of cloth which, under euphoric scrutiny, is translated, in the mock-epic manner of Cyclopean interpolations, into a precious, unique, *objet d'art*:

> The muchtreasured and intricately embroidered ancient Irish facecloth... was then carefully produced and called forth prolonged admiration. No need to dwell on the legendary beauty of the cornerpieces, the acme of art, wherein one can distinctly discern each of the four evangelists. ... The scenes depicted on the emunctory field... are as wonderfully beautiful and the pigments as delicate as when the Sligo illuminators gave free rein to their artistic fantasy. ... Glendalough, the lovely lakes of Killarney, the ruins of Clonmacnois, Cong Abbey... all these moving scenes are still there for us today rendered more beautiful still by the waters of sorrow which have passed over them and by the rich incrustations of time. (*U* 12.1438)

The whole insertion takes up close to 300 words—a comic exaggeration of 'hold up on show' indeed. There are now four cornerpieces with artful embroidery. Stephen's prosaic dirty handkerchief has here escalated to an 'acme of art' with an extended list of Irish beauty spots. What started out as a derisive 'snotgreen' has now pompously become an 'emunctory field' with 'rich encrustations of time'. The handkerchief on display, in other words, can no longer be overlooked.

cinematographic perception

The early chapters of *Ulysses* seem to render the perception of occurrences in what has been called 'imitative form'. This is especially true of passages featuring Leopold Bloom, a man given to close, often curious, observation of ordinary events. Watch him crossing O'Connell bridge:

Looking down he saw flapping strongly,...

What is 'flapping strongly'? An impression of motion precedes whatever is flapping; the sequel simply extends the impact and gives it a location:

wheeling between the gaunt quaywalls,...

It is only then that what Bloom sees (and we anticipate to be some kind of bird) is spelled out:

wheeling between the gaunt quaywalls, gulls. (*U* 8.51)

In a saliently cinematographic mode, attention moves from flapping and wheeling to the flapping and wheeling gulls, as though the birds were not recognized, or registered, before the end. Empirically we may well notice something *moving* before the *thing* moving is determined—motion before identification. For one fleeting moment, at least, the purely sequential reading 'Looking down he saw flapping' (as though a gerund) makes independent, transient sense. English gerundival and participial forms allow for much more gliding, in-between states than other languages. French grammar, in particular, does not easily tolerate a postponed object:

Il aperçut sous lui des mouettes qui battaient des ailes véhémentement, et tournoyaient entre les parois de pierre. (*Ulysse* 148)

We see the gulls right away, who then, in a separate clause, are doing something with their wings, and our gaze comes to rest finally on solid stone (an uncalled-for addition which, however, demonstrates a tendency towards solid fixation). There is instant ornithological recognition, and correspondingly far less of an initial indistinct general flutter. The point of this close inspection is not to fault the translation (which was certainly not objected to by Joyce), but to show that syntactical subtleties did not yet occur to the hard-pressed translators in the twenties. Half a century later a matter like word order was no longer to be neglected. An endeavour to recreate—in motion-writing—what Joyce had meticulously charted shows in the Italian version of 1960; it cannot have been easy in a Romance language to postpone the object to the end of the sentence, far removed from its verb:

Abassando lo sguardo vide con vigoroso palpito d'ali, roteanti fra i tetri muraglioni, i gabbiani. (*Ulisse* 206)

Even the pause before 'gulls' is reproduced, but not the momentary indetermination after 'flapping'. The original text makes Bloom pass through several cognitive phases from the perception of strong flapping to flapping and wheeling, then to something yet unclassified flapping and wheeling and finally to its identification as gulls—a gradual, groping recognition, a gradual act of apprehension.

The overemphasis on cinematographic, perhaps perceptional, phases is only part of what such a singular sentence achieves. By its arrangement it self-consciously juxtaposes two similar words: 'walls, gulls'. This anticipates Bloom's meditation on a related pairing: '*The hungry famished gull/Flaps o'er the waters dull*' (*U* 8.62), using 'similar sounds' ('That is how poets write', *U* 8.64). The sentence that introduced the gulls was already mildly poetical. An earlier poet had sung, centuries ago, about two eagles, not gulls, that were sent down by Zeus to an Ithacan assembly as an omen, something to be closely watched for its predictive significance. The movement of those homeric birds was rendered by Butcher and Lang in words that resurface in the Joycean sentence under discussion:

they *wheeled* about and *flapped* their *strong* wings (*Od.* 2:150).[9]

The echo may be wholly coincidental, the result of stereotypes habitually applied to bird flight.[10] Or it may mean that an expressive turn of phrase has great power to invoke literary memories. Apart from the homeric birds, there is also an eagle that was once combined with another choice adjective of our sentence. Ben Jonson's *Catiline* mentions the bird that feasted on Prometheus: 'His owne gaunt Eagle' (III, i, 1.200).[11]

Joyce's sentence, then, points two ways: on the one hand it seems to simulate through words the way in which a visual impression might affect a bystander; on the other hand it points to itself as a contrived artefact, which may in turn call up previous ones. It points both towards empirical 'real' life and towards its own place in a tradition of literature.

deviant sequences

Once we have noticed the close adherence to minute chronology—even against syntactical norms—each departure from it invites attention and becomes potentially meaningful. Otherwise one would hardly stop at a sentence like,

Buck Mulligan suddenly linked his arm in Stephen's and walked with him round the tower, his razor and mirror clacking in the pocket where he had thrust them. (*U* 1.147)

Temporal awareness ('suddenly') and chronological unfolding are well in evidence. Two objects, which become acoustically noticeable, have figured prominently in the preceding scenes: to wipe the razor Mulligan has usurped Stephen's handkerchief, as shown above; the mirror was looked at and has just served to initiate the stream-of-consciousness technique, *U* 1.134ff). The relative clause, however, though narrative routine, is out of sequence: mirror and razor had been put away in the pocket before their noise was noticed. This is the first pluperfect tense in the descriptive sections of the book. The pluperfect is a narrative intervention, an epic updating. Action told in the pluperfect cannot be observed, it has always already happened. Anterior supplementation is one of the oldest narrative necessities; relative clauses often fill us in about the past. If we consider the perspective to be Stephen's, as we have been conditioned to imagine in *Ulysses*, we may translate the temporal inversion into a succession of impacts.

The clacking may have lead him to conclude that the utensils had been put in the pocket earlier on. Or else, and more likely, Stephen might now remember something he noticed before, but did not consciously register—some peripheral perception, one that took place 'on the side': *paraesthesis*.[12] Such perception, since not part of the main line of attention, is almost impossible to handle in realistically linear narration. During the time when Mulligan was stowing his shaving gear into his pocket (a marginality that went unrecorded), Stephen was listening to Mulligan quoting Wilde (probably shaping his aphorism about a cracked mirror being a symbol of Irish art), which would have absorbed most of his concentration. There was also some emotional tension, so that little attention was given to a mere pocketing of objects, though it may have been vaguely glimpsed in that paraesthetic twilight zone of the mind.

The choice of the dramatic verb 'thrust' (rather than a noncommittal 'put') seems to disclose that attention, however marginal, was in fact given; 'thrust' is appropriate to Mulligan's histrionic behaviour.[13] Alternatively Stephen may internally dramatize everything his opponent is doing. Perhaps we remember that Mulligan, irritatingly assertive, has already been 'thrusting a hand into Stephen's upper pocket' (*U* 1.67). In the light of Stephen's fencing metaphor immediately following ('Parried again. He fears the lancet of my art as I fear that of his', *U* 1.152), 'thrust' acquires an even more psychological, aggressive force.

Given the suppressed tension between the two characters, we may appreciate the rightness of that theatrical 'thrust': it signals, after all, the stage exit of razor and mirror that were ceremoniously introduced into the book's very first sentence. They have had their dramatic moments and deserve a departing flourish. What must appear an overestimation of trivial details, at this early point in the book where it still behaves like a novel, will come to be actually staged in 'Circe' where simple things like a bar of soap or mirrors may attain their apotheoses (*U* 15.3821ff.). Such later grandiose performances are mutely foreshadowed in the language of the opening pages.

some little time subsequently

The early, more realistic style is practically discontinued after 'Wandering Rocks' and 'Sirens', when other, more parodistic modes take over and 'realism' is shown to be one judiciously confected illusion among others. In many ways, 'Eumaeus', the first of the three Nostos chapters, is a return, a stylistic homecoming—but with a difference. It still evidences a very close concern for minute chronology, but there are also startling lapses. The sailor Murphy leaves the shelter:

He made tracks heavily, slowly[,][14] with a dumpy sort of a gait to the door, stepped heavily down the one step there was out of the shelter and bore due left. (*U* 16.922)

There is still in part a cinematographic progression and what pertains to be imitative form; the language in its turn correspondingly assumes a dumpy sort of gait, making tracks heavily. The next sentence signals temporal awareness in its opening conjunction and a minute advertence to simple acts:

While he was in the act of getting his bearings[,] Mr Bloom...

The neat sequentiality, however, is disrupted and a long digression separates the predicate from its subject:

... Mr Bloom[,] who noticed when he stood up that he had two flasks of presumably ship's rum sticking one out of each pocket for the private consumption of his burning interior, saw him produce a bottle. (*U* 16.924)

Clearly the digression takes us back to an anterior phase, coterminous and congruent with an earlier 'the sailor vacated his seat' (*U* 16.919). The relative clause ('who noticed when he stood up') is out of sequence, probably another peripheral perception moving into consciousness. We need a slight adjustment; 'who noticed when he stood up' is momentarily misleading—not Bloom is standing up, but Murphy *was*. Actually and functionally 'who noticed when he stood up' is 'who *had noticed* when he *had stood up*'. The pluperfect tense is what the French translation silently and correctly substituted, probably out of instinctive regard for the *concordance des temps*. Meticulously this version takes us back to that earlier moment:[15]

M. Bloom qui avait remarqué quand il s'etait mis sur ses jambes qu'il avait deux fioles sortant de ses deux poches... (*Ulysse* 563)

The Eumaean style seems to be more concerned with rhetorical flourishes ('the burning interior') than with successive niceties. Seeing the sailor 'produce a bottle' may have turned Bloom's thoughts back to a paraesthetic observation of just a few moments ago. But then even the *associative* order is out of line; the triggering cause 'saw him produce a bottle' is preceded by its effect. Such fumbles are typical of the lax syntax of 'Eumaeus', a chapter of slackness and failed intentions. Its ambition to observe a strict chronology can be seen from the context: towards the end of the same paragraph, 'the noise of his bilgewater *some little time subsequently*' (*U* 16.939) follows close upon '*after a brief space of time*' (*U* 16.937); even brief spaces of time can be recorded redundantly. The endeavour to adhere to a strict chronology is foiled by disturbing associations and a more psychological progression. The style of 'Eumaeus' is also characterized by the incongruous fusion of dignified epic recording and an associative ramble. In his well-publicized schemas, Joyce named the 'technic' of the first chapter 'Narrative young', that of 'Eumaeus' in analogy 'Narrative old'.[16] The young, brisker, morning style is characterized by tautness, by sharp and often cinematographic precision. This has changed in the small hours of the following day, where a kind of nervous energy is at work in an elaborate but thwarted attempt to keep close track of events, when concentration fails and vagrant digressions keep interfering, as though the vigour of youth had passed, leaving behind a wobbling kind of comprehension and a haphazard kind of alertness.

that is when

'Eumaeus' still aims at mimetic narrative accordance; but at variance with this is a whole array of stylistic embroidery, in which process the early morning vivacity has been lost. There is a constant dichotomy between epic control and the caprice of a wandering mind. The typical bumbling maladroitness is well in evidence when early in the chapter a dark figure salutes Stephen Dedalus, and Bloom moves discretely aside in protective apprehension. The story then switches back to Stephen.

Stephen, that is when the accosting figure came to close quarters, though he was not in an over sober state himself[,] recognised Corley's breath redolent of rotten cornjuice. (*U* 16.128)

Something has happened to the telling, which is once more out of sequence, as it might well be in oral, improvised storytelling, where second-thought material has to be accommodated extemporaneously (the sort of thing that would be edited and rephrased in a written composition). The subject is introduced, but the verb ('recognised') has to wait all through a slightly redundant common-sense remark that recognition depends on proximity. An awkward, self-conscious pause after 'Stephen', with an annotative 'that is', signals the irregularity and defines the fronting of the subject as a wrong start. No wonder that early translators, not yet sensitive to the chapter's glorious ineptitude, rearranged the sentence in conventional improvement:

Als die grüssende Gestalt näher kam, erkannte Stephan, wenn er auch selbst nicht grade ganz nüchtern war, Corleys Atem... (Goyert 617)

The elision of the clumsy, gear-shifting 'that is when' streamlines the diction and de-Eumaeanizes the wording.[17] Rectifying the syntax and translating the partly associative jumble into a lucid period[18] deprives it of atmosphere and mood, of its incongruities with the constant need for readjustment. The mention of Stephen's own not 'over sober state' makes sense in relation to what is yet to come, that Corley's breath is 'redolent of rotten cornjuice'. Once more, the effect has been put before its cause, the cart before the horse, another slight sequential disarray quite in keeping with the dis-sequential jars of the chapter.

contretemps

A final resurgence of realistic description, reminiscent of the first *Ulysses* chapters, are the doings of a real horse (some are purely metaphorical) towards the end of 'Eumaeus'. After an abortive start, 'The horse was just then', trailing off unfinished, and a few lines of indirect speech, it re-emerges into Bloom's and our vision:

The horse[,] having reached the end of his tether, so to speak, halted[,] and, rearing high a proud feathering tail, added his quota... (*U* 16.1874)

After this medley of description, ornamentation, narrative comment (with a comment on the phrasing itself), and the epic uplift of a preparatory 'proud feathering tail', we descend for the last time to the Dublin of here and now when the quota that has been announced is particularized:

by letting fall on the floor[,] which the brush would soon brush up and polish, three smoking globes of turds.

Similar to the example first adduced ('Stephen suffered... hand-kerchief'), an action is carefully drawn out and comes to rest when an object looms into delayed view. The delay in this case is no longer a perceptional imitation, but a prospective look into the imminent future (the horse is drawing a sweeper car, cleaning the street). Before the yet unspecified thing has reached the ground we antici-pate its impending removal, a wholly premature cleaning, not yet necessary at this miniphase of the close-up. An observer like Bloom might well have a passing thought to some such effect, which has precipitately intruded into a sentence whose overt purpose is to depict a natural occurrence. Between a reared tail and the expected impact something contrary to realistic narration has intervened.

But in the continuation another quota is added in narrative replay, a variant report; the identical action is reassembled into different items and an alternative arrangement:

Slowly[,] three times, one after another, from a full crupper[,] he mired. (*U* 16.1877)[19]

A lovingly redundant account of an act not often delineated in fic-tion; three 'times' are explicitly distinguished. The careful and some-what superfluous notation 'one after another' communicates an awareness of sequence more than anything useful ('three times' is always in succession), a sequence that has already been reversed. We can also consider the retelling a summary or a variation on a theme. The two sentences, a twice-told tale with varying highlights (both tales scrambled), are in parallactic diversity, partly chiasmic: 'The horse—letting fall—three... globes of turds—three times—he mired.' Attention is drawn both to the occurrence and to the manner of its telling, a demonstration, incidentally, of how a simple and natural act might be epically translated, into how many possible words and how many sequences.

The horse has been personified into 'he' (suggesting Bloom's cus-tomary empathy), but the next sentence already qualifies this deter-mination of sex as unwarranted, a mere thoughtless assumption:

And humanely his driver waited till he (or she) had ended, patient in his scythed car. (*U* 16.1878)

This also reminds us that all this while we, like the driver, have been waiting patiently, detained by a marginal spectacle closely observed, in a few instances of epic leisure and self-conscious artistry. The following paragraph begins

Side by side[,] Bloom, profiting by the *contretemps*, with Stephen passed through the gap of the chains, divided by the upright, and, stepping over a strand of mire, went across... (*U* 16.1880)

Again it instantly contradicts a pointed 'side by side' by verbally severing Bloom from the companion at his side, by a clause which calls the foregoing incident a *contretemps*, something inopportune and out of order, unexpected, as in fact it was. Odysseus, we might remember, profited by multiple *contretemps*. But to pedantic close readers the term appears to suggest what has been under scrutiny all along: a literary discomposition of phases and their artful (or else clumsy) redisposition *contre temps*, against the order in which they occur or might be observed or might logically make sense.

In its descriptive passages, *Ulysses* seems to move from a more imitative cinematographic mode to increasingly overt artistic manipulation and reprocessing. But even the later temporal transpositions could be termed cinematographic with emphasis on *graphic* (the process of verbal depiction). The new medium film also instantly proceeded to take movement apart and reassemble it in artful ways, for example showing it in reverse or by contracting or extending time. The horse's repetitive antics at the end of 'Eumaeus' might be rendered cinematographically by judicious cutting and by montage. Joyce, at any rate, just like the new film makers, was fascinated by how movement evolves in time, how we come to perceive it, and how in artificial recreations we can manipulate it.

NOTES

1 James Joyce, *Dubliners* (New York: Viking Press 1967 [1916]), 119.
2 James Joyce, *Ulysses* (1922); references are by chapter and line, following the Corrected Text edited by Hans Walter Gabler with Wolfhard Steppe and Claus Melchior (London: Bodley Head 1986).
3 Frank Budgen, *James Joyce and the Making of* Ulysses *and Other Writings* (London: OUP 1972), 20.
4 James Joyce, *Ulysse*, traduction française intégrale d'Auguste Morel, assisté de Stuart Gilbert, entièrement revue par Valery Larbaud et l'auteur (Paris: Gallimard 1948 [1929]), 9.
5 James Joyce, *Ulisse*, traduzione di Giulio de Angelis (Milano: Arnoldo Mondadori 1968 [1960]), 11.
6 James Joyce, *Ulysses*, übersetzt von Hans Wollschläger (Frankfurt: Suhrkamp Verlag 1979 [1975]), 9.
7 James Joyce, *Ulysses*, übersetzt von Georg Goyert (Zürich: Rhein Verlag 1956 [1927]), 9.
8 James Joyce, *Stephen Hero* (New York: New Directions 1955 [1944]), 211.

9   *The Odyssey of Homer*, S.H. Butcher and A. Lang (trans.) (London: Macmillan 1987), 21.

10 A later collocation of 'sea eagles, gulls' (in a cataclysmic cluster of birds, *U* 15.4668) may also be gratuitous.

11 Quoted from *Ben Jonson*, C.H. Herford and Percy Simpson (eds) (Oxford: Clarendon Press 1937), vol. 5. Whatever the source, the adjective fits the Lestrygonian theme of the chapter. Joyce uses it in the sense of 'desolate', but it could mean, as it does in Jonson's line just quoted, 'emaciated, lean'. Bloom makes the gulls, in his fiction, 'famished, hungry'.

12 Greek *par-aisthanomai*: remark or hear by the way; the noun *paraisthesis* could also mean an illusory perception.

13 In the stage directions of *Exiles*, both Richard Rowan and Robert Hand 'thrust' their hands into their pockets. James Joyce, *Exiles* (New York: Viking 1951 [1918]), 51, 58.

14 The commas in 'Eumaeus' present a textual problem. It seems that Joyce originally punctuated very sparsely, but that a typist added hundreds of commas with good and misguided intentions, that Joyce at a revision stage deleted a number, but by no means all of them, and therefore many were left standing in all editions except the *Critical and Synoptic* one by Garland Publishers (1984). Commas or ellipses put between brackets '[,]' indicate their precarious status; see also note 19.

15 So does the German translation of 1927: 'Bloom, der, als er aufstand, bemerkt hatte' (Goyert 642). Translators make such modifications almost automatically; the syntactic rules of the target language usually override the niceties or the sloppiness of the original.

16 Stuart Gilbert, *James Joyce's* Ulysses: *A Study* (London: Faber & Faber 1930), 92, 340.

17 The French version follows the inelegance: 'Stephen, quand le survenant fut à proximité, mais alors seulement, et bien que lui-même ne fut pas précisément à jeun, reconnut l'haleine de Corley qui sentait le moût pourri', with a deferred marker, 'mais alors seulement' (*Ulysse* 541).

18 Wollschläger's translation of 1975 replaces the initial Eumaean fumble by a rearranged period of epic management: 'Obwohl er selbst sich in einem alles andere als nüchternen Zustand befand, erkannte Stephen, das heißt, als die Gestalt, die ihn angesprochen, in größere Nähe kam, daß Corleys Atem stark nach saurem Fusel duftete' (Wollschläger 764). This also changes the nature of the recognition.

19 Pre-Gabler editions retained some commas that make the dissection of the continuous occurrence even more emphatic: 'Slowly, three times, one after another, from a full cropper, he mired.'

REMODELLING HOMER

The topic is Modernism. I begin, a true pedestrian, with a footnote in *Finnegans Wake*, one that can be conveniently misappropriated.

This is modeln times (*FW* 289.n6)

Modern times is what the spelling seems to aim at. The footnote is attached to 'the reptile's age'. *Finnegans Wake* spans such periods, from prehistory to modernity, with nonchalant ease. 'Modern' is a strange word, by its very nature something relative and mobile, by grace of literary fashion the portion of twentieth-century conventions for which Joyce has been selected as prototype. 'Modern times' is continually possible as a boast, a program or a lament, at *any* time; but 'Modernism' can become outdated. Joyce's phrase, added to his work in progress during the heyday of that movement, may antedate the title of a famous movie by one of the outstanding leaders of that up and coming medium, Chaplin's *Modern Times* (1936). It is a matter of manuscript evidence whether this reference would be within the author's intended range; but we have learned that texts, especially accommodating ones like the *Wake*, are not bound by their creator's legislation. Nowadays it would take a conscious effort to *dis*sociate Joyce's 'modeln times' from a cinematic fiction, a pictorial evocation of the hazards of survival and the rhythms imposed by modern mechanization. Chaplin's Bloomian resilience among the wheels within reels of the movie are now integrated in the *Wake's* clockwork. A Wakean consciousness permits the past to be affected by the future.

So far I have been so concerned with the temporal setting of the phrase that I overlooked the mechanics of the graphic actuality of 'modeln', and the models they suggest. Maybe someone—an exiled foreigner?—is having trouble with the liquids and takes an *r* for an *l*. A German foreigner would be using a native verb, *modeln*, and changing the syntax. *Modeln* means to 'change the shape of', 'modulate'; it is of course derived from Latin *modus* (measure or manner), and related to 'modern', an offshoot of the same family. Family members quibble and quarrel, have different manners or moods (another cognate of 'mode'), want to form the world according to their own divergent views. *Finnegans Wake* is energy that modulates itself, that modulates times and reshapes words. It was written, at a time of vigorous disruptions and new starts, by a man whose works were considered novel, progressive, revolutionary, but who had steadily been reshaping classical models. They also modeled new types of readers—or revived obsolete reading skills.

At this point I should fulfill my cultural obligations and casually work in Bergson, Einstein, Husserl, Heidegger, Russell, Proust and, certainly, Wyndham Lewis. Instead, I had rather stick to Joyce's pliable 'modeln times' to lead gradually to my subject, the modernist reformation of the past. New movements have always affected old ones. The Middle Ages exploited Antiquity within their own frames, and they were succeeded by a new departure which rediscovered more of Antiquity differently, and was aptly named Renaissance. Ultramodernist Joyce always turned back to the classics, Aristotle, Homer, Ovid; to medieval figures like Augustine, Aquinas, Dante; and later to Giordano Bruno, Nicolas of Cusa, Pico della Mirandola, or Shakespeare. History, Vico, and *Finnegans Wake* all say that each impulse of new life is a *revival*. Some such revivals, like the Irish Renaissance, appeared to Joyce too narrow-mindedly nostalgic. His backward looks were far more radical. If anyone, Joyce was always altering, remodelling times, including his own past. *A Portrait* puts this into words and style. *Dubliners* went into *Finnegans Wake* and *Finnegans Wake* changed *Dubliners* for us.

In this essay I will look back to Homer's metamorphoses, not to find out, once again, how Joyce adapted them for himself, but to figure out (or to feign) how Joyce influenced *them*, the classics. Such retrospection may unearth old chestnuts, or make tiresome rediscoveries, or it may resurrect dormant ghosts. I am confident that this will happen to some degree. The classics may not be quite as staid as they have appeared; they may be more dynamic and full of 'Modern' tensions. So the result may produce necessary adjustments but also, just as likely, falsification. Since no one knows how the Greeks (which Greeks? Homer's audience, fifth-century Athenians, Alexandrians?) responded to the epics, we may simply add one more specious reading to the conventional ones. A lay reader conditioned by Joyce, deformed by *Finnegans Wake*, will naturally project features that historical philologists may disprove.

Joyce could intentionally imitate stilted recreations of heroic styles ('A many comely nymphs drew nigh...' *U* 12.1774). He even set out to fake the more recent past of English literature in a series of blatantly flawed forgeries, fashioning, in the wake of Daidalos, the sacred cows of Helios. By artificially fathering the fathers of English prose, he meddled in their ancestry and perverted it, so that Carlyle or Bunyan may never be quite the same again in the eyes of the corrupted beholder. Irrespective of intention, Joyce also agitates the *Odyssey* (as did the Grimm brothers, Schliemann, Frazer, Jung). The title 'Ulysses' is here used as a signpost—not to go and re-explain the new by the old, but to look at the old as though it were modernist. The title gently advises us to do what Homeric agents do: *peiraein*—test, try out, inquire, experience. Such backward glances at an epic are not to be trusted, all the less so since that author left behind no eyewitnesses like Stanislaus or Frank Budgen for corrective common sense.

The areas touched will be Functionality, Semiotics, Ambivalence, Self-Reference, and Listener Response or, to put it plainly, a few samples will be inspected *as though* they had been composed by James Joyce.

each adventure... should not only condition but even create its own technique (Letters 1, 147)

There are no conspicuous similarities in the *Odyssey* to the narrative variation of *Ulysses*, certainly not those highly idiosyncratic chapter modes and the stylistic orchestration. Joyce could have found his models in the past, but he hardly needed any. His devices appear to have evolved in the workshop, almost naturally. What could be more naturally conforming than that a chapter about music should contain songs, have a vocabulary in tune with it, with appropriate metaphors, and be made, more and more, to comport itself *like* music? Such increased styling in fact moved the novel away from the Greek groundplan. Homer's poem cannot have corresponding scope. An epic diction had shaped itself out of centuries of a bardic tradition we can only guess at. The language is generally elevated, 'noble', artistic, with a great store of ready-made, but still flexible, formulaic supports. That would not allow for too much variation, though there is a lot more of it than some translations would have us believe.

In *Ulysses*, to move from the end of 'Nausicaa' into the next chapter and then into 'Circe', is quite a jolt, with instant changes of scenery, idiom, atmosphere, arrangement.[1] Not so in a classical epic. One vague impression we often get is of an extended uniformity, accentuated by metre. But there are considerable shifts. The transition from omniscient narrative (*here* the epithet makes sense) to personal tale is the best-known variation. Beyond that, the disparity between the time actually passing and the narrative expenditure for it may be very effective. Many lines may be lavished on an exact movement, or a well-wrought object; then again time can be crowded —one whole year's stay on Kirke's island takes up slighly more than a single line (10:469). Another long detention, on Kalypso's Ogygia, is handled quite differently. We first hear, through several sources, of Odysseus pining there; then we ourselves watch him leave; later on, on two separate occasions, he tells of his arriving there: so the seven long years are suggested by a circumfluent vacuum. Not even *Ulysses* can boast of such a model of splitting time; the *Wake* seems to make the time potentially passing from the final 'the' to the initial 'riverrun' somehow meaningful. So the adventure part of the *Odyssey* doubles back from the end of Book Twelve to its opening at 1:14.

I will now briefly compare two adjacent episodes. The escape from the Laistrygonians is told rapidly, succinctly. In the preceding disasters (the Kyklopes, Aiolos) we were sharing the thinking and wavering of Odysseus and his emotions: he was terrified, courageous, cool, crafty, miserable, considering suicide. Of such feelings the Laistrygonians episode is stripped; there are hardly any superfluities, no glimpses into the psyche. There is the habitual geographical outline, one remark about the closeness of day and night (and a very Bloomian reflection on someone who could do without sleep, being able to earn double wages). The description of an excellent harbour remains factual, but Odysseus, contrary to epical practice, fails to reveal why he alone did not moore his ship in the harbour, but stayed outside. As usual some companions are sent out to reconnoitre, and the story takes its quick course. Not a single spoken word is quoted. One Greek messenger is seized and eaten; the other two escape, followed by the natives who hurl down rocks and spear the men like fishes from their boats. Odysseus, with his ship and his crew, can flee. The whole episode, containing the largest massacre in the whole poem, takes up less than sixty lines (10:76–132); the report is so objective, almost neutral, that the loss of eleven ships and of several hundred men is tucked into less than one full line, one austere sentence. But we can feel a powerful undercurrent not stated, in the sound as well as the shape of the words, even in transliteration:

autar hai allai aollees autoth'olonto (but these others altogether there perished) (10:132)

We need not know Greek in order to get some impression. The adjective *aollees* (in a body, a mass, close together), of four syllables, seems to add assonant reinforcement to an implicit warning against being herded together.

After this the remaining Greeks came to Aiaia, where they lay for two days, and everything (although nothing very exciting for a while) is told in far greater detail. There is much talk. As though in compensation, the pent-up grief and shock finds belated expression: now we hear of weariness, grief, despair, encouragement—and hunger. We share the doubts and fears of Odysseus, and also his deliberations. There is perhaps even subliminal psychology in a straightforward epithet for the harbour: it is *naulochos*, which means safe or 'ship-sheltering', where, literally, ships (*nau-*) can lie (*lochos*, from *lecho*, 10:141). As it happens, *lochos* alone would mean a special kind of lying-down place, in concealment for an attack, an ambush. Odysseus has learned his lesson about ambushes in caves or in harbours surrounded by cliffs; he may be cautious of even an echoing word.[2]

Exploring the new territory, Odysseus comes upon a magnificent stag, a welcome prey, which he kills and carries back to the camp. It looks as though the compassion withheld from the hundreds of Ithacans who had been harpooned and eaten by the cannibals in the previous episode is now transferred onto the hunted animal as it is turned into food for humans. The individual's plight is brought out. The stag has been drawn to a spring by the heat of the sun, the spear strikes him, he falls into the dust with a moan; it is all vivid, like the death of an Iliadic hero, full of empathy. We even learn how the animal is carried, and what Odysseus does with the spear at each moment. All is told with the loving care that is so patently absent from the previous episode (10:156–72). Throughout, much attention is devoted to eating and its effect on human beings. We have another focus: close-ups in a different narrative 'style'.

Parallax stalks behind (*U* 14.1089)

It is difficult to talk about *Ulysses* without posing the question of narrative trust. There is a lot that we know merely through associations or memory, highly unreliable sources. Much information also comes through hearsay, in a city which is particularly given to gossip, rumor, and the production of what Hugh Kenner has termed 'Irish facts'. One safeguard is the multiple reference from different sources or places. Joyce has Bloom introduce the scientific term for the analogous method in astronomy, *parallax*, the key principle of stereoscopic vision based on at least two different reports. If an improbable claim—like Bloom giving 'the ideas for Sinn Fein to Griffith' (*U* 12.1574)—is not supplemented elsewhere, we tend to disbelieve it. On the other hand we can fairly trace Bob Doran's meteoric progress through a Dublin afternoon by matching displaced observations, and we can form some conclusions about his domestic situation. What we learn in the novel also parenthetically serves as parallactic external confirmation of what we might have surmised from a set of reports in an earlier short story, 'The Boarding House' (which in itself consists of three sequential views grouped around a narrative void—a past event and a present decision). If all we knew about Doran only derived from the unknown narrator of 'Cyclops', we would have our doubts as to what to make of it.

The Homer of the *Odyssey* knew too that reports do not automatically deserve credence. We can mistake appearances, we have devious motives, a lie is as easily phrased as a truth, and it is ever impossible to tell a whole truth. Distrust in words is built into the poem, with great emphasis on something being told *kata moiran* (in a proper way, accurately), *kata kosmon* (truly, in order), or *atrekeos* (truly, exactly); some statements are labelled *nemertea* (unerring, infallible, in acccordance with reality). That such expressions have become stereotypes (compare 'as true as I'm telling you', 'I'm told for a fact', or 'declare to God', etc., especially in 'Cyclops'), does not make them less functional as signals or reminders.

Odysseus' return is set in motion by benevolent dissemblance. The gods decree it at a meeting, at a moment when Poseidon's back is turned, and Athene has set off for Ithaka. She takes on the appearance of Mentes. When asked her name and origin ('declare it truly'— *atrekeos*, 1:169), she 'truthfully' (*atrekeos*, 1:179) makes up the first fictional biography, to urge Telemachos on. Some time later when Penelope is visited and advised by her sister in a dream, it is a phantom sent by Athene. Hermes, dispatched to Kalypso to proclaim the will of Zeus, pretends he does not know the name of the man she keeps on her island. Kalypso in turn says nothing of a divine threat, but tells Odysseus of his release as though it were due to her own generous nature. He does not believe her, doubting not so much her motivation as her intention, rightly, though misdirectedly, suspecting her of not meaning what she says.

The *Odyssey* is full of deceit. Without it Penelope or the kingdom of Ithaka could not have been won back (nor Troy captured). It is fitting and significant that the final reconciliation with Poseidon should be contingent upon future misrepresentation. When an oar that Odysseus will have to carry inland shall be mistaken for a 'winnowing fan', then he can make his peace. This harmless deception will be the 'manifest sign' (*sema... ariphrades*, 11:126–9). Practically all translations render the landlubber's misinterpretation as 'winnowing fan' (Butcher and Lang, Murray, etc.). A reader of *Ulysses* and its chapter of illusions might mistake Bella Cohen's 'large fan winnows wind' (*U* 15.2752), and dislocute two words into a sign of something—Kirke's magic wand, perhaps.[3] The last person we hear of in the poem is Mentor, and he once again is an impersonation of Pallas Athene's; the last words we read are *demas* and *auden*—a (spurious) shape and (an assumed) voice. In *Ulysses* the first shape is stately Buck Mulligan, masquerading as a priest; the first sound heard is his dissembling voice. He proceeds to mentor Stephen, not too seriously, to go with him to Athens.

As listeners, or readers, we have to be circumspect like Odysseus, alert for verification. What about that famous web that Penelope reputedly wove by day and unwove at night? Did it happen? We might not believe the suitors, for they want to brand her in public for treachery; nor would we necessarily (having been warned that her mind may be set 'on other things', *passim*) trust her own telling to the stranger, since her motive is to show herself as loyal in adversity. But together the two equivalent reports bear each other out from different points of view (2:92f., 19:137f.; see also 24:128f.).

At times there is intriguing parallactic doubt. At the palace of Menelaos and Helen, Telemachos is treated to reminiscences of Troy. Helen recalls Odysseus, how he once sneaked into the besieged city, diguised as a beggar. We know that he will do this again later, and since Helen cannot know that, the story sounds very plausible. She then recognized him and he, binding her by an oath, 'told her all the purposes of the Achaeans'. If *that* is true, Odysseus may have forgotten his proverbial caution and endangered the Greek cause; or it may

prove how greatly he trusted the one woman whose elopement
started the whole war; or it may show she was simply too charming
to resist—in any case, the anecdote which is offered to demonstrate
Odysseus' cunning shows her in a favorable light, and at the centre
of attention. There were, naturally, no witnesses (4:240–66).

Her husband (who had been in the other camp when all this
occurred) immediately remarks that Helen has spoken 'aright' (*kata
moiran*), and goes on to tell another war story, perhaps the most decisive moment of all. When the Greek leaders were in ambush (*lochos*)
inside the wooden horse, she came along with the Trojans and
walked round it, three times. She tempted the Greeks. 'You must
have been urged by some *daimon*'—he surmises, speaking no doubt
with utter courtesy—'who made you call the Greek chieftains by
their names, imitating the voices of their wives.' Odysseus, not taken
in, handled the dangerous situation with customary aplomb, so that
the invaders did not give themselves away. And Athene took care of
Helen (4:265–89).

This illustrates the resourcefulness of Odysseus, but also a different Helen. Both stories fill us in on incidents of the siege that are not
otherwise reported. They are also comments on Helen's character
and her adaptive skills that seem to match those of Odysseus. The
two anecdotes do not quite tally, but need not contradict each other.
They are full of domestic decorum and connubial tensions. And
there is enough for us to wonder at and to interpret. If we are modernist interpreters we may puzzle whether this staging of several
Helen *personae* (sophisticated hostess in the present; confidante of
Odysseus, artful temptress, in the past; perhaps also clever inventor
of fictions) should systematically be aligned with the sequel, a story
which Menelaos introduces with the words 'I will not deceive you'
(4:348). It is the story of changeable, wily, adaptable Proteus, master
of many roles and appearances.

This is a story that we hear twice. First, in a more general way, his
daughter predicts what will happen and gives advice. This advice is
put into practice, and Menelaos' own account, much more comprehensive, then also includes what Proteus, once caught, reveals. This
is a frequent doubling device. Often a goddess foretells what we will
ourselves witness later on. Kirke carefully instructs Odysseus about
the Sirens, and he follows her counsels. We get both her description
and his own chronicle. There is some overlapping as well as complementation. Odysseus quotes what the Sirens sang to him (which
Kirke did not anticipate), but Kirke tells him (and us) some facts

from her divine and multiscient perspective that were not within the range of his vision (the mouldering bodies of former victims). The seduction of course was vocal, so he only reports what he heard. So we have a perfectly stereoscopic-stereoacoustic impression.

Almost everything important outside of our range is either parallactically confirmed, or implicitly questioned. All of the adventures of Odysseus are listed once more, in due order, when he tells them to Penelope in a brief summary (23:310–41). Of course these are the words of the cleverest inventor alive. We can detect some minor, uxorious abbreviations in his tale. But we do have independent narrative or Olympian testimony at least for the most crucial adventures, the blinding of Polyphemos and the slaughter of the sacred cows. So all his accounts may well be true, which is not to say that he might not have touched up some exploits, for better effect upon the Phaiakian hosts.

What is claimed here is not an 'influence', that Joyce should have picked up some clues from the *Odyssey*, but, perhaps vaguely, some kinship. Steadying our post–Ulyssean lenses 'to a new focus' (*U* 7.811), we may uncover, or invent, features in an older text that we might otherwise not have cared to notice.

in medios loquos (*FW* 398.8)

Self-reflexiveness is a trademark of much recent story-telling. Joyce's later works, in particular, seem to have a self-awareness of their being artifacts. *Finnegans Wake* comments continually on its own nature, and infelicitous exculpations are never far off. *Ulysses* also more and more denounces itself as narrative scheming. Asides like 'As said before' and even 'as said before just now' (*U* 11.519, 569, 763) are conspicuous avowals of the creator's handiwork. As against such narcissism, the *Odyssey* will appear simple and nobly primitive. On the other hand, its temporal arrangement is intricately contrived, in fact much more so than sequential *Ulysses*. The beginning, an address to the Muse, follows an epical convention. The goddess is to tell the story of that versatile man. After a brief plot summary the Muse, daughter of Zeus, is entreated to 'tell us too' about the events just indicated. There is one little word, unstressed, in the closing line of the evocation, *hamothen*, and it stands for something like 'from anywhere'—it is a little hint that narratologists should jump at. Perhaps they have.

It occurs here only and, unfortunately, it does not travel too well and is easily neglected in translation, or it is treated merely quantitatively (in 'some part left', says Chapman; 'snatch some portion of these acts', enjoins Pope). It may be taken to denote the origin of the information ('from whatsoever source you may know them', Samuel Butler), or else it is turned into a ponderous subordinate clause or a sonority like 'beginning where thou will' (Palmer). Homer is much more casual, as though one professional were nudging another. The bard knows the Muse knows that the epic disposition of ten years and several strands of action is a formidable order, and that the handling of time alone entails many choices. In the *Iliad* the matter was easier to settle. For reporting the Anger of Achilleus it suffices to propose a starting point: 'from where' (*ex hou, Il.* 1:6) the two heroes began to fall out. For the more intricate *Odyssey* the Muse is relieved of compositional deliberation, and we can almost hear a reassuring: 'Don't bother—start any old place!'⁴

So there is a touch of artlessness which we realize is studied, a pretense; and the little adverb *hamothen* disguises and thereby signals both craftmanship and narrative consciousness. Odysseus himself is conscious of the same problem, where to begin, when about to tell his own adventures. 'What shall I tell you first and what last?' (9:16), he asks and decides to begin with the end of the Trojan war, and to follow a straightforward chronological order. His sequential account is embedded in a complex time scheme, and this admirable Homeric manipulation is an instance of, as the *Wake* has put it, 'modeln [in that German sense of shaping to specification] times'. This can furthermore be echoed in the microstructure because of the multiple tenses and moods of the Greek language.

Epic bards were sometimes told where to begin. Odysseus had already directed the local singer, Demodekos, to 'sing of the building of the wooden horse'. This is worth a little digression. In a text scrupulously structured by a modernist we might be justified in treating

hippou kosmon aeison (the horse's building sing) (8:492)

as a recall of the opening of the *Iliad*: '*Menin* (the anger) *aeide* (sing... of Achilleus' (1:1). Odysseus is asking, after all, for a continuation of those earlier events. But Homer might not be like Joyce, who can use Howth as a site to end *Ulysses* and to start off *Finnegans Wake*, or who might, in his cyclical joining of the ending to the beginning of his last work, 'along the... riverrun', not only echo a Coleridgean sacred, subterranean river, but also the origins of his own published works, 'There's music *along the river*' (*Chamber Music*, I). That may not be plain-spoken Homer's incidental linking. Still it is odd to find a minor invocation of a tale within a tale imitating, perhaps by chance, the beginning of its twin epic. And by one more chance, since the demand is for *hippou kosmon*, the stratagem about the horse, we might remember the *last* word of the *Iliad* as well: *hippo-damoio* ('Thus they held the funeral of Hector, tamer of horses', *Il.* 24:804). Maybe coincidence, and maybe simply post-Joycean zealous projection? Still, from the safe ignorance of three millennia later, we can always posit, for the sake of an argument, that Homer (or his latest editor) knew what he was doing. Homer used *kosmos* here, just three lines after Odysseus praised Demodokos for his competence, having sung the fate of the Achaeans *kata kosmon* (accurately, in due order: 8:489).

The submission here is that Homer might in fact have contrived what the text synecdochically suggests in the best Joycean fashion—*kosmos* (that is to say adornment, arrangement, stratagem, order, fashioning). If the Greeks had a word for structuring, it could have been the verb *kosmeo*.

Very orderly himself, Odysseus ends *his* tale with the arrival at Kalypso's island and his stay there; and he breaks off quickly, for he has told that story already to a portion of his audience. 'It is irksome to tell a plain-told story a second time', he says, all but doing it (12:453). By this negation, the *Odyssey* acknowledges its own narrative principle, the parallactic doubling already referred to. We have in fact heard the Kalypso affair not only twice by Odysseus, but before that by the poem's narrative voice, and twice by Athene. The story of the adventures is brought back to its starting point, where it was set in motion by that almost offhand *hamothen*. We are now at the end of book twelve, exactly halfway through the epic, at its structural middle.

And the identical same (*U* 16.1331)

I now go on to report for the second time on the Proteus incident, the one of which we have two accounts as well. Proteus is *nemertes* (unerring, 'who tells the truth', 'whose speech is sooth'), he 'knows' the depths of all the seas. A seer himself, he becomes visible in changing forms. We hear this, first, through his daughter (or rather, she indicates wisely, 'he is said to be her father'). Her name is Eidothea, the goddess of *eidos* (shape, appearance, what can be seen). Dealing with illusions and reality, sense perception and knowledge, identity, likeness, trickery and disguises, the whole theme to be mythologized appears like an etymological deployment of the Indo-European root *weid* (to see), which lost its initial to become the Greek verb *eid* or *id*. Some forms of its elaborate system retain the old meaning of sight (as it is preserved in Latin *videre*, vision, etc.), while its perfect *oida* (I have seen) came to mean *know* (compare also its Germanic relatives 'wit', 'witness', 'wise', German *wissen*, or even a semantic reunion like the *Wake's* 'wiseable', 16.24). The passive *eidomai* means to appear, to seem. Other relatives are *eidos*, *eidolon*, idyll, or idea. What we see is what we think we know, it belongs to the ineluctable modernity of the visible, 'thought through my eyes' (*U* 3.1). 'Proteus' is full of forms for seeing and knowing (and so is 'Nausicaa', Joyce's second Sandymount strand scene).

Eidothea proposes concealment and a fake appearance to trap the old wizard. She predicts that he will first (*proton*) count (*arithmesai*) all his seals (4:411; the adjective *protos* seems to be used here recurrently for homonymous reverberation). When Menelaos tells what actually happened, the wording varies slightly. Proteus, coming up to the seals, counted their number: '*lekto d'arithmon*' (4:451; *lekto* is an aorist form of the verb *lego*, to pick, number, count, recount, tell—*logos* was to become the most renowned member of the family). And as the first ones (*protous*) he counted (*lege*) the Greeks in ambush hidden under the sealskins: here *lege* is the imperfect tense of the same verb. And then, right after, we read, Proteus '... *lekto*...' So he is counting some more, and what might it be? The sentence continues: '... *kai autos*' (he himself). A jolt, and we need readjustment. He is not counting, but he himself *lies down* among the seals. The verb is from another root: *lech* (cognate with 'lie' or *liegen*). The semblance was deceptive. We might have been misled.

It is not that this clash of two *lekto*-forms has never been noticed, but somehow commentators did not know what to make of it.[5] Of all the translators only Rouse at least tries to capture some link: '... counted the number; counted us first... he lay down himself *in the count*'; but even the addition does not tempt us with a wrong lead. For a Joycean what happens is simply that the listener has been drawn into the game of deceit. The reader has to sort out substance or accidents, truth or deceit, seals or human intruders, concealment and detection. The theme is acted out in the language, and the Greek inflection effortlessly offers a variety of forms, so that an identical activity can be expressed in different ways (*lekto/lege*); and the same phonetic appearance (or shape, *eidos*) does duty for two distinct doings. An identical *lekto* is not the same as another *lekto*; you cannot trust words ('lie' may not be 'lie'). That, moreover, the shape *lekto/lech* is related to *lochos* and *lochao* (a lying down in ambush and to ambush), links up with the ruse through which the tricky seer himself has been tricked, adds to the etymological functionality.

The device that Joyce used, and used widely in 'Proteus' (think of 'lap', 'strand', 'see', 'close'; perhaps also 'I, eye', 'sea, see', and all the rest), may be three thousand years old and has been largely over-looked in the meantime, to judge from the commentaries we have. I am fairly sure that Joyce, cunning or 'knowing (*eidos*) crafty tricks' like Proteus (4:460), never set eyes on the doubling of *lekto*. He did not have to, and neither did Shakespeare.

What do they think...? (*U* 11.1049)

One reason why ambiguity, often mistermed 'pun', tended to be disregarded or simply not registered for long periods, may have been its supposed ignobility. It is my guess that teachers of Greek may also have been responsible for its neglect. Teachers have to drive home distinctions, very often crucial trifles, like accents or the length of a vowel. Preoccupied as they would be with the niceties of Greek inflection, they would not have a class pause over the question why Homer, reputedly no mean manipulator of words, used the aorist *lekto* once only in the whole poem in the sense of counting, and almost juxtaposed it with an unaffiliated likeness, just in this passage. A pedantic, staid (let's think of our Victorian stereotype) teacher of old languages might not have encouraged observations like the following.

Agamemnon, a shade in Hades, speaks to Odysseus and monomaniacally dwells on the wrongs done to him by his treacherous wife. Sweepingly, but understandably, he curses the whole sex, excepting only Penelope. His motive may be genuine, if envious, admiration, or it may be mere courtesy towards an old companion who now stands before him soon to depart on his protracted way home. Penelope, Agamemnon concedes, is 'discreet and prudent in all her ways' (Butcher and Lang), 'a very admirable woman and has an excellent nature' (S. Butler), 'too wise, too clear-headed, sees alternatives too well' (Fitzgerald). What a student has to spell out is something like: she is wise and knows (*oide*) well (*eu*) in her mind (*phresi*)—*medea* (11:445). That has to do with *medomai* (plan, plot, consider); 'knowing *medea* (counsels, prudence)' is a tag quite frequent. And it applies to Penelope, who *is* shrewd and loyal. But a lewd student might spot an alternative word, identical, also *medea*, in the dictionary, and apply that. It has occurred in the poem before. When Odysseus is about to brave Nausikaa and her maidens on the beach, he covers his *medea* with a twig, the first gentleman of Europe (6:129). To cut off a man's *medea* will later be a threat to a beggar and a real punishment for disloyal Melanthios (18:87, 22:476). So what is it that Agamemnon indicates that Penelope knows so well? Surely our old schoolmaster would not incite a sniggering class into probing this off-possibility too thoroughly. But what did Homer, who knew and used both homonyms, have in his subtle mind? Are we perhaps anachronistically psychologizing a formulaic phrase with post-Freudian nastiness? Is it fair to imagine that Agamemnon, in his morbid preoccupation with his wife's sexual infatuation, could spitefully or unwittingly try to disquiet a former war companion (whom he did not always trust or like, see *Iliad* 4:339, and who is still alive)? Who is to decide? Verbal suspicion, justified or not, at any rate invigorates an otherwise routine phrase and makes it disturbing. Joyce's Penelope is one who does have a fair knowledge of male *medea* (*U* 18.143, 542, *et passim*), and this in the sense that modernist writers seemed to devote so much attention to. Molly's familiarity with *medea* helped to have *Ulysses* banned.

If *you*, having become duly suspicious, should now turn the various alternatives and aspersions over in your mind (as you should), you would be living up to the activity of *medomai*—to take counsel, meditate, measure, consider.[6]

produce your credentials (*U* 16.1342)

All signals have to be treated with caution, and we also cannot tell what is or is not a signal, sign or *sema*. Odysseus, on his return, has to disguise himself and to fake names and origins in order to find out whom he can trust. It takes skill to hide one's identity, but it is also difficult to prove it. Names are particularly unreliable, for anyone can make up a story. One's looks change with age, naturally or by divine interference.[7] Some bodily marks, however, remain as tokens of recognition, like the scar the nurse Euykleia discovers in one of the most memorable scenes. The scar does what a name cannot do. Names can be arbitrary or significant (*Odysseus—odyssamenos* is both, 19:407–9), but scars or, for that matter, tattoos, are silent and truthful testimony.[8] The feet of Odysseus are about to be washed, the nurse prepares cauldron and water (Leopold Bloom, at home in his kitchen, puts the kettle with the water on and then washes his hands, and the secrets of the Dublin waterworks are revealed (*U* 17.160–

229—an entirely different story). All of a sudden Odysseus remembers his scar: if the nurse touches it, she will recognize the wound and everything might come out. In one of the most evocative lines:

oulen amphrassaito kai amphada erga genoito (scar would recognize and manifest truth [literally, *works*] would become) (19:391)

the alliterative force is evident even to the Greekless reader, and the two *amph-* words become more significant when we learn that both of them are *hapax legomena*, that is they occur here only. Joyceans might even become excited over a scene as trivial as a foot-washing, where an old wound is recognized (as it immediately will be) and something startling, a whatness, is revealed. Stephen Dedalus can get eloquent over such cases (*Stephen Hero* 213). Being revealed is to be made *amphada*, a dialectal or even colloquial derivation of the verb *anaphaino* (to make appear, reveal, display, show forth). Homer, a moment before the hazardous disclosure, happens to use a near-synonym term of the one that young Joyce, and many later critics, was so fond of. The scene that follows literally and polytropically *is* an epiphany, and by some lucky chance, Homer almost called it so.

The (non)recognition fluctuations in Book Nineteen of the *Odyssey* are so subtle, both linguistically and psychologically, that they would need separate and extensive attention. Here I can only focus on that scar, *oulé*. Since it leads almost instantly to the naming of Odysseus, it would be tempting to link *oulé* to one of the non-Homeric variants of the name (which basically splits into an *Od-* and an *Ol/Ul*-lineage)—*Oulixes*, but there seems to be no philological evidence for this. Sounds and shapes, we know, are impostures. The scar will be mentioned seven more times, with one exception always in the accusative (since the scar is noticed, known, covered, inflicted, or suffered)—*oulén*.

Before the famous foot-washing there has been a bristling first encounter between Odysseus, still a beggar, and Penelope who, most likely, does not yet recognize him. She is wary about anything reported about her lost husband. Calling himself Aithon and inventing some Cretan descent, he says that long ago Odysseus, on the way to Troy, had been his guest. Penelope wants some evidence: How did he look, what clothes did he wear, who was with him? Now Odysseus, making up fictional memories of meeting himself, is at his dexterous best. It is not easy, he says, you see, to remember things of twenty years ago, but he will try. And proceeds to recall the cloak Odysseus wore—it had a most marvellous brooch—and his doublet, and the one companion whom he can still name. But of course how is he to know that those actually were the clothes that his wife gave him for the journey; he might have gotten them from someone else along the way (19:218–48). It is all very common sense and most crafty. We also detect a Bloomian touch in the impression of the doublet being 'like the skin of a dried onion'. Penelope is convinced.

What clinched it is clearly that brooch of unique design and workmanship, with a 'curious device' (*daidalon*). There is little doubt that the detailed description of the artwork—the earliest piece of pictorial life-like realism (19:226–34)—is the best proof of his veracity. Odysseus had begun, however, almost offhandedly and hesitantly, with a cloak, an unexceptional one. Unfortunately now, my presentation reverses the emphasis, directing attention precisely where it would not have been. I read the passage almost as a show Odysseus puts on of gradually remembering something from the past, not important at the time, in paraphrase like: Let me think. Ah! 'A cloak (*chlainan*)—purple (*porphyreen*)—made of wool (*oulén*) he was wearing, of double fold' (*diplen*, 19:225–6).[9] And no one, surely, hearing the story for the first time, would give much thought to the common garment which only serves to introduce a marvel of epic acknowledgement, the depiction of the splendid brooch. It is not until a few minutes later, when we have come upon the revelatory scar, *oulen*, that we can turn the commonplace adjective woolly, *oulen*, into a potential identifying device, perhaps an auctorial overtone. Mind you, *oúlén* (from *oúlos*, related to our 'wool', occurring in its feminine accusative singular form only here), is slightly different from the noun *oulén*—a matter of accent, well discernible to a Greek ear, something that students of the language have to distinguish the hard way.

If Odysseus had wanted to signal, subliminally, a secret to his wife, or if Homer had wanted to communicate with his audience, that muted *oulen* would have done the trick, a word that claims or proves nothing, yet spells a tiny message. All of this within a context of disguise and identification. Is this a cunningly wrought (*daidalon*) strategy? Penelope, we are told, 'recognized the tokens' of circumstantial evidence, and the word for token is *semata* (19:250).

Semantic deviation of a phrase from its denotation is a technique that Joyce taught us. The signatures of the *Odyssey* are not usually read like that. We do not know whether we can take a slightly unnecessary remark, 'and another thing will I tell you, and take it to your heart', occurring halfway through the listing of the clothes of Odysseus, at its below-surface level: *allo de toi ereo...* (19:236). If we take to heart what he said in his very first spoken words in the poem, in partly identical phrasing: *allo ti... medeai* (5:173), we get into deep waters. For there *allo ti* meant also something other than what has ostensibly been said. If we now take *him* at *his* own previous word, an ordinary woollen cloak may be refunctioned into an incidental epiphany.[10]

previous intimations of the result (U 17.327)

Even *primarily* understanding Joycean phrases may depend on a second exposure later on, which is to say that reading, re-reading too, changes what we have read. It can clarify or add complexities. We cannot possibly account for the strange behaviour of Bantam Lyons, who cryptically says 'I'll risk it' and speeds off (U 5.541). That 'it' will make belated sense when Bloom's 'throw it away' has been drawn into a racing environment and accreted more fortuitous meaning from a religious pamphlet, so much so that even a wholly juxtapositional 'hardly a stone*throw away*' (U 16.9) may set an already intricate net of correspondences into motion. Retroactive semantification is vital in *Finnegans Wake*. We do not expect it in Homer, though the Greeks were later to attribute ambiguity to their oracles, where decoding often tragically trailed behind.

I can think of at least one miniature example of delayed enlightenment. In the second book of the *Odyssey* an Ithakan assembly has been convened. The first person to rise is old, sage Aigyptios. Before he speaks, we are told that one of his sons, Antiphos, had gone away with Odysseus, and that the savage Kyklops had killed him in the hollow caves, and—

pymaton d'hoplissato dorpon (last [he] prepared supper) (2:20)

The Kyklops had 'prepared (a, the) last meal.' According to unstated laws of narrative pertinence, there must be some connection, but we are unable to deduce what it is. Translations, here representing reader response, go several ways. But one has to roam far afield to find versions that limit themselves to the simple statement of the original: A nineteenth-century German rendering is: 'das Mahl sich, das letzte, bereitend' (Hubatsch); and the same is expressed in a more recent French form: '... mais ce fut son dernier repas' (Jaccottet). Buckley needs a pronoun: 'the Cyclops... prepared for his last supper'. The majority translate a different story, augmented by a decisive link: '... *on him* made a supper last of all' (Palmer); '... and made *of him* his latest meal' (Butcher and Lang).

In this view Antiphos is 'last' in a meal as a passive victim. These readings are of course correct, but they are not what a novice listener to the tale could pick up. Translators anticipate and gloss, sometimes in creative amplification: '... who had cooked him too, and eaten him for his latest, and his last, feast' (T.E. Shaw); 'The ravenous Kyklops in the cave destroyed him/Last in his feast of men' (Fitzgerald). Pope gave freest rein to his imagination:

> But (hapless youth) the hideous Cyclops tore
> His quivering limbs, and quaff'd his spouting gore.

All of this is in full, but predictive, awareness that the Kyklops used to feed on guests that dropped in. Of the companions of Odysseus, he took two at a time, on three recorded occasions. One might reopen the old question of *verbatim* against 'free' translations, but what the responses bring out here are shifts in interpretation, all the way from a fairly innocuous domestic meal to a gruesome spectacle, and not, for example, a metaphoric licence, as in 'The Russians, they'd only be an eight o'clock breakfast for the Japanese' (*U* 4.116).

It is the dangling adjective *pymaton* that seems to cause so much divergence in translation and to provoke officious paraphrases. What does the phrase really say? It has both an uninformed (present) and an enlightened (future) meaning, and this latter one is let out of the translators' bag too soon. Reviewed from the later perspective of the Kyklops adventure, *pymaton d'hoplissato dorpon* appears as a shorthand version of the much more detailed later report. After attending to several chores in the case, the Kyklops 'seized two men' (*dyo marpsas*), and made ready (*hoplissato*) his supper (*dorpon*); this is the final one of three such outrages, the one, as we now can conclude, that involved hapless Antiphos (9:344). The first and most shocking demonstration of cannibalism, however, is the one most drastically evoked: it shows the victims' brains flowing forth, their limbs being cut, with mention of entrails, flesh and bones, all this around another *hoplissato dorpon* (9:29–3):[11] here clearly is the source for Pope's transferred quivering limbs and spouting gore. The visualization has been anticipated.[12] The meal we first heard of was not the last one for the dining host, but the last feasting on the Ithakans—or else it was the last one Polyphemos could still enjoy seeing. The translations already quoted by Fitzgerald and Shaw, as well as Rieu's 'when he made the last of his meal off Odysseus' men', are explicitly adequate synopses, but not what Homer said in less than half that many words.[13]

We may note in passing that a phrase for taking a meal, which could easily be dismissed as a bardic routine, has become full of suspense. There is at least one more retroactive overtone to *pymaton*. The Kyklops had guilefully promised a 'guest-gift' in return for the stranger's name and then, when 'Outis' introduced himself, craftily answered him: '*Outin* I will eat *pymaton* (last)... this will be your gift' (9:369–70). The threat will not be fulfilled, but the adjective has acquired more reciprocal punch. The more we read and remember (or, like good modernists, cross-reference), the more ominous each single term becomes. The suitors too will suffer their fateful last supper, as Odysseus announces to them before he takes up his bow: 'now it is time to prepare *dorpon* for them...' (21:428). These meanings are not just 'there' from the start, but gradually accrue, just as Joyce's words ('home', 'key', 'jingled', 'four', or even 'up') grow in resonance as we go along.

So the question has turned into what does our phrase mean *when*, and to *whom*? Time, reading time, is modelling our understanding in progress. We are given two accounts, only minimally overlapping. Odysseus, maybe in heroic caste-consciousness, has not mentioned the names of any of his subordinates in a conflict which is between an anonymous Kyklops—whose name will be revealed accidentally by his compatriots ('Polyphemos', 9:403, 407)—and a pseudonymous 'Outis'—who finally gives away his identity in an uncautious lapse. The much more concise epic digression in Book Two supplements the self-centered story of the titular figure and shows, more humanely, the reverse of heroic survival—an individual with a name, a qualification (he was a spearman), and a bereaved father.

There is also parallactic ignorance. The novice reader is told that Antiphos has been killed (which he could never learn from the extensive Kyklops episode alone), but is unable to understand the exact nature of the meal. Aigyptios, the father, does not even know that his son is dead. In poignant irony the father is called 'sage', literally 'who... knew—*myria*' (2:16), but for all the 'numberless' things he knows, he cannot know what he would care most about, what happened to his son, and he still hopes the assembly might hear news of the expedition force coming back. Homer has deftly sketched a subsidiary tragedy of a father and a son. And once more a formula that has all the visible signs of a cliché, 'knowing—*myria*', has become almost harrowing.

A commentator, far less deft than Homer, has to muster an inordinate amount of verbiage and quotations (and, excuse me, transliteration), to show how 'understanding' may come about slowly, sequentially, chancily, parallactically.

The above readings are all modelled on techniques that we may call Joycean. Joyce, at any rate, helped to teach them to us. As might be shown in much more ample detail, some of these techniques were already Homeric, and may have been overlooked. But, inevitably, I have offered not only interpretations, but also metachronic figments, or feints—for that is what fiction means: Latin *fingere*, 'feign', or figure (all cognates of English 'dough') go back to a root meaning to knead, mold, form, or what in German could be expressed by *modeln*.

Which brings me commodiously back to the modernist fiction of the arch-modeller Joyce. In his last work, after *Ulysses*, he wrote that 'Temp untamed will hist for no man' (*FW* 196.22). In the history book of Everybody no man may be Outis, and the author might condone the dislocution of a phrase close by (the context is a trial) into a comment on my own illicit tampering with an ancient model—'illysus distilling'.

NOTES

1   Homeric names are closely transliterated here so that figures or places (Kirke, Eumaios, Ithaka) are easy to distinguish from the Latinized forms Joyce used in his schema to refer to *Ulysses* chapters ('Circe', 'Eumaeus', 'Ithaca').

2   I may be making too much of a lexical suspicion nowhere recorded. The epithet *naulochos* turns up only once more, at the end of Book Two, where the task force of the suitors found a convenient harbour 'for ships to lie in' (*naulochoi*, 4:846). The next lines say that the suitors are waiting for Telemachos to kill him, 'ambushing (*lochoontes*) him'.

   Before Odysseus leaves for Kirke's house he falls out with the lieutenant who cautiously had not entered her place but came back to report. He now refuses to join the rescue party, for fear of being trapped again. Odysseus seems to over-react to the one companion who shares so much of his own prudence. His name is Eury*lochos*.

3   Joyce may have inverted this misconception in his Book of Deceptive Signs. Instead of a final reconciliation, we read of the origin of Earwicker's agnomen, an episode, with 'a high perch atop of which a flowerpot was fixed'—a strange landlubber's device to trap earwigs which is mistaken for an aquatic implement, part of a fishing rod—'paternosters and silver doctors' (*FW* 31.2–8). In *Finnegans Wake* this is how the troubles *begin*.

4   Robert Fitzgerald shifts the choice of a starting point from the Muse addressed to the invoker, who specifies: 'Begin when all the rest... had long ago returned.'

5   The most recent gloss on this that I could find says: 'Il giocco di parole e chiaramente intenzionale'. Omero, *Odissea*, vol. I, Testo e commento a cura di Stephanie West (Milano: Arnoldo Mondadori 1961), 356.

6 That words like *medomai* and *medea* are related to 'measure', 'metre', 'meditate' and, moreover, cognate to 'mode', 'modern', 'modality' and *'modeln'*, merely shows that this is a small world of Indo-European roots. But it is intriguing to notice that the first instance of dubiousness by Odysseus is connected with *medomai*. When Kalypso, out of the blue, announces his sudden return, he says distrustfully: 'Something else, goddess, you have in mind (*medeai*) than my return' (5:173). He knows, no one better, about the disparity of what people say and what they intend. I think it significant that the first words Odysseus ever speaks are *'Allo ti'*—'something else'. Something-elseness is characteristic of his mind and his cunning, it is a feature of the *Odyssey* and of Joyce's works, it is the life-force of *Finnegans Wake*. When I speculated on the *pars pro toto* validity of this opening hint ('Paratektonik oder Nichts gegen Homer', in *Nichts gegen Joyce: Joyce Versus Nothing* [Zürich: Haffmans Verlag 1983], 155–6), I had not even noticed that the first, exemplary speech is actually sandwiched between this common word denoting otherness: *'Allo ti... allo'* (5:173, 179).

7 Leopold Bloom's incongruous measurements have been explained in various ways. Mythologically, some obvious discrepancies in the size of Bloom's 'chest... biceps... forearm... thigh... calf' (*U* 17.1817) need not worry us, for Pallas Athena can diminish Odysseus for his role as a beggar (13:430f) and, at need, enhance his appearance: 'Odysseus... showed his thighs, comely and great, and his broad shoulders... his chest and mighty arms. And Athene... made greater the limbs...' (Murray, 18:67–70).

8 Maud Ellmann has written about the linking of the scar with the naming of Odysseus in 'Polytropic Man: Paternity, Identity and Naming', in Colin McCabe (ed.), *James Joyce: New Perspectives* (Brighton: Harvester Press 1982), 81ff. Her excellent essay relies on translations, in which identifying features get easily blurred.

9 The cloak is *diplen*, 'worn double'; another cloak that Odysseus (disguised) claims he was given by Odysseus (real) in a Trojan fictitious exploit, creating a lie of fascinating duality in order to wheedle a *real* cloak from Eumaios, is also 'of double fold' (*diplaka*, akin to Lat. *duplex*). Twofoldedness is typical of the Nostos-books of the *Odyssey*, but duplicity also suffuses Eumaeus, with its doubling of roles, events, identities, etc.

10 As though to reinforce such suspicions, the last description of the companion that the beggar remembers, Eurybates—who is 'so much like-minded with Odysseus'—is *oulokarenos*, literally 'woollyheaded' (19:246). Because of the phonemic and semantic functions indicated, accents are provided for *oulé*, but not for all the other transliterations from the original Greek.

11 Line 311 is identical, only the meal this time is *deipnon* (taken in midday or, here, in the morning). A similar formula is used for the meal that the Laistrygonians make of one of the Greeks (10:116), so that this further disaster may become part of an expanding aura of secondary associations.

12 Homer is modelling times. Odysseus' report of the Kyklopian adventure narratively *succeeds* the brief mention in Book Two, but *precedes* it in actual time. Translators remodel the tidings for the reader's comfort and for facile instant consumption.

13 It is congruent that Joyce translators too are occasionally inclined towards glossing amplification. If my somewhat excessive listing of metaphrastic evidence

should undermine the readers' trust in translation generally, then we have to be grateful to Homer and Joyce for showing us *that*, too.

QUOTED TRANSLATIONS OF *THE ODYSSEY*

Most of these translations are available in several editions. Since the citation of the original (5:173 = line 173 of Book Five) can always guide a reader to the corresponding passage, the page numbers have not been given.

Buckley: *The Odyssey of Homer*, Theodore Alois Buckley (trans.) (London: Bell & Daldy 1867).

Butcher and Lang: *The Odyssey of Homer*, S.H. Butcher and A. Lang (trans.) (London: Macmillan and Co. 1887).

S. Butler: *The Odyssey of Homer*, Samuel Butler Roslyn (trans.) (NY: Walter J. Black, Inc. 1944) (dated July 1900).

Chapman: *Chapman's Homer*, vol. II, *The Odyssey*, Allardyce Nicoll (ed.) (Princeton University Press 1958) (first published 1614–15?).

Fitzgerald: *Homer: The Odyssey*, Robert Fitzgerald (trans.) (Garden City, NY: Doubleday 1981).

Hubatsch: *Homers Odyssee*, Oskar Hubatsch (trans.) (Bielefeld & Leibzig: Velhagen & Klasing 1892).

Jaccottet: *Homère: L'Odyssée*, Philippe Jaccottet (trans.) (Paris: François Maspero 1982).

Murray: *Homer: The Odyssey*, A.T. Murray (trans.) (Loeb Classical Library, Cambridge, Mass.: Harvard University Press 1910).

Palmer: *The Odyssey of Homer*. George Herbert Palmer (trans.) (Boston and New York: Houghton, Mifflin and Co. 1899).

Pope: *The Odyssey of Homer*, Alexander Pope (trans.) (London: Frederick Warne & Co. *c*.1725–6) (the translators were Pope, Elijah Fenton and William Broome).

Rieu: *Homer: The Odyssey*, E.V. Rieu (trans.) (Harmondsworth: Penguin Books 1946).

Rouse: *The Story of Odysseus*, W.H.D. Rouse (trans.) (New York: Modern Age Books Inc. 1937).

Shaw: *The Odyssey of Homer*, Newly Translated into English Prose by T.E. Shaw (Lawrence of Arabia) (New York: Oxford University Press 1932).

PROTEAN INGLOSSABILITIES:
'TO NO END GATHERED'

Readers of Joyce depend on the mediators of background information, the commentators, annotators, source tracers, scholiasts. Reading Joyce is, in part, to play such roles. But no matter how superior
we may comport ourselves, we need co-operation; no single reader
knows enough. Group readings, pooled experience, are one antidote,
printed notes or glosses another. They also invade the class-room
when the teacher supplies comments, and as soon as 'Any questions?' becomes the question. The mediation of background and
intertextual sources—whether the results are called 'Annotation',
'Notes for Joyce', 'Allusions', 'glosses', 'scholia', 'commentaries' or
whatever—is both necessary and problematic. We may not give
much thought to what kind of notes, exactly, we need for which
occasion. Once we stop assuming that all a student/novice needs to
be told is the sum total of the notes that happen to be in mainstream
currency, the misgivings become intriguing. The following remarks
will take cautious common sense looks at some of the issues.

No doubt, we want our glosses to be accurate, correct, reliable.
Not all of the ones in circulation are. If a note for 'Schwanzenbad-
Hodenthaler' (*U* 12.560) reads: 'German: Idle-about-bath-Inhabitant-
of-the-valley-of-testicles'[1] then it is unreliable, incorrect and not
accurate, and one might wishfully imagine such sloppiness to be a
rare exception. No matter what the practice is, at least we have an
ideal of 'correctness' against which to measure shortcomings. Correctness in itself is already quite a tall order, requiring serial safe-

guards of double-checking. For certain occasions, say for a very advanced level, we might even want commentaries to be reasonably complete—more of an aspiration than a possible achievement, already beyond the reach of any one expert or small team. Ideally we should all collaborate in the supremely consequential task. Which, in a scattered sort of way, we do, but then the editorial and organizational problems become formidable.

Beyond correctness and inclusiveness we want the notes to be relevant. Relevance is a less objective notion even than accuracy, it already belongs to the realm of interpretation. Notes should enable interpretations, not predispose them, but in incommodious vicious recirculation they are already part of what they help to bring about. Every item in a note is interpretation by its tacit assumption of deserving a place there; every note is also, by nature, a meddlesome intermediary. Readers, Joycean ones in particular, are note-creating beings. All these dilemmas are certain to remain, Protean insolubilities. Meddlesome interpretation will inevitably lead to disagreement. No wonder, Joyce's works are essentially also *about* this problem—the mind interpreting the world and words. An interior monologue or a Shakespeare theory or a nationalist harangue or a Circean phantasy or an Ithacan list are abristle with running notes and comments. Our notes are (sorry!) meta-notes.

In the following queries particular stress will be put, furthermore—and principally—on a didactic aspect: At what time is what kind of information profitable; or can information be, on occasion, premature and detrimental? Notes, in other words, should also be expedient (should, etymologically, 'free our feet' for exercises of our own) and stimulating, not blunting. They should open, not close. This has to do with time, the appropriate moment, *kairos*, and the time devoted to our own, unaided, primary interaction with the text. Notes deceptively posit the simultaneous availability of all information.

Questions of this kind could be tackled systematically. Principles could be established, perhaps; but they might either be too rigidly cramping, or else too vaguely flexible for precise application. Principles usually have the advantage of revealing more about their own metaphysics than the perennial uniqueness of each individual item. The approach taken here is purely pragmatic, what has been done, and what might be done in specific cases (all cases are specific)—exemplified frustrations. A few inductive nongeneralizations will be tried. The trial runs are selected from the chapter which above all

others acts out mutability, the elusive 'Proteus'. This suitably highlights the problems at hand. Implicit in all will be the overall concern of *how* to gloss the most pervasive drive, change itself, not just
its single manifestations. Notes have a way of securing and fastening
their objects, treating them *as* objects. Such fixation is often betrayed
in the wording of a note: 'this is an allusion, a reference to...' We
entangle ourselves in an inherent contradiction. 'Put a pin in that
chap, will you' (*U* 3.399), Stephen addresses himself when he tries to
fix fleeting thoughts, ideas, inspiration, into the stability of letters.
(How, by the way, would we gloss the odd word 'chap'?) Pins are, or
were, proverbially put into butterflies for their exposition. What gets
lost in doing this is the flying, the flutter, the motion, whatever characterizes butterflies. In trying to put pins in the chapter we may lose
nothing but its 'proteity'.

ineluctable dilemma
What words in *Ulysses* should be glossed in the first place? Surely
words like 'diaphane' or '*Frauenzimmer*' (which has been wrongly
glossed as meaning 'midwife', an annotation that has sporadically
survived lexical truth). Perhaps 'modality' in the first line, and
already this would not be too easy to pin down in a manner that is
both precise and intelligible. What about 'Ineluctable'? It means, we
know and sometimes read, unavoidable, inevitable. Should we tell
those who might pass by heedlessly that an appropriate image is hidden in the rare adjective—that which cannot be struggled out of: '*in-
e-luct-abilis*'; the verbal form *luctari* actually means 'to wrestle'.
'Ineluctable' is what you cannot get out of by wrestling.[2] It was Proteus, the versatile wise man of the sea, who wrestled out of anyone's
grip by changing his form into such volatile things as fire or a running stream. How can you hold, or, as Leopold Bloom puts it, 'own
water really'? (*U* 8.95). Joyce began with the right word, which has a
way of becoming alive beyond its merely epistemological niceties
once its inherent metaphor is brought to light. And should any note
indicate that for an older generation, brought up on the classics,
'ineluctable' would have had two strong possible echoes? It was Virgil who used the adjective in a prominent position. It became a
winged word, part of our heritage. Aeneas is told that the fall of Troy
is imminent, in fact has already occurred, in these portentous words:

Venit summa dies et ineluctabile tempus
Dardaniae. Fuimus Troes, fuit Ilium... (*Aeneid* 2:324–5)

At this point Troy (Dardania) has become a matter of the past, the ultimate day (as prophesied in the *Iliad*) has arrived. There is no struggling out of it (the struggle about the city has at this moment become nearly pointless). Time is in fact ineluctable, it always is. Another part of the passage cited will turn up later in *Ulysses*: '*Fuit Ilium!*' (*U* 7.910). Elsewhere in the *Aeneid* it is destiny that cannot be wrestled against: '*fortuna omnipotens et ineluctabile fatum*' (*Aen* 8:334: 'almighty fortune and ineluctable fate'). In such radiation the first word in 'Proteus' calls up Fate and Time.[3]

All very well, but is it mandatory to force these classical ghosts on an unsuspecting reader who wants to go on with a rebarbative chapter and is content enough, at a first reading, to figure out what Stephen has in his complex mind? Certainly not, and certainly not too soon. If the above suggestions were to be condensed into a short annotative entry, some dim-witted user might come along and claim: 'Ineluctable' is an allusion to Virgil; or to Swinburne.[4] It is not, really, an allusion or reference, or even a 'quotation', but perhaps the effective part of an aura. The word, unusual enough, has its own karma: in a former incarnation it served a Roman poet to designate momentous turning points. Some words too 'remember their past lives' (*U* 4.365). It is wrong and heavy-footed to insert Virgilian ineluctability in a canon of comment; it is equally not quite right to leave it out and not to give readers a chance to tax its vibrations, or simply to appreciate the vividness of 'wrestling out of'. It may be worth knowing that the first word of the chapter has potential associations with Time and with Fate. Previous literary uses of a word conduce to our understanding of, or at least feel for, the context. Or else, this may lead us astray and clog our minds with gratuitous trivialities.

We have not even yet done with the first word in the chapter of change: the beginning is also a contrast: 'ineluctable' is a word that has remained stable with the passing of time. For practical purposes it is still identical in shape with its Latin ancestor. Scholars took it over as it was from the classics. As a bookish term it did not have to undergo the metamorphoses that just before Joyce's age were being traced and reconstructed. The last word in the first 'Proteus' sentence, 'eyes', would be aligned by etymologists with the German *Auge*, Latin *oc-ulus* or Greek *os-somai*—forms that do not appear to have much in common with each other. Etymology is the unveiling of past Protean shapes. Yet it should not therefore clutter the entries of notes even in a chapter whose 'Art' is philology, or should it?

Potential Virgilian ('SAYS PEDAGOGUE', *U* 7.1053) echoes are definitely not allusions in any narrower sense. They are not part of the primary equipment we need to wrestle with the chapter's opening. They are not quotations like '*maestro di color che sanno*' (*U* 3.6) soon to follow, which clearly derives from Dante's *Inferno* and would be obscure without knowledge of that source. The original context determines, identifies, fixes the person referred to, Aristotle, a professional knower. This we accept, as Hugh Kenner reminded us,[5] through a concatenation of commentaries that have come down through the centuries: Aristotle is not named in the *Divina Comedia* either. Ironically, a reader has to be master of a little knowing (or to be informed by one). None of the presiding thinkers in the first paragraph—Aristotle, Berkeley, Jakob Boehme—are nominally present. One thing the Dantean line does is play with knowledge (personified by the arch-philosopher, 'master of those who know') and with our ignorance (most of us do not recognize a line we never saw before). Among other things, '*maestro di color che sanno*' is a comment on commentaries and their tradition.

In that line, which a commentator will translate and put within a pertinent framework, at least one word other than '*maestro*' is tricky—'*color*'. It is our natural reflex to connect it with a preceding thought: 'Then he was aware of them bodies before of them coloured?' Colour, of course; but no, the Italian '*color*' is—or rather: was—a demonstrative pronoun, merely pointing forward: 'those'. 'Colour' is wrong, and yet it is hard to resist the idea that the antecedent 'coloured'—and, of course, the fact that Stephen is meditating on colour which is an Aristotelian *accidens* (and not substance)—helped to call up the Dantean phrase in which the shape, body, appearance, *color* may be as effective as the actual (purely grammatical and hardly noticed) meaning. 'Proteus' is about the treacherous relation between appearance and essence, semblance and reality. The wrong sense of '*color*' seems to be more vital than the essential one. What kind of shape is one grappling with by finding in the correct reading of '*color*' (a demonstrative, something you can point out to be seen) and the false one just once again the opposition Stephen is thinking about? Paradoxically in '*color*' we may be aware of the erroneous colour before (we are aware of) the functional body (*U* 3.5). Such dynamic intricacies would exceed the requirements or feasibilities of annotation. Practically speaking, can we imagine, or accept, a gloss that would say that '*color*' does not mean colour but energetically calls up the misleading vision all the same? '*Color* = colour' is not a favourite, but a throwaway.

Notes, whose essence it is to be functionally brief, moreover, if they truly attempt to struggle, *luctari*, with the text, become unwieldy and cumbersome, laborious to digest, an obstacle rather than an impetus. With all the necessary speculation and hedging, they tend to get too long for convenience; but it is again a Joycean fact that micro-notes strive towards comprehensive exhaustion. A few further proliferations of that sort will now document the inherent impossibility of solidifying metamorphoses. Examples are easy to find, they are everywhere.

common searches

Stephen imagines his uncle, Richie Goulding, whom he might visit:

He lays aside his lapboard whereon he drafts his bills of costs for the eyes of master Goff and master Shapland Tandy, filing consents and common searches and a writ of *Duces*[6] *Tecum*. (*U* 3.80)

Who are masters Goff and Shapland Tandy? Goff, Tandy, Shapland— uncommon, striking, names. There is something quaint, antiquarian, memorable about them; we can understand that they would occur to Stephen. So we look around and might find, antiquarians ourselves, for example, one 'Matthew Goffe' in Shakespeare's 2 *Henry VI* (IV, 5, 10) who would help nothing. Our existing reference works and annotations offer items like this: 'Goulding was a law clerk with Messrs Goff and Tandy' (*Norton Anthology of English Literature* 224)—a possible explanation, except that we know that Richard Goulding is employed by Messrs Collis and Ward, solicitors, 31 Dame street. John Vandenbergh, the Dutch translator of *Ulysses*, who compiled a volume of annotations, expands this non-fact into a corrective gloss: 'In reality the solicitor's office of Collis and Ward' (my rendering of *Aantekeningen bij James Joyce's 'Ulysses'* [Amsterdam: De Bezige Bij 1969], 35). This still leaves Goff and Tandy unaccounted for. Most Joyceans turn to the *Notes for Joyce* by Gifford and Seidman:

Goff—one who is awkward, stupid, a clown, an oaf. Master *Shapland Tandy*—combines Irish revolutionary Napper Tandy (1740–1803) (see 45:2–3n) and Laurence Sterne's eccentric hero from *Tristram Shandy* (1760–7). (35)

All such information consists of, no doubt, true facts, reflections or possible associations, but the commentaries amount to no more than guesses of some probability: Napper Tandy, for instance, takes us by the hand soon after (*U* 3.260). Sterne's Shandy is a bit removed from Tandy, however, but then Shandy's tale is at least proteanly confusing in perhaps fitting analogy. 'Shapland', by the way, is still left dangling.

We would be on more solid ground consulting the entries on Goff and Tandy in the factually oriented *Thom's Dublin Directory* for 1904:

Goff, James, esq., taxing master, Supreme Court Judicature—res. 29 Leeson street, lower. (1882)

Tandy, Shapland Morrie, taxing master, Supreme Court Judicature, and com. for affidavits—res. Clarinda park house, Kingstown. (2022)

We also find them under Supreme Court Judicature (Chancery Division) as members of the 'Consolidated Taxing Office':

Taxing Masters, Jehu Mathews, esq. J.P.; Shapland Morris[7] Tandy, esq.; James Goff, esq. (898)

So these two are real civil servants, taxing masters ('master' or '*maestro*' at this stage in the book is already a reverberating complex, a word of apprehension for Stephen Dedalus). We will in fact see 'Richie Goulding carrying the costbag of Goulding, Collis and Ward'—most likely in a professional pursuit—'pass from the consolidated taxing office to Nisi Prius[8] court' (*U* 10.470). Appearance led most of us to believe the names belonged to fiction or history, now they turn out to be part of existing legal institutions—Dublin surface, not historical embroidery. Goulding in a manner of speaking does work for master Goff and master Shapland Tandy, in the sense that the two are part of a supervisory board. We might now even detect Goulding's own voice as a reading possibility: just as he calls the firm he works for 'Goulding, Collis, and Ward' (we learn later: *U* 6.56), he might facetiously claim to be working 'for the eyes of master Goff and master Shapland Tandy', his superiors somewhere in the hierarchy; or else, such a phrase might be a scathing remark passed by Simon Dedalus on his brother-in-law.

The 'correct' information would derive from a source like *Thom's Directory*. The correct information is trivial, but to the point. It clarifies something, not everything. (How exactly do these taxing masters affect Goulding's work? Would Dublin folklore of 1904 have something worthwhile about them? Whose voice is being echoed?) If we do not know the identities of Goff and Tandy, as most readers obviously did not, not much is lost. Our understanding of *Ulysses* does not—*must not*—depend on it. In such a case the question mainly turns on *when* such correct annotation should be imparted to new readers. If *Notes for Joyce* informed us right away in civil service terms (as it no doubt will in a future revised edition), it might also instantly lay all those ghosts from the past: Napper Tandy, the Goffs of yesteryear, and all sorts of maybe vague tentative overtones. The right information might lull the explorative urge which, especially in 'Proteus', is as much part of the active meaning as the correct factual answer—which *does* belong in a note. Instant facts may curtail the richness of associations in—mind you—the 'interior monologue' which consists *of* associations. Associations are never wrong, but notes, even notes of associations, may be.

The struggle for meaning is more than a terminative gloss of resolution may seize. To put it differently, even when the local Dublin habitation of master Shapland Tandy has been determined, when we solve that little puzzle for good, the taste of that 'Shapland' should linger disturbingly—for it is evidently also some such pulsation that made Stephen evoke it. 'Tandy' will be redefined by the recall of a stereotyped consciousness of 1798 nationalism, the legendary Napper Tandy. 'Napper' and 'Shapland' are at least introspectively connected. The legendary rebel of a hundred years ago might be disheartened to see a Sassenach namesake firmly instituted in the levying of taxes and the dispensation of justice. So the entries above that actually were associative shots in the dark do add their quota, they lend '*color*' to the passage as literary reverberations. But even the factually appropriate gloss may lead us into tangential bypaths: Stephen Dedalus seems to be beset by masters that are taxing him. Joyce, of course, is a taxing master for annotators.

The point is that even undoubtedly correct, that is verifiable information, notwithstanding its indispensability, may be hermeneutically ill-timed. A gloss has a levelling effect: it puts all its consumers in the same position. It induces a state of knowledge which would precisely not have been identical for, say, Richie Goulding himself, or Stephen (who may never give any thought to the legal institution), or an ordinary Dublin citizen of 1904. Meanings change, and ought to, with the accidental state of our knowledge. New knowledge does not automatically replace former guessing. In *Finnegans Wake* a residual and often dominant element of guessing remains.

Stephen conjures up Dean Swift, 'his mane foaming in the moon, his eyeballs stars'. This leads to 'Houyhnhnm, horsenostrilled' and then to:

The oval equine faces, Temple, Buck Mulligan, Foxy Campbell, Lanternjaws. (*U* 3.111)[9]

The meaning we get out of this list differs according to what we bring to it. Every reader of *Ulysses* will recall Mulligan and may, but already less likely, remember one of Stephen's creditors, out of a given list of ten: 'Temple, two lunches' (*U* 2.257). In *A Portrait* (which no reader is obliged to know, or memorize) a fellow student Temple featured often in the fifth chapter, so the reader of the previous novel will be at an advantage. A very attentive one may call to mind 'eyeless faces' and:

Was it not a mental spectre of the face of one of the jesuits whom some of the boys called lantern Jaws and others Foxy Campbell? (*P* 161.25)

So the sum of four names refers to three people, all summoned from Stephen's past. 'Lanternjaws' and 'Foxy Campbell' are alternative appellations for the same person, a priest. If we did not know all this, if it were not served up ready-made as it is here, we might be more likely to wonder about 'Lanternjaws'. If it is not recognized as a nickname, it might be many things, as is borne out by the two translations Joyce was alleged to have supervised:

Têtes chevalines, Temple, Buck Mulligan, Foxy Campbell, lames de couteaux.[10]
Die ovalen Pferdegesichter, Temple, Buck Mulligan, Foxy Campbell, hohle Gesichter.[11]

In both renderings the last item is not treated as a name at all. Once the correct designations are revealed to us, lanterns and foxiness subside, and may well be overlooked. One need not inspect what is familiar. If the list is still partly cryptic, there seem to be at least four interwoven clusters worth our attention: 1 and primarily) *persons* that have impinged on Stephen at one time or another; 2) there are *priestly* traits: one person *is* a jesuit, Mulligan played the role in mockery, Temple's name is sacerdotal; 3) description of *faces*: equine, lantern (=hollow) jaws, temple; 4) there are *animal* features: equine, foxy, buck. The Protean role of an item like 'Temple' is more vital at the speculative stage. A certain amount of guessing, before the nominal identification brings it to an end, may be aptly fruitful. External complications may play their part: a textual corruption formerly separated 'Lantern jaws' into a sentence all of its own, turned the passage into a more Protean one than its author may have contrived. But Joyce on the whole tended to push names back towards their primordial meaning by often putting them in lower case. The Dublin district called 'Liberties' is invested with more original freedom in 'From the liberties, out for a day' (*U* 3.33); the lower case letters at least make us stop and wonder. The text takes liberties with names like 'the dead sea' (*U* 4.219); this is a bit of water that by its spelling becomes deader than an orthodox Dead Sea would have been.

What deserves inclusion? When a trite French '*Bonjour*' follows right upon '*Et vidit Deus. Et erant valde bona*. Hlo!' (*U* 3.440), does the *Bon* in the salutation echo *bona* from Genesis? Is '*Bonjour!*' supposed to be spoken not (only) by or to Kevin Egan, perhaps, in Paris, but by God in prophetic French, God who after all first created the day (Gen. 1:5) and certainly found it good? Would such ripples be part of the commentator's job? Most likely not.

patient groans

Beware of foreign languages, they may be traps; and make sure which languages *are* foreign. German '*Frauenzimmer*' (*U* 3.30) is not a room, '*Zimmer*', but, oddly, a woman irrespective of where she happens to be. Before the Critical and Synoptic Edition of *Ulysses* settled for 'Los *demiurgos*' (*U* 3.18), a phantom Spanish configuration ('*Los Demiurgos*') added some congruous trickery to the phrase. On the other hand the bride in 'Bride street' (*U* 3.34) is spurious[12] but psychologically effective; this is an Irish saint Brigid turned into a location. 'Romeville' (*U* 3.375) does not contain Rome, but a variant of 'rum lingo' (*U* 3.378), not to be confused with the one in 'rum tum tiddledy tum' (*U* 3.392), and again distinct from 'mulled rum' or even 'Rum idea' (*U* 8.196, *U* 5.352). Beware of wrong *colours*. Beware of translations. It is fitting that Stephen's exploits in Paris should be observed and mocked by Irish missionaries to Europe: 'Columbanus. Fiacre and Scotus on their creepystools' (*U* 3.193). Especially St Fiacre, a vehicular saint, for in France he has become, by a series of random transversals, a hackney coach. A Protean fate. Is it significant enough for acknowledgement in Ulyssean glosses that 'navel' and '*omphalos*'—only a few lines apart (*U* 3.36, 38), two words that share but one single letter—are akin, derived from the same ancestor, linked by etymological navelcords between them?

Annotation should not, presumably, take care of non-meanings: if '*ponton*' were French (it is Homeric Greek), it would mean something else, something that floats *on* the 'windedark sea'—'*oinopa ponton*' (*U* 3.394); if 'Algy' (*algae*?) or 'mare' (*U* 3.31, 22) were Latin, illegitimate overtones would accrue, not to be accepted or perpetuated, but somehow in line. '*Prix de Paris*' (*U* 3.483, recalling *U* 2.302) is undoubtedly French but has a way of seducing us towards the unfaithful Helen who was offered as a prize to Paris of Troy in a mythological French triangle (Helen is the wife of Menelaos, who tells of his encounter with Proteus in book IV of the *Odyssey*). When 'Faces of Paris men go by... curled conquistadores' (*U* 3.215), we may think of the capital of France and of the Trojan beau. In other words, 'Proteus' is also about selecting and refusing meanings, about semantic weavings and undoings. According to location, an identical verbal shape, or sound, would have different significance. Joyce's next work, *Finnegans Wake*, will brazenly exploit allotopical non-meanings of this sort.

No language is said to be more precise than Latin, one reason why students once had to learn it as a mental discipline. So nothing should be more facile than to clarify the significance of a short Latin passage, late Latin at that, marked, indirectly, as a quotation of Saint Ambrose who heard the 'sigh of leaves and waves, waiting, awaiting the fullness of their times':

diebus ac noctibus inurias patiens ingemiscit. (*U* 3.466)

As it happens, several English renderings exist in print, not all of them agreeing with the others. The views given differ: *Who* is groaning/sighing? *What* is '*inurias*' the object of? What is the determination of '*patiens*' etc.:

A—Night and day he patiently groaned forth his wrongs (St Ambrose).[13]
B—Days and nights it patiently groans over wrongs.[14]
C—He who suffers injuries complains day and night.[15]
D—Day and night it [the Creation] groans over wrongs.[16]
E—Suffering injustice days and nights it sighs.[17]
F—Suffering wrongs by days and by nights it sighs.[18]

Not all of these paraphrases can be equally correct, though there seems to be a vague consensus (D, E, F). It is the departures that are interesting. A and B seem to construe *iniurias* as dependent on *ingemiscit*; *patiens* has naïvely created its English surface semblance 'patiently', which all the other glosses think of, rightly, as an active participle: 'suffering wrongs'. A and C have a personal subject for the verb, the other versions a neutre 'it'. Most interestingly, C stands aloof as an autonomous and sententious rendering.

Most commentators take account of the patristic context (already indicated by 'Saint Ambrose'): Stephen calls to mind a fragment from the saint's *Commentary on Romans* 8:22: '*Scimus enim quod omnia creatura ingemiscit et parturit usque adhuc*' (for we know that the whole creation groaneth and travaileth in pain together until now). The subject of the Latin clause is, therefore, 'it' ('*creatura*', the result of creation), certainly not 'he'. But in ignorance of the original background we may naturally assume a personal agent, all the more so since the preceding specifications of '*creatura*', 'weeds, fonds, leaves and waves', are all in the plural.

The transformations give evidence of '*diebus ac noctibus inurias patiens ingemiscit*' as a very Protean appearance. Six Latin words with their inflexion produce various English forms, grammatical relationships, differences of word order, alternatives like groan or sigh; wrongs, injustice, injuries, etc. Taken by itself, the sentence might mean something like version C: 'He who suffers injuries complains day and night'. There is some psychological veracity in this, and somehow it might apply to Stephen. It might co-explain why this particular echo and no other occurs to him now. His own mood is reflected, and the erroneous translation emphasizes this. Actually Saint Paul will continue: 'And not only they, but ourselves also... even we ourselves groan within ourselves...' (Rom. 8:23). Stephen groans/sighs and projects this onto creation: 'they sigh' (*U* 3.464). The Latin must have some meaning taken by itself, in its newly transferred context.

It is part of the trickiness that two of Saint Ambrose's Latin shapes, *iniurias* and *patiens*, have English equivalents, so the text teases and misleads us with the phantoms *injuries* and *patient(ly)*, untrustworthy appearances. Paradoxically, the wrong, ignorant, translations are the most Proteanly revelatory ones.

For the conscientious commentator a few questions arise. We know the source of Stephen's echo: how profitable is it? The late Father Noon, SJ, who traced the phrase, speculated that 'Joyce probably came across this in some choir manual or sodality manual', and not in Migne's voluminous *Patrologia Latina* (*Allusions* 65). At the same time the source is 'written into' the passage by way of an intertextual link. Not knowing whether the author ever set eyes on it, should we revert to the fountainhead? For the sake of the experiment, it shall be given here, from *Commentaria in Epistolam ad Romanos*:

Scimus enim quod omnia creatura ingemiscit et parturit usque adhuc. Parturire dolere est. Ipse sensus est, quia omnis creatura per quotidianum laborem ingemiscit et dolet usque modo. Usque modo tamdiu significat, quamdiu legitur. Ipsa enim elementa cum sollicitudine operas suas exhibent, quia et sol et luna non sine labore statuta sibi implent spatia, et spiritus animalium magno gemitu artatur ad exhibenda servitia; nam videmus illa gementia cogi invita ad laborem. Haec ergo omnia exspectant requiem, ut a servili opere liberentur. Si autem haec esset servitus, quae ad Deum

proficeret promerendum, gauderet, non doleret creatura; sed quia nostri causa sub-
jecta est servituti corruptionis, dolet. Videt enim quotitie opera sua interire; quotidie
enim oritur et occidit opus ejus. Recte ero dolet, cujus operatio non ad aeaternitatem
pertinet, sed ad corruptionem. Quantum ergo datur intelligi, satis de nostra salute sol-
licita sunt, scientes ad liberationem suam proficere maturius, si modo nos citius
agnoscamus auctorem. Haec itaque scientes, omni cura diligentiaque dignos nos prae-
beamus, aliis quoque ut exemplo simus, non nostra solum miseratione commoti, sed
et ejus causa quae diebus ac noctibus injurias patiens ingemiscit; solemus enim in
alienis causis propensius vigilare.

(For we know that the whole creation moans and is giving birth up to this moment. To
give birth is to suffer; the exact sense is that all creation, in its daily labour, is moaning
and suffering up until now. 'Until now' means however long as the moment in which
this is being read. The elements themselves perform their works in anxiety: not without effort do sun and moon occupy the room assigned to them; and the breath of life
must be forced to do its duty with a loud moan, for we see it driven to work unwill-
ingly, with a cry. So all these things are awaiting their surcease, when they may be
freed from their servile toil. Yet were this a service directed toward winning to God,
the creation would be glad in it, not suffer: the reason it suffers is that it is in servitude
for our own sake. For every day it sees its works perish: daily its work is born, daily
dies. It has a just complaint, having its labour directed not towards eternity but decay.
So far, then, as is given us to understand, they [the elements, the creation] are quite
deeply concerned with our welfare, knowing as they do they can the sooner attain
their own freedom the sooner we are brought to acknowledge our creator. And we ourselves, knowing this same, ought to use every care and pain to become examples to
others, not only out of compassion for our own kind, but for the sake of that which
'moans', bearing its harms day and night; for it is normal for us to pay more attention
to others's troubles [than our own].)

This *is* the context. Is it enlightening as a note, or just pedantic
dead weight? Who will actually read—and not skip—it in the first
place (as you did just now, gentle reader)? If all glosses were thus
laboriously detailed, any commentary would swell to unpractical
proportions. What might we gain? The Ambrosian passage happens
to contain coincidental echoes: '*Et vidit Deus*' (*U* 3.440); the creator's
satisfied look contrasts with its opposite, after the fall: '*Videt enim
quotidie opera sua interire*'; Ambrose's '*Occidit*' may be in some relation to a subsequent quote: '*Lucifer, dico, qui nescit occasum*' (*U*
3.486). Anyone interpreting, that is to say trying to make out 'exact
sense', might find many motives in the theological sources that surface in the *Ulysses* chapter. Stephen thought the weeds were swaying
'reluctant arms' (*U* 3.462); Ambrose finds nature driven to work
'unwilling' (*invita*). In a later patristic recall, Stephen will think of
'corruption' (*U* 7.843). That all is '*labor*', toil, is immediately taken
up in Stephen's 'loom of the moon' with a 'toil of waters' (*U* 3.469,
whether 'toil' does duty as labour or as texture). The groaning con-

nected with parturition (for which in English the Latin 'labour' now
does multiple duty) is connectable with Bloom's empathy with
women's lot, ('groaning on a bed... her belly swollen out... Life with
hard labour. Mina Purefoy swollen belly on a bed groaning to have a
child tugged out of her', *U* 8.373, 378, 480). The saint points out several times that these things happen every day: '*quotidie*'.

Professor Alan Brown, of Ohio State University, who kindly supplied the translation and background information, suggests the relevance of a passage immediately following, one of Saint Ambrose's
most famous metaphors or similes:

Post creaturam mundanam adjecit etiam nos hoc exspectare, et ingemiscere ad Deum,
ut hinc liberemur cuncti destinati ad vitam; quia christianis mundus his pelagus est.
Sicut enim mare adversis excitatur procellis, insilit, et tempestatem navigantibus facit;
ita et saeculum perfidorum conspiratione commotum, perturbat fidelium mentes: et
tanta diversitate hoc agit inimicus, ut quid prius evitandum sit, ignoretur.

(Following the universal creation, [Saint Paul] adds that we ourselves await this event
and bemoan to God that we may be set loose hence, all of us who are ordained to life.
For to Christians the world is the deep sea. For as the sea is whipped up by contrary
winds and rises and storms upon sailors, so the world, stirred about by the councils of
faithless men, tosses the minds of the faithful, and the Enemy brings it all upon us to
turn and turn about that one cannot tell which way to flee first.)

Saint Ambrose's simile seems in part to derive from the *Odyssey*
itself and its (also) symbolical adventures on the sea, at the mercy of
contrary winds. (Conversely this remote part of a potential gloss
belongs to the noxious councils that toss and agitate the minds of the
faithful.) The original context potentially contributes (or we co-cre-
atively make it contribute) to the imagery or atmosphere. The whole
Ambrosian passage is in itself an interpretation. In cultural transformations we find an apostle commenting in Greek on the world's suf-
ferings in the light of a new belief, which in part is based on Hebrew
scriptures. A fourth-century theologian interprets Saint Paul's commentary in Latin. Stephen Dedalus in turn meditates upon it, and
ultimately it is up to us to find out what, as St Ambrose puts it, '*Ipse*
sensus est'. The results of such processes are always arbitrary and
selective. Commentaries offer verdicts and, as the illustrative groanings here show, it may be hard to decide which of them are pertinent
and valuable—and to whom, at which stage.

Interpretation—or minds tossed, like the sea, by contrary winds—
does not naturally stop at any given place. A phrase like '*iniurias*
patiens' has its own scriptural history, layers to be uncovered: we
find it inflected in Acts 7:24, or in the Psalms (145:7, for example).

The psalms also provide a precedent for Stephen's 'Lord, they are weary' (*U* 3.464): 'I am weary with my groaning' (*'Laboravi in gemitu meo'*, Ps. 6:7). The New Testament recirculates and recontextualizes material from the Old.

The sum total of all possible glosses is not to be confused with the 'meaning' of any passage, a platitude that practically all Joyceans and certainly most recent theorists would pay lip service to. In practice, however, texts are still reduced to what happens to be conspicuous in print about them. Every gloss tends to be too much and yet not enough. Apart from the wealth of directly adducible commentary, with the ever intriguing problem of relevance, there are the possible refractions. Everything in the mind is refracted: Stephen's interior shorthand is not exact quotation ('to no end gathered'); thoughts are transformed into new shapes. Evidently the sighing over wrongs touches a chord in Stephen. The first chapter has displayed injuries to his self-esteem, grievances; one such indignity was afflicted in painful protraction by Buck Mulligan: 'Stephen suffered him to pull out and hold up on show by its corner a dirty crumpled handkerchief' (*U* 1.70)—this is suffering: *'patiens inurias'*. In *Ulysses*, however, it is mainly Leopold Bloom who suffers wrongs. Bloom indeed 'sighs' several times in the next chapter; he is a 'muchinjured but on the whole eventempered person' (*U* 16.1081). These epithets are Homeric: *'polytlas'* (*Od.* 5:171, and *passim*) and, perhaps, *'echephron'* (*Od.* 13:332). Transversal links are part of the reading experience, though these particular connections, being at best anticipations, looking ahead into territories yet to come, should emphatically not be put into a running commentary.

The Proteus episode in the *Odyssey* tells us about the fate of distant Odysseus. The sea god Proteus, once caught in a firm grip, reveals that he saw Odysseus on Kalypso's island shedding tears (*Od.* 4:555ff). Structurally Book 4 of the *Odyssey* is also in dramatic preparation for the appearance of Odysseus in person, in the next book, where indeed he is called *'polytlas'* (*Od.* 5:171, 354, 486). When we first meet him in person, he is groaning:

dakrysi kai stonachesi kai algesi thymon erechthon ([with] tears & groans & pains [his] soul racking) (*Od.* 5.83)

A Latin translation says *'lachrymis et gemitibus et doloribus animum macerans'*.[19] The Greek for groans (*'stonache'*) is the same root Saint Paul used in Romans 8:22; *'ingemiscit'* translates *'systenazei'*, from *'stenachein'*. These are not relations Joyce ever knew or cared

about; they just occur in the reshaping of similar themes. But even so
it is obvious that *iniurias patiens* would render what we learn about
Odysseus right from the start and in many formulaic repetitions: he
is introduced as suffering many wrongs: 'polla... pathen algea' (*Od.*
1:4; 'plurima... passus est dolores' in Clarke's Latin).[20] There are tantalizing coincidences. Menelaos, who reports the encounter with Proteus, was approached by Eidothea, daughter of the unerring old man
of the sea, and addressed like this: Are you foolish or 'do you take
pleasure in suffering woes—*terpeai algea paschon*'? (*Od.* 4.372). She
hints at a masochistic indulgence. Then again there is the recognition
scene between father and son in the *Odyssey*, where much-enduring
(*polytlas*) Odysseus says to Telemachus: 'I am your father, for whose
sake you suffer many griefs with groaning.' This is Telemachos himself '*iniurias patiens*'; several motives come together: '*sy stenachizon
pascheis algea polla*' (*Od.* 16:188–9; Clarke: '*suspirans... dolores
multos, injurias sustinens*', II:86).

What such philological evidence would show, once more, is the
strandentwining of Judaeo-Christian and Hellenic chords, and the
inexhaustibility of affiliations—irrespective of what the author may
ever have had in mind. No reasonable and appropriate completeness
could be achieved; just to gather all potential interlinkings would be
a laborious accumulation of groans. Again our efforts mirror those
under discussion: saint Ambrose (whose name means 'immortal' and
remains in fact the same Indo-European shape in merely a different
transformation) tried to determine the meaning of words in scripture.

Extensive glossing can be intimated in exemplary selection only,
as has been done here; one consequence is that it instantly becomes
its own parody. Negative examples could be cited as well. In no matter how thorough a Homeric commentary on the Proteus chapter, an
important figure like Eidothea, Proteus's daughter who advises and
helps Menelaos,[21] in the role that Athene plays to Odysseus, may
never register at all. There are no 'allusions' to her, only her attitude
can be felt. It is she who says that her father will 'try to assume all
manner of shapes of all things that move upon the earth, and of
water, and of wondrous blazing fire' (*Od.* 4:417–8). It is she who
counteracts the stench of the seals under whose skins the Greeks lay
in ambush with ambrosia (*Od.* 4:445). There is stench in the chapter,
but no such sweet fragrance; but there is, as seen before, a saint who
bears the name Ambrose, unrelated, and unrelated also to Homer's
'immortal night—*ambrosie nyx*' (*Od.* 4:429). There is, strictly anno-
tating, no need to mention her, and yet her function pervades the

episode. She outsmarts her father, she teaches not to be misled by appearances, to persist in the attempt. She is the goddess (*thea*) of appearance: *eidos* is outward form, shape, that which is seen: her name could also be read, as it has been, as meaning 'the goddess who sees, or knows'. 'Proteus' opens on that note, the 'visible', 'thought through my eyes'. The root that spawned 'visible' and the Latin *videre*, generated the Greek *idein* (to see), and *eidos*; but also—in words like 'idea', or 'wit', in German *wissen*—the thought that arrived through the eyes, for 'to have seen' has become 'to know' in some languages.

To change to other shapes, is it worth taking up 'a maze of dark cunning[22] nets' that Stephen observes in Ringsend (*U* 3.154) and to gloss the obvious? Stephen Dedalus aimed to fly by nets, using 'cunning' and two other weapons; Daedalus the artificer built a maze or labyrinth: Stephen's past seems to meet him once more. So far, so trite (commentators are afraid to spell out what everyone would notice unaided). But why should—against English usage—nets be 'cunning'? Well, in Greek '*daidalos*' could mean (and did in Homer) 'cunningly wrought', and be applied to artefacts; '*daidalos*' of course is 'cunning' and therefore became the name for the mythological craftsman. Allusions to Daidalos-Daedalus-Dedalus? No. Dynamisms perhaps.

The enemies of the heresiarch Arius attributed a disgraceful end to him: 'In a Greek watercloset he breathed his last: *euthanasia*' (*U* 3.52). Does the ironic comment '*euthanasia*' (a happy, good, death) somehow also suggest the name of the principal opponent of Arius—Athanasius, a notable Greek Father of the Church, after whom one of the Creeds was named, but whose name is not in the text? Prefixes have to be shifted: a bad death is euphemistically turned into its opposite ('good-death') and may turn associatively to no-death (*athanasia*). The point is that such possibilities can very well be flashed in discursive equivocation (the purpose of this exercise), but that annotation has to be more responsibly decisive, with a responsibility, however, that is more towards the tradition of glossing than to Ulyssean polymorphism. In any case there will always remain a limbo area of mere potentiality. Some possibilities may be so vigorous that they too are 'not to be thought away' (*U* 2.49); it may be hard ever after to unthink that 'euthanasia' insinuates (or does *not* insinuate) Athanasius.

a maze of dark cunning nets

put a pin in that chap, will you? (*U* 3.399)

The examples were all taken from the third chapter, the one that
compounds the problems, as its thematic concern *is* Protean change.
How can change be fixed? The preceding remarks are less a sweeping
complaint against existing annotations or future attempts, than exemplars of an inherent predicament. It is difficult—in some essential
way impossible—to handle processes, transformation, becoming.
Proteus of many shapes, true to his nature, keeps eluding us.

Parenthetically again: Proteus is not limited to the *Odyssey*. Ovid
proposes a changeful or ambiguous sea-god: '*Protea ambiguum*' (*Met.*
2:9), he adds a few transient shapes of his own to Homer's, enumerat-
ing a youth, a lion, a raging boar, a serpent, (and prefiguring a Wakean dichotomy:) a stone or a tree, flowing water, a stream, fire (*Met.*
8:731–6). Virgil's list includes a tiger, a scaly dragon ('*squamosusque
draco*'), a lion*ess* with a mane (*Georgica* IV:406–10). Horace has a
'scoundrelly Proteus' who is, as Stephen Dedalus once wanted to be,
not confined by nets or ties: 'slipping through all those nets—*effugiet
... haec sceleratus vincula Proteus*' (*Satires* II, iii:71). Proteus was
developed long before Joyce, and again one might ask if these post-
Homeric elaborations ought to be part of a commentary on the third
chapter of *Ulysses*.

If the Protean dynamisms, not any particular situational 'parallel',
are of value—and they seem to be ubiquitous—then it is good to take
Homer at the words he gives to his characters. Eidothea, daughter of
Proteus, cautioned Menelaos that her father, when seized, would

panta ginomenos peiresetai (try [3] to become [2] everything [1]) (*Od.* 4.418)

including fire and water, and when it happened, he did become a
bearded lion, a snake, a pard, a boar, then running water, and a tree
(see above, and *Od.* 4.456–8). The emphasis is here not on the various incarnations (corresponding, as they would, to the single identifications in our Glosses), but to the inconclusive actions of becoming[23] and trying ('*peiresetai*'). The verb *peiraein* (related to em-pir-ical
and to ex-per-ience) is one of the key activities in the *Odyssey*: to
find out, examine, get information, to test, to make a trial of ('to try
conclusions'[24]), to endeavour.

Proteus *can* be caught, by diligence and perseverance, but even
then only for a short while. He answers a few questions (usually only
those that are put to him), then he plunges out of sight. Information

provided by him is important, reliable, but inevitably partial. Notes are such information, selected for pertinence. As long as we know that their finality (having to stop somewhere) is treacherous, no harm is done, as long as they are not taken, as in fact they often are, for conclusive truths.

Notes are what is known, *(g)nota*, the results of knowing. Paradoxically, knowledge is ongoing: one can always know more, and better, and differently in widening or changing contexts. New theories, for one, add new questions, new answers, and new mysteries. The ancients were aware of this, it was reflected in their language. Verbs for knowing are inchoative, inceptive (a form marked by an 'sk/sc' suffix), that is to say they denote a beginning: *co-gno-scere in* Latin, *gi-gno-skein* in Greek. The meaning in the present tense is not 'to know' but 'get to know'. The Greek verb *gi-gno-skein* is furthermore reduplicated in its initial consonant: *gi-gno*, as though in imitation of the process, which demands a repeated effort (an effort that in Greek would take at least three syllables). One single attempt, the shape of the verb itself seems to imply, is not sufficient. The German verb *erkennen* (with its derivation *Erkenntnis*, so all-important in philosophy) has a prefix that suggests a forward or outward motion, something in progress, a way rather than a goal. Notes have an air of finality which belies the inchoative process.

Perhaps that early Joycean signpost in *Dubliners*, which has so often been critically discussed, fits in here, 'gnomon' (*D* 9), a Euclidian form which, however, is marked by a trace of a cognescent activity. A *gnomon* is one who knows, judges, interprets, discriminates. It may be one who can read oracles—a skill the chorus in an Aeschylus play pointedly disclaims:

ou kompasaim' an thesphaton gnomon akros / einai (I do not boast to be an acute interpreter of oracles) (*Agamemnon*, 1130–1)[25]

Joyce began his prose with a story in which we tentatively learn something and fail to learn as much as we need for our comfort. The agent of the story himself gets to know more and more by cautious deduction from observation or from questionable utterances, but never enough. His and our efforts are, at best, *cognoscent*; we still argue our findings. That same story exposes 'gnomon' as a strange and fearful word which in the exact science of geometry has been redefined to mean something highly specific and exact: a form characterized by incompletion.

Reading and interpreting are in essence *cognoscent*; notes in contrast are fixed with a semblance of determinacy. What is by nature cognescent is replaced by specific *cognita*, things now known. This is unavoidable. A pin *has* to be put in that chap if fleeting verbal inspiration is to be noted down (*U* 3.399).[26] For catching hold of processes, or associations, notes are a contradiction in terms.

This inchoative nature of knowledge, its cognescent quality, is at the pulsating core of what has been vaguely termed the 'uncertainty principle'; it is not some stable principle or discovery once hit upon by Joyce or anyone else. Uncertainty is an epistemological condition, as well as a humanistic stock-in-trade, which we all, and Joyceans in particular, are glib to acknowledge and which we easily lose sight of when our interpretations and annotations, in their dazzling splendour, are to be revealed to the world.

The dilemma can be phrased in variable ways. It is the function of notes to abbreviate, condense, summarize, give the gist—this is what they are paid for, to save us preparatory labour. They are products, conclusions, outcomes. They emphasize the goal, often assume it has been reached, and must neglect the evolution. Notes are resultative, not processive. The 'Result of Gold Cup races!' (*U* 13.1174) is not identical with the actual race, its waverings, developments, the ingenuity of its prophets, the tensions and expectations, the chanciness of what eventually took place.

Notes, glosses tend to to freeze, fix, make static and factual. They offer things, facts, data, substances. They lose their edge if they are hedged in discursive qualifications, such as are possible in an essayistic probe. They tend to concentrate on WHAT and let go of HOW. The least we can do to counteract the inherent falsification of putting a pin into Proteus is to indicate from time to time, by whatever signals, that our offerings are stages or phases at best, that the results are discretionary, arbitrary, the semblance of chimerical relevance. It is true, presumably, that St Ambrose lived '*c*.340–97' or '340?–97', but it is false to assume that these dates are in any way more to the point than the many data that might have been adduced with equal justification. Notes tend to become canonical material, solidified into spurious truths by routine transmission.

Readers have to de-reify the glosses, and annotators should help this process along more than has been usual up to now. We need commentaries and glosses. No single reader knows enough. Who knows, to take the chapter at hand, about the controversies of the Fathers of the Church, the Old and the New Testament, Shakespeare, Ovid, Virgil, Homer, Dante, Blake, Aristotle, Berkeley, Jakob Boehme (and commentaries on all these), Joachim Abbas, Thomas Traherne, *Thom's Directory* of Dublin, Latin, legal terminology, heraldry, and all the abstruse rest? So we depend badly on the experts and their mediators. But what Joyce also teaches us in *Ulysses*—and diffusively in the *Wake*—is that you can never trust any messenger, no matter how well-disposed, even if he/she is doing his/her best, seems ideally equipped (no-one is), and has no axe to grind (all communication is a grinding of axes). We cannot rely on the experts and messengers we need so desperately.

A serious drawback of even ideal annotation, a perfect compromise of conflicting demands, would still be that time is taken away from the reading process. It is possible to know too much too soon, before our minds have begun to revolve the possibilities of the text. None of the above suggestions, for example, should ever be proffered to novice readers of 'Proteus'. Not only might it confuse them, it would litter their minds. What is even worse, it might make them imagine that the proposed intertextual echoes could replace their own essential, incubational, Odyssean, explorations, searches, adventures. Even the most optimal note is wrong when it stifles curiosity and puts a stop to further inquiry.

All Notes are liars—useful, incomplete, overdone, misconceived, partly irrelevant, and unseasonable liars. The previous sentence is a note. So is the whole of this essay.

January 1988

NOTES

1   The note (never mind where) is quite on target, except that it misses a German vulgarism '*Schwanz*' (penis) to match the testicles in '*Hoden*', and that 'Idle-about-the-bath' is entirely unfounded: '*Schwanzen*' is not a verb, the suffix '*-en*' links composite nouns [there is, however, a verb, one with a morphemic difference, '*schwänzen*' (what's in an umlaut?), which indeed means 'play truant, shirk' (a dictionary may give an intransitive 'idle about') and has blatantly nothing to do with the name], and that note is insufficient also since it does not tell us that the whole matrix 'the Archjoker Leopold Rudolph von Schwanzenbad-Hodenthaler' is a common one for the old Austrian aristocracy (Archduke).

2   A swamp can be *ineluctabilis*, or serfdom, and literally so. Out of a certain type of soil, Virgil instructs us, water may have to 'force its way out': '*aqua eluctabitur omnis*' (*Georgica* II, 244).

3   Time and Fate are at least implied in 'That lies in space which I in time must come to ineluctably' and 'Self which it itself was ineluctably preconditioned to become' (*U* 9.1200, 15.2120).

4   'With all strong wrath of all sheer winds that blew,/All glories of all storms of the air that fell/Prone, ineluctable,/With roar from heaven of revel...' These lines are from a sea poem 'Thalassius' (220–3). Swinburne, alias 'Algy' (*U* 3.31) is all over

the first chapters. Many thematic relations might be listed.

5   'Who's He When He's at Home?' in Heyward Ehrlich (ed.), *Light Rays: James Joyce and Modernism* (New York: New Horizon Press 1984), 60.

6   The misleading nature of '*Duces*' (*ducere*: Latin for to lead, guide) has been dealt with in *Joyce's Dislocutions*, John Paul Riquelme (ed.) (Baltimore: Johns Hopkins University Press 1984), 31.

7   The discrepancy between the two entries: Morrie—Morris, due to typographical chance, adds a minor Protean touch to the identifications.

8   Perhaps a shade of master Goff of the Nisi Prius court appears in *Finnegans Wake*: 'growing the goff and his twinger read out by the Nazi Priers' (*FW* 375.17).

9   Pre-Gabler editions were further confusing by an intrusive period: '... Campbell. Lantern jaws.'

10 James Joyce, *Ulysse*, Auguste Morel (trans.) (Paris: Gallimard 1948), 42.

11 James Joyce, *Ulysses*, Georg Goyert (trans.) (Zürich: Rhein-Verlag AG 1927, rep. 1956), 48.

12 Or, to put it differently, a disguise, just as 'the head centre got away... Got up as a young bride' (*U* 3.241).

13 David Daiches, *The Norton Anthology of English Literature* (New York: W.W. Norton & Co. 1968), 2454.

14 Weldon Thornton, *Allusions in Ulysses* (Chapel Hill: University of North Carolina Press 1968), 65.

15 L. Arnold and N. Diakanova, *Three Centuries of English Prose* (Moscow 1967), 267. Bernard Benstock compares several glosses of the Latin sentence in 'Redhoising JJ: USSR/II', *James Joyce Quarterly*, 6, 2 (Winter 1969), 177–80.

16 Don Gifford with Robert Seidman, *Notes for Joyce: An Annotation of James Joyce's Ulysses* (New York: E.P. Dutton 1974), 46.

17 Harry Vreeswijk, *Notes on Joyce's* Ulysses, Part I (Amsterdam: Van Gennep 1971), 190.

18 Brendan Ó Hehir and John Dillon, *A Classical Lexicon for Finnegans Wake* (Berkeley: University of California Press 1977), 538.

19 *Homeri Odyssea Graece et Latine*, Samuele Clarke (ed.) (London: Longman & Co 1828), 174.

20 Alexander Pope: 'On stormy seas unnumber'd toils he bore'; Thomas Hobbes: 'suffer'd grievous pains'; William Cowper: 'He num'rous woes on Ocean toss'd, endured.'

21 This happens when Menelaos, like Stephen Dedalus, is walking on the beach, alone, 'as I wandered alone apart from my company' (*Od.* 4:367).

22 Compare 'A darktongues kunning' (*FW* 223.28).

23 Even the verb forms change: they *become* different (which is easy in Greek and may often be also metrically determined): '*ginomenos, genet, gineto*', in three lines. Interestingly the lion becomes bearded: '*genet, eügéneios*' (4.456). This form has nothing to do with '*gen-*' becoming; '*geneion*', beard, is related to *genys* (=chin), it is merely a similar, deceptive, shape. See in this context my speculations on Protean features, 111ff.

24 Significantly, these 'conclusions' are not the final judgements of logic, but 'experiments', the outcome of which is not yet certain (*Hamlet* III, iv, 194).

25 Why work in Aeschylus? *Gnomon* is not an 'allusion' to *Agamemnon*. The word is, however, part of a literary heritage. Clearly such a lexicographical antecedent

of Euclid's term ought not be part of annotations of 'The Sisters'. Yet not to go beyond the merely geometrical range would arbitrarily curtail the potential radiation of the signal.

26 As it turns out when the poem, temporarily fixed in Stephen's mind, is made known (*U* 7.522), it is in a form that we could not possibly know from the thoughts out of which it arose.

'ALL KINDS OF WORDS CHANGING COLOUR': LEXICAL CLASHES IN 'EUMAEUS'

The remarks in this extended note deal exclusively with the delightful incongruities in the diction of 'Eumaeus' and how they derive in part from words that are used in different senses and at times jostle with each other. The following may be representative:

Mr Bloom promptly did as suggested and removed the incriminated article, a blunt hornhandled knife with nothing particularly Roman or antique about it to the lay eye, observing that the point was the least conspicuous point about it. (*U* 16.817).
Being a levelheaded individual who could give points to not a few in point of shrewd observation he also remarked... (*U* 16.218)

In either case, 'point' does not quite equal 'point', which makes the sentences less than esthetically pleasing, they contravene stylistic precepts. With its bumps and jars, 'Eumaeus' is not always quite to the point, it consistently grates on our refined tastes. A certain inertia seems to govern the choice of words, some of them tend to linger in the mind for handy but malappropriate repetition (notice the reiteration of 'about it' in the first sample). The episode is characterized by a strange lassitude and a warped vitality.

In particular, many words, dispersed over the whole chapter (and of course all of *Ulysses*), are used both literally and figuratively. The text confesses itself in excusatory self-awareness as 'figuratively speaking' and '(metaphorically)' (*U* 16.607, 1597).

figuratively speaking
Towards the end a horse, in a late reassertion of the novel's initial

realism, a horse 'of bones and even flesh' (*U* 16.1783), thrusts itself upon Bloom's and our notice, by depositing, in narrative slow motion, three memorable turds on the ground. This is not the only horse in the chapter; somewhere in the distance a 'horse of the cabrank' is being woken (*U* 16.940); others are featured in the report of the Gold Cup race. But many are purely figurative, rhetorical devices: 'but it's a horse of quite another colour to say you believe in the existence of a supernatural God' (*U* 16.770). Belief in supernatural existence is not exactly a horse, and yet English usage allows abstract notions to incarnate themselves in vivid illustrations. 'Eumaeus' itself, in analogy to its phrasal horses, varies its colour; all of *Ulysses* does. So do words. In the same chapter, synesthetic Stephen Dedalus can hear 'all kinds of words changing colour like those crabs about Ringsend... burrowing quickly into all colours of different sorts' (*U* 16.1143). Those, by the way, are colours of a different sort again from any that would modify a phantom horse. The 'blind horse' that is given a 'strong hint' in Bloom's internal comment (*U* 16.1192) owes its existence to the proverbial expression that a nod is as good as a wink to a blind horse. The *Evening Telegraph* recalls a 'dark horse' of 1892 as an analogy to the 'outsider *Throwaway*' (*U* 16.1243). In 'Cyclops' Throwaway, an outsider, was compared to Bloom, 'a bloody dark horse himself' in yet another trope that originates from the race track (*U* 12.1558). We do not share Stephen's thoughts about an exemplary horse in an *ad hoc* philosophical 'dagger definition': 'Horseness is the whatness of allhorse' (*U* 9.84). Ulyssean horseness goes a long way, as an earlier chapter unwittingly has it, an 'equine portent grows again, magnified' (*U* 14.1097). The multiple horses are indeed all 'of quite another colour' and we cannot trust any of them, which may be appropriate in a story that has umbilical connections with the classical semblance of a horse carved in wood which brought about the fall of a city. The point of these trite collocations is simply that Joyce exploits the whole range of words, and this in 'Eumaeus' probably more than elsewhere, and more farcically. This may also have something to do with the chapter's 'Technic' in Joyce's well-advertised schema, 'Narrative (old)'. Metaphorical use of language is, presumably, secondary, a later development in semantic evolution: *horse*, one would imagine, was first the name of a useful animal before analogous and figurative extensions were thought of. Changes of meaning in all their vagaries are historical events, some can be documented, others only guessed at. The style of 'Eumaeus' allows obsolete spectral meanings,

troublesome semantic phantoms, to discompose the surface of stereotype usage.

Horses have bred many metaphors in the British culture which
dominated Ireland. 'Nestor', presided over by horse-loving Mr Deasy,
testifies to this. Even a lexical heritage tells its political story. The
names of horses and their owners, 'lord Hastings' *Repulse*, the duke
of Westminster's *Shotover*, the duke of Beaufort's *Ceylon, prix de
Paris*', also catalogue imperialism. The Irish who attend races are
inevitably 'backing king's colours' (*U* 2.301). The Gold Cup with the
reflected glory of Royal Ascot casts its minor shadow over Dublin.
Against heavy odds, Throwaway wins the race and multiple misin-
formation turns Bloom, the person least interested in the event, into
a supposed beneficiary. The event itself is featured in the *Evening
Telegraph* report, where we learn that the peculiar but felicitous
name 'Throwaway', in accordance with rules of equine nomencla-
ture, is an offspring of 'Rightaway' (*U* 16.1278). The name of the Gold
Cup winner is accidentally echoed in 'hardly a stonesthrow away' (*U*
16.9); this is no overtly meaningful recall of the horse, but, once
observed, difficult to put aside, especially since 'Eumaeus' is an
episode full of vacuous throwaways as well as of erratic innuendoes.

Gumley, now a night watchman, was, as Bloom reflects, 'at the
end of his tether' (*U* 16.952), and this tether is purely metaphorical.
But towards the end we come across a real horse, whose doings are
lovingly scrutinized, and it is reported as 'having reached the end of
his tether, so to speak' (*U* 16.1874). What kind of tether is that? A figurative one, no doubt, but somehow it is doubled back to a horse that
might potentially be tethered, yet manifestly is not. Eumaean incongruity reaches one of its intriguing convolutions. The apologetic 'so
to speak' signals that Bloom's—or the chapter's Muse's—idiomatic
instinct feels something slightly amiss in the phrasing. 'Eumaeus' is
very much 'so to speak'. It highlights the pitfalls of speaking and
writing, of using Protean words of changing colours and non-existent
yet conceivable tethers.

As prefigured in 'Circe', Joyce is 'doing the hat trick' (*U* 15.195).
Both Stephen and Bloom, like everybody else, wear their hats. A
streetwalker peers into the shelter from 'under a black straw hat' (*U*
16.704); we can identify this as a 'black straw sailor hat' already
noticed during the afternoon (*U* 11.1252). Bloom, always observant,
'remarked on [Corley's] very dilapidated hat' (*U* 16.220). This would
have been a hat from which, etymologically, stones are taken away,
for this is what 'dilapidate' once indicated. The stones, of course,

have long since left the word and remain a spectral skeleton in the closet for pedantic commentators, as idle perhaps as the stones which the watchman Gumley is minding in his sleep, 'having a quiet forty winks for all intents and purposes' (*U* 16.214). (Whatever 'for all intents and purposes' is meant to stand for, it now mainly underlines the lack of any intent or purpose). Another piece of headgear, a very specific one, looms large in the episode, Parnell's 'silk hat' that was knocked off his head, then picked up and returned by Bloom when he was rubbing elbows, for one glorious moment, with Irish history. That one moment is reported twice, with slight modifications ('changing colour'). The incident is compared to the episode with John Henry Menton, whose 'headgear Bloom also set to rights earlier in the course of the day' (*U* 16.1524). Such hats, including one on a stage ('the Lazarillo-Don Cesar de Bazan incident depicted in *Maritana* on which occasion the former's ball passed through the latter's hat', *U* 16.492) provide a framework for two quite different uses. In an exemplary mixture of metaphors Bloom considers the *Gloria* in Mozart's *Twelfth Mass* 'the acme of first class music as such, literally knocking everything else into a cocked hat' (*U* 16.1739). This is quite an achievement for either an 'acme' or else a piece of music—whether that piece exists or not—and to do so 'literally' would be even stranger if 'literally' had not come to mean, in current use, 'not literally'. The wording conjures up a surrealist vision. Literally, such a 'cocked hat' is not to be confused with what the Blooms once sold or rented: 'Balldresses... and court dresses... Any God's quantity of cocked hats and boleros and trunkhose' (*U* 11.493). Somehow the shade of Parnell's hat once *knocked* off still hovers over the beautiful malapropism. Observations of the nature made here amount to facile stylistic faultfinding, and we have it on the chapter's own authority that 'Faultfinding' is 'a proverbially bad hat' (*U* 16.790). So far no annotator seems to have unearthed the underlying proverb. Eric Partridge lists *bad hat* as a catchword that may be 'Irish in origin, "the worst Hibernian characters always wearing bad high hats (caps are not recognized in kingly Ireland)".'[1] The Odyssean versatility of hats in 'Eumaeus' seems to match what can be done, and is being done, on the stage with them, as was exemplified in the preceding chapter, 'Circe'.

Boots are no less versatile, real ones to wear (or else by grace of idiom: 'He could spin those yarns for hours on end all night long and lie like old boots' [*U* 16.823]). Under the scrutiny of Sherlock Holmes, to whom, by the way, Bloom feels some affinity a few lines later ('Sherlockholmesing him up...' *U* 16.831), old boots, of all

things, would never lie. To the sharp mind of a detective they reveal
a detailed background. Bloom has a sharp eye for footwear as well,
he noticed a priest 'showing a large grey bootsole' (*U* 5.370) and that
Stephen in the morning, had 'a good pair of boots on him today. Last
time I saw him he had his heels on view' (*U* 7.985). The phrase 'lie
like old boots' appears more out of line once we call up a memory of
the inquest of Bloom's father: 'Boots giving evidence' (*U* 6.361).
Boots can tell or hide the truth, except that 'boots' of course does not
equal 'boots', a conflation that is in lexical analogy to questions of
identification of the kind that Odysseus had to contend with in his
native land after his return. In *Ulysses* identical shapes are unreliable. It is a sobering thought, incidentally, how much cross-referen-
tial dynamism must be lost by translation into languages where a
hotel bootsboy is unlikely to be shortened to 'boots', and where
horses may not have different colours, or cocked hats are idiomati-
cally unfit for knocking. Joyce uses the potential of his language to
breaking point. Bloom admonishes Stephen not to trust Mulligan—'if
I were in your shoes' (*U* 16.281), not suspecting that Stephen is wearing, of all people, Buck Mulligan's boots, or shoes: 'My two feet in
his boots are at the ends of his legs, *nebeneinander*' (*U* 3.16), in fact
the identical boots that Bloom has looked at in the morning.

The chapter sports an early exemplary trial run of associative
divergence when Bloom's mind is stimulated by 'the very palatable
odour indeed of our daily bread' arising from James Rourke's city
bakery. He runs through a short list of practical, metaphorical and
parodistic phrases: 'Bread, the staff of life, earn your bread, O tell me
where is fancy bread, at Rourke's the baker's it is said' (*U* 16.58).
This paves the way for 'He [Mulligan] knows which side his bread is
buttered on' (*U* 16.282) and all other similar figurative deviations. As
we may remember, Mulligan quite literally had 'filled his mouth
with a crust thickly buttered on both sides' (*U* 1.446); Bloom is more
on target (or is it off target?) than he knows. In such ways do the
book's phrases scuttle blatantly or imperceptibly from the literal to
the figurative, buttered, so to speak, on both sides. While on the subject of 'mouth', compare 'He took out of his mouth the pulpy quid'
with '—You just took the words out of my mouth' (*U* 16.468, 1109);
and again with 'being not quite so down in the mouth after the two
and six he got', or else 'open thy mouth and put thy foot in it' (*U*
16.204, 1269).

There is real bread in 'Eumaeus', at least in the shape of a 'socalled
roll' (*U* 16.366), but no real salt, which is of another order: 'Salt junk

all the time' (*U* 16.622), and a few lines later Bloom thinks of an 'old salt' (*U* 16.630, also 'old salt of the here today and gone tomorrow type', *U* 16.1223); the keeper of the shelter considers 'no Irishman worthy of his salt' that serves the British empire (*U* 16.1024). Such is the spectrum of meaning. Homeric Greek already used *hals* (salt) as a metaphor for the sea (as in *Od.* 1.162, etc.). Nautical language allows for an easy transition from rocks that have to be steered clear of, 'Daunt's rock' (*U* 16.906), and all the rest, to figurative ones: 'God knows I'm on the rocks' (*U* 16.155); 'all at sea' (*U* 16.380) is on a par. All of those are again not to be confused with Molly's exclamatory 'O, rocks!' as a rude comment on Bloom's didactic efforts (*U* 4.343), and yet they form a tenuous link to 'all them rocks in the sea' that the sailor Murphy, if he is the sailor Murphy, professes to be tired of and which, with some geographic latitude, seem to include the rock of Gibraltar where Molly Bloom spent her youth (*U* 16.622). Subsidiarily, all these rocks may also call to mind the native land of Odysseus, 'rocky Ithaka' ('*krananae Ithake*', *Od.* 1.247, 14.124, 21.346, etc.).

Homer used terms like *kradie* or *hetor,* usually translated as 'heart', to personify various emotions. In 'Eumaeus' we find 'he was at heart a born adventurer' only a few lines before 'breaking Boyd's heart' (*U* 16.502, 507). Faces are adaptable too. Stephen was 'rather pale in the face'; Bloom imagines a 'face at the window' and is flustered by the 'face of a streetwalker' (*U* 16.15, 430, 704). More metaphorically, we find 'the face of God's earth' (*U* 16.988), and one particularly delightful conflation: 'there was nothing for it but put a good face on the matter and foot it' (*U* 16.32). Somebody or other, we learn, 'had to sail on' the sea 'and fly in the face of providence' (*U* 16.639). 'It was a subject of regret and absurd as well on the face of it' (*U* 16.539); the phrase is echoed in 'a patent absurdity on the face of it' (*U* 16.1101). As for Molly's appearance on the photograph that Bloom displays to Stephen, 'it was a speaking likeness in expression' and it is then the *expression* 'speaking likeness' that seems to trigger off its sequel 'and leave the likeness there for a few minutes to speak for itself' (*U* 16.1444, 1457). The episode is very much based on deceptive likenesses finding voice. Footsteps can be matter of fact, as when 'a brazier of coke... attracted their rather lagging footsteps', or else a visual illustration: 'high personages simply following in the footsteps of the head of the state' (*U* 16.101, 1200). Contrived metaphorical lapses can as easily equip heads with footsteps as it allows, in the sample quoted above, to put 'a good face on the matter and foot it'.

Eyes have a wide reach in most languages. In 'Eumaeus' there are many; the real ones that can be looked at, like 'drowsy baggy eyes' (*U* 16.375), tend to be in the plural. Eyes in the singular are more singular, the chapter features a 'practised eye' (*U* 16.230), a 'weather eye' (*U* 16.367), 'Stephen's mind's eye' (*U* 16.269), a 'lay eye' (*U* 16.819) as well as a 'public' one (*U* 16.1486), an 'eagle eye' (*U* 16.1796), and an odd variant—'He threw an odd eye' (*U* 16.215), which manages to underline the act of throwing. No wonder then, with such licence, that Bloom and Stephen 'didn't see eye to eye in everything' (*U* 16.1579). The listing also shows how tedious a complete enumeration of every single instant of semantic variation would be.

There is nothing unusual for a piece of fiction to contain a real cat in a kitchen, like the one remembered by Stephen—'the cat meanwhile under the mangle devouring a mess'—as well as a more tropological variant: 'that turned out to be how the cat jumped' (*U* 16.274, 1036). 'Eumaeus' seems to turn such low key contrasts into a stylistic device. In the latter example the reader, as well as Bloom, may recall what he thought about his own live cat in the morning: 'No, she can jump me' (*U* 4.29); the cat's Eumaean antics are linked, incongruously, to the 'idea... that... the coal seam of the sister island would be played out' (*U* 16.1034). The horse seen in the street makes Bloom think: 'even a dog... would be a holy horror to face' (*U* 16.1790). On one occasion 'he misguidedly brought home a dog (breed unknown)' (*U* 16.1607). That was a very general species, as against a particular breed that is imagined for an unexpected return home after a long absence: 'You were a lucky dog if they didn't set...' Let us wait a moment to watch this sentence slipping into the danger of having a real, houseguarding dog biting a purely figurative—'lucky'—one; at the last moment disaster is averted by the substitution of a particular variety: 'You were a lucky dog if they didn't set the terrier at you directly you got back' (*U* 16.1339). This terrier now adds an ironic touch to the parenthetical 'breed unknown' in the previous illustration. Somewhere in the background we may bring to mind the Homeric dogs that Eumaios kept and that fiercely attacked Odysseus, but recognized Telemachos, as well as the faithful Argos who died at the sight of his master (*Od.* 14.29ff, 16.4ff, 17.291ff).

This lexical probe began with a few examples of 'points' at conspicuous variance. 'Eumaeus' is full of them, no fewer than twenty-three occurrences of *point(s)*, out of a total of seventy-one in all of *Ulysses* (this amounts to 32 per cent, the chapter by line count takes up some 7.5 per cent in bulk). Out of these, five are 'Bloomian': '(in) point of fact' (*U* 16.195, 686, 877, 1068, 1335). Some are geographical or geometrical: 'the starting point—Between this point and—beyond a certain point where he invariably drew the line—Europa point' (*U* 16.46, 51, 92, 614). Others are mental and abstract: 'to concede a point—On this knotty point—sticking to his original point—Another little interesting point' (*U* 16.765, 774, 777, 1040), or a more literary 'not to put too fine a point on it' (*U* 16.60). Point becomes verb: 'to point a moral—point a finger' (*U* 16.126, 1302). The finest example juxtaposes Hellenic mythology with the human physique:

Brummagem England was toppling already and her downfall would be Ireland, her Achilles heel, which he explained to them about the vulnerable point of Achilles, the Greek hero, a point his auditors at once seized as he completely gripped their attention by showing the tendon referred to on his boot. (*U* 16.1002)

Vulnerable point indeed. We know that the demonstration backfires, at least for Bloom, who will turn the tendon referred to into the 'most vulnerable point too of tender Achilles', and 'his right side being, in classical idiom, his tender Achilles' (*U* 16.1640, 1716). The point, at any rate, seems to have been lost, either by inattention and psychological revelation, or else in an echo of a once current joke. The quotation above shows that inexpediency need not be limited to the repetition of an identical signifier, but that near synonyms like 'seized as he completely gripped' may be just as quaintly gauche. Lapses of language have produced a tender Achilles, which is ironic in view of the wrath of the hero that sets a whole epos in motion in which his ferocity looms large. It is possible to find a few hints in the *Iliad* of an Achilles motivated by tenderness (his relationship with Patroklos comes to mind). At the same time the fact that warlike, destructive (*oloos*) Achilles is mentioned only in connection with vulnerability, tenderness or in the company of women (*U* 9.350) is mutedly symptomatic of *Ulysses'* drift away from macho heroism.

Greek myths and parts of our anatomy—such is the span of *Ulysses*. 'Eumaeus' in particular thrives on the semantic tension of words operating in various and at times conflicting contexts. Imagine for a moment the Homeric equivalent situation, and remember that in the hut of Eumaios Odysseus prepares himself for the final showdown, the trial of the bow and the slaughter of the suitors with his arrows. For the sake of the experiment imagine also what epic, Homeric, constellation might be contrived out of martial or active words like *shot, stir, venture*: a vocabulary of potential heroism, and then appreciate their bathetic application:

—Have a shot at it now, he ventured to say of the coffee after being stirred. (*U* 16.807)

Mind you, this is also epic style in feeble imitation, for in Greek you might easily append a perfect participle meaning 'after being stirred' to an inflected noun without violating grammatical rules or provoking 'apologies to Lindley Murray', a grammarian whose rules the 'Eumaeus' episode goes out of its way to break (*U* 16.1474).

Since 'figuratively speaking', which the chapter does with gusto, has been taken to be one of its trademarks, the word 'figure' itself deserves passing attention. It is a pliant, versatile word and quite in tune with its origin, something fashioned, shaped, a cognate of *feigned* and of *fiction*. In the Library chapter the word can come closer to the original meaning of Latin *figura*: 'Our young Irish bards... have yet to create a figure which the world will set beside Saxon Shakespeare's Hamlet' (*U* 9.43). At the beginning of 'Eumaeus' 'the darker figure' of the corporation watchman is made out (*U* 16.105), then a 'figure of middle height', 'the accosting figure' (*U* 16.112, 128) of Corley. Towards the end Stephen and Bloom themselves become 'the two figures... both black, one full, one lean' watched by the driver of the sweeper car (*U* 16.1886). This looks like a carry-over from 'Circe' where unidentified appearances were referred to as 'figure(s)' in stage directions (about fifteen of them). On the sailor Murphy's chest, we get a full view of a figure, which is here not the shape of a young man, but 'the figure 16' (*U* 16.675). This follows closely upon 'He'd be about eighteen now, way I figure it' (*U* 16.665). Molly's photograph, in quite another context, 'did not do justice to her figure' (*U* 16.1445). Parnell was once 'a commanding figure' (*U* 16.1326) and then, a few pages later, 'still a commanding figure' (*U* 16.1505): and it seems that this stereotype helped to phrase a wholly different strand of thought: if Stephen were to train his voice, Bloom advises, 'he could command a stiff figure and, booking ahead, give a grand concert' (*U* 16.1854). So figurative bifurcation can interact and interfere, even where no misconstruction is possible. Lifted from its environs, the 'unmistakable figures' which Bloom reads on the pricelist and refers to ('coffee 2d, confectionery do', *U* 16.1699) might well be enlisted as an inverse Eumaean self-reflection. No figures seem unmistakable, identifications become a perennial problem, identical shapes, appearances of letters, are leading us astray. A 'point' is not quite a 'point', nor a horse a horse, and the 'John Bull' that Stephen Dedalus has in mind is not 'the political celebrity of that ilk' (*U* 16.1769, 1774). On the other hand a 'bibulous individual' may be practically identical with a 'communicative tar-paulin', a 'doughty narrator', a 'friend Sinbad', an 'old seadog' or an 'impervious navigator' who metamorphoses into a 'rough diamond' in the next sentence (U 16.337, 479, 570, 858, 653, 1011). Elegant variation amounts to a series of different roles, comparable in this respect to the rapid costume changes that are staged in 'Circe'. An 'entelechy' of the sailor remains 'under everchanging forms', in the words of Stephen, who has given philosophical thoughts to the ques-tion of 'I am other I now' (U 9.205). Or perhaps, the glib verbal muta-tions indicate, there is no such entelechy.

Not that roles are clear cut or that primary and figurative uses are always easy to keep apart. A pliant word like 'shape' can be out of tune for almost opposite reasons. It is inappropriate in a formula like 'drinkables in the shape of a milk and soda' (U 16.10), and involun-tarily suggestive in 'the counterattraction in the shape of a female' (U 16.930); milk definitely has no shape, in contrast to an attractive female. Parnell, we read, had 'what's bred in the bone instilled into him in infancy at his mother's knee in the shape of knowing what good form was' (U 16.1520). This may lead to speculation about the kind of 'shape' that 'knowing' can have. A view of the shape of a mother's knee may briefly intervene, and 'shape', moreover, grates on its potential synonym 'form' (compare 'intolerance in any shape or form', U 16.1100). While on the subject of infelicities, we may also note the semantic rivalry of breeding ('bred in the bone') and instill-ing, which was, at least originally, an infusion by means of drops (Lat. *stilla*), and such instillation is not located at the 'mother's knee'.

Words are misplaced, and yet 'Eumaeus' is also a lesson in applied shifts of meaning as they occur in all languages so that there are no longer any etymological stones in 'dilapidated' or drops in 'instilled'. Even so forgotten or dormant sources can be aroused. When Joyce is at such pains to make his first character feel his skin 'with stroking palps' (U 1.123), the vacuous repetition of the derivative 'palpably' (what can be touched or is perceivable by touch), though it has lost its anchorage, may cause minor irritation: The prostitute who looks into the shelter, is 'palpably reconnoitring on her own' (U 16.705), yet she hardly incites contact, nor does the sailor, 'that rough dia-mond palpably a bit peeved' (U 16.1012); no-one would seem inclined to touch either the man or, for that matter, a real rough dia-mond. 'Though palpably a radically altered man he was still a com-manding figure' (U 16.1505) refers to Charles Stewart Parnell, who, of all people, was known for his aloofness. The adverb 'palpably' is a choice, educated, word employed with the wrong feeling, out of touch.

what construction to put

The contrived oddities of the Eumaean style have been subsumed here under the heading of lexical clashes. In practice such clashes manifest themselves usually when they are clustered together, as were the different 'points' that have been mustered, or when 'he had hurt his hand' is followed by 'On the other hand...' (*U* 16.1608), and in specimens like 'there were on the other hand others' (*U* 16.1213). Often the divergences clamour stridently for attention. An example already quoted in part, is here repeated in its totality:

> This was a quandary but, bringing common sense to bear on it, evidently there was nothing for it but put a good face on the matter and foot it which they accordingly did. (*U* 16.31)

The surreal jostling of 'face' and 'foot' tends to eclipse the metamorphoses of a simple word like 'it', usually a place-holder or a referent. The three 'it' seem to have nothing in common: the first one ('bear on it') refers to the situation outlined before or else the 'quandary'; the second one ('there was nothing for it') is part of a formula and bears hardly any relation to quandary; the third one ('foot it') is part of a verbal phrase. It definitely does not take up 'the matter', though a spectral connection may trouble us for a moment. Reading 'Eumaeus' is largely also to confront and discard obtrusive grammatical misdirections. An assembly of disparate 'it' is nothing extraordinary in speech or writing, and linguists could put distinctive tags on the three that infest this particular sentence, but the low-key incongruities play their role in the meticulous orchestration of wrong touches, a world that is stylistically out of joint. 'Eumaeus' is right, 'all *kinds* of words' are changing colour. Language itself is in a 'quandary'. That term occurs three times, and only in 'Eumaeus'; at least in one case the quandary again affects the syntax:

> Mr Bloom, to change the subject, looked down but in a quandary, as he couldn't tell exactly what construction to put on belongs to which sounded rather a far cry (*U* 16.1172).

The patched construction of the sentence imitates Bloom's bewilderment over the construction of one of Stephen's sentences: 'Ireland must be important because it belongs to me': (*U* 16.1164). That Bloom would worry over a phrase like 'belongs to' is subconsciously linked to his fellow Dubliners' aspersion that he, a stranger, does not belong to Ireland, as was driven home in 'Cyclops', where Bloom also contended: 'And I belong to a race too... that is hated and perse-cuted. ... Persecuted. Taking what belongs to us by right' (U 12.1467), with the further irony that he does not quite belong to *that* race either. If we recall Ben Dollard's prominent genital 'belongings on show' (U 11.557, 1027, 1056) which once amused Molly so much, we realize that a simple word like 'belong' can be so emotionally charged that it causes psychological and syntactical turbulences.

At this point in the story Bloom is set back by Stephen's unwill-ingness to engage in conversation, in particular, by the snub 'Let us change the subject', and does not quite know how to deal with it. The construction of the sentences that render his multiple discomfi-ture is revealing:

With a touch of fear for the young man beside him whom he furtively scrutinized with an air of some consternation remembering he had just come back from Paris, the eyes more especially reminding him forcibly of father and sister, failing to throw much light on the subject, however, he brought to mind instances of cultured fellows that promised so brilliantly nipped in the bud of premature decay and nobody to blame but themselves. (U 16.1179)

What exactly is 'failing to throw much light on the subject'? Presum-ably the expression of Stephen's eyes or the family likeness or the fact of Stephen's recent return from abroad. The phrase itself fails to throw much light on its own subject, with the added turgidity that the subject referred to is not the subject that Stephen has just wanted to change (though perhaps his motivation for doing so). The minor clash of a subject of conversation to be changed and a subject for reflection may sharpen our awareness that the convoluted sentence, up to that point, has not yet revealed its own grammatical subject. It has merely paraded a ramble of tangential offshoots, until the sequence reveals the subject as Bloom: 'he brought to mind'. The sen-tence climaxes in a 'bud of premature decay' that has to be savoured at leisure. Alternative expressions for a similar effect ('to nip in the bud' and 'premature decay') are almost incestuously mated and result in an oxymoronic blend. Somehow many sentences of 'Eum-aeus' appear indeed to be nipped in the bud of premature decay.

Exploitation of non-meaning: PEN SOMETHING
Imagine being given just one isolated phrase from *Ulysses* and having to figure out its import. It might consist of two words presented neu-trally as PEN SOMETHING. *Ulysses* makes some readers aware of

detachable units, but of course no one separates them out of their immediate context. The phrase occurs within Bloom's recall of earlier and, in retrospect, happier days of connubial life, not without disturbances:

> Stream of life. What was the name of that priestylooking chap was always squinting in when he passed? Weak eyes, woman. Stopped in Citron's saint Kevin's parade. Pen something. Pendennis? My memory is getting. Pen...? (*U* 8.176)

'Pen', it turns out, is the first part of an elusive name, which occurs to Bloom some moments later when the blind stripling he has been escorting and watching for a while brings to his mind both the face and the name.

> Bloodless pious face like a fellow going in to be a priest. Penrose! That was the chap's name. (*U* 8.1112)

One connection is that Penrose with his weak eyes squinted at Molly, which the blind man could never have done. In the sudden recollection, 'something' is revealed, by hindsight, to be a memory blank for '-rose'. According to inclination we may or may not connect this missing part with 'rose' as theme, motive, or symbol, or again, wondering what in this particular name is likely to cause a psychological block. One might construe it as a subliminal 'pen rose' of disquieting overtones. The name Penrose resurfaces twice in 'Circe' and later in the Ithacan list of men, hypothetical lovers of Molly, who have caused Bloom unrest at one time or another (*U* 17.2133). The last chapter provides parallactic complementation from Molly's point of memory:

> that delicate looking student that stopped in no 28 with the Citrons Penrose nearly caught me washing through the window only for I snapped up the towel to my face that was his studenting. (*U* 18.572)

The same event with different emphasis: Molly remembers 'that delicate looking student', Bloom 'that priestylooking chap... Weak eyes, woman: bloodless face'; the two parallactic views can tally.

'Pen something' has nothing to do with a writing pen, it is a truncated part of a name, has otherwise no independent semantic existence. The truncation (making the name incomplete like Home Without Plumtree's Potted Meat) is due to defective memory, a failure which Bloom attributes to the passing of time and interfering street noises. There is no writing pen in the name. Or not yet. In a constellation within *Finnegans Wake*, there might be, for we have conditioned ourselves to read the *Wake* by semantic side-tracking. It is hard to overlook something to write with in 'he would pen for her, he would pine for her' (*FW* 301.11), even though the major direction of the word may be wholly different. In *Finnegans Wake* we tend to hesitate about elimination. A mere similar shape, as in 'A penn no weightier' (*FW* 13.28), not even spelled correctly, can act as a name and still forcefully call up a mighty pen. Bloom's wrong guess 'Pendennis?' coincides with part of the name of a society novel (*The History of Pendennis*). The gratuitous 'Pen' would fit into such a context and implicate an author like Thackeray. The wrong association has a way of radiating beyond lexical confines. We can imagine a context of memory and pen. Pens are instruments to write what otherwise might be forgotten. One function of writing is to substitute for memory.

The graphic unit PEN was also featured in the heading of the previous chapter, in a prominent, conspicuous position, in capital letters. For uninitiated readers the word must appear puzzling: 'ITHACANS VOW PEN IS CHAMP' (*U* 7.1034). Nothing preceding can quite explain that PEN. In the seventh episode we find an artificial, editorial, fragmentation of the narrative and interspersed anticipatory labels that in themselves seem to get out of hand. We generally account for them as newspaper headlines or captions, features of communication as events in printed type. By the time we come to the end of the chapter they have become, in a Joycean process that I call 'provection', more aggrandizingly distracting. Stephen, with a 'sudden loud young laugh', has just finished his story of the two old women climbing to the top of Nelson's pillar, and by abruptly coming to an end, surprised his audience. A prospective headline intervenes (*U* 7.1032):

SOPHIST WALLOPS HAUGHTY HELEN SQUARE ON PROBOSCIS. SPARTANS GNASH MOLARS. ITHACANS VOW PEN IS CHAMP.

It projects a Hellenistic flavour and seems, at first blush, to move from the immediacy and everydayness of the story and the manner of its telling to a Greek mythological past that is adumbrated in the book's title. On the other hand the presentation deviates into physiology: 'molars' and 'proboscis' (originally the trunk of elephant, then in jocular, hyperbolic transference the human nose). The two directions, towards the human or even animal body, and towards classical antiquity, have been major ingredients of the book all along. Literary parallax emerges: hypothetical journalism differs from the custom of ancient writers. Journalism retained rhetorical figures of antiquity; such figures may now in turn change the fictional situation that may have given rise to the rhetorical forms.

But that is looking ahead. When considered by itself, the 'PEN IS CHAMP' headline contains vague suggestions. The dangling indecisiveness of 'PEN' is part of its function, to create suspense and raise expectations. It would be interesting to stop novice readers experimentally at this point and enquire what the headline seems to promise. Pens have been around. One newspaper man is seen with 'a pen behind his ear' (*U* 7.34), a tool of the trade. Gallaher, we read, 'was a pen' (*U* 7.630); and here pen is a figure of speech, as it is in the headline 'THE CROZIER AND THE PEN' (*U* 7.61). Quite evidently, neither PEN as a writing utensil nor the metonymic function of the word supply the clue. Of course in some figurative way the writing pen, precursor of movable type and the printing press, is implicitly championed in the newspaper episode. Joyce, incidentally, added the headline, like all others, on the proof sheets, with his pen. Anyone is of course free to rearrange the spaces between letters (the way typesetters would handle characters in lead). Leslie Fiedler, for one, found it 'tempting... to read "PEN IS" as the single word "PENIS", which would translate the sentence into a phallic boast.'[2]

'CHAMP' is most likely interpreted as a newspaper shortening of 'champion' and not as something connected with horses, as in a previous 'champing' (*U* 3.56; 5.214). However, an attentive reader might be forgiven for linking a recall of 'the gently champing teeth' (as noticed by sympathetic Bloom in the morning) with 'SPARTANS GNASH[ing] MOLARS' in the immediate context. It might be an irrelevant linking. The classical Ithaka, by the way, was not suitable for horses, as Telemachos explains in the *Odyssey* (4:606).

When we read on we find that, after the overgrown headline, the text is mainly devoted to a comment on Stephen as the author of an *ad hoc* story; his bitterness is linked to the cynic Antisthenes, whose alleged views on the competitive beauties of Hellenic mythological women—'he took away the palm of beauty from Argive Helen and handed it to poor Penelope' (*U* 7.1038)—becomes a wholly tangential issue. But it is this aside, this afterthought, that provides the extended headline. As a representation of the main text to follow it is out of focus, an almost autonomous diversion or titillating digression. It enables us, perhaps, at leisure, to connect Stephen's two fictitious elderly women with Helen and Penelope of Homeric fame and splendour.

'PEN IS CHAMP' resolves itself by typical hindsight illumination: we read the headline from the end of the body of the text and not, as would seem more natural, the other way round. 'Pen' translates into a non-classical abbreviation of Penelope who, in the views of professor MacHugh, was considered more beautiful than Helen of Troy. Even so, by the way, the two versions given, the disproportionate title and the one sentence in the paragraph, do not match: All that is said in the conversation is that the sophist Antisthenes, who was not himself from Ithaka, put Penelope above Helen (for which so far no documentation from antiquity has been found). The headline statement shifts the supposed beauty contest into a matter of nationalist pride. Of course, we might now take our cue from the *Odyssey* and consider 'ITHACANS VOW PEN IS CHAMP' a transposition of a scene where Penelope enchants all assembled suitors with her appearance, and where one of their leaders says:

epei periessi gynaikon/eidos te megethos te (since you excel all women in comeliness and stature). (18:248–9)

So this particular Ithacan, speaking for all the others, did put on record long ago that the local Pen was champ; Odysseus on occasion said the same (though not referring to beauty). In one sense, the catchy line takes us nearly home to Ithaka, we are in sight of the island, as was Odysseus before the winds released from the bag by his companions blew him into another nine years of adventures. The point is that a preceding headline and the subsequent text interact: 'Penelope' post-identifies 'PEN'; and once we can compare the two accounts, all kinds of disparities may lead to hermeneutic concatenations and seductive marginal irrelevancies. The headline has moved far away from Stephen and his story. Yet Stephen's patron artificer championed 'pens' in their original sense. When he sent out his mind towards arts not yet known, as the *Portrait*'s motto has it, the first thing he did was to arrange feathers ('*pennas*') to build wings; '*et ignotas animum dimittit in artes/naturamque novat. Nam ponit pennas in ordine*' (*Metamorphoses* 8.188–9). The word 'pen' as a metaphor for writing derives from the feathers, *penna*, of large birds. Interpreters can make non-existent pens go a long and fanciful way.

The headline is multiply imaginary. True to type, it dramatizes, exaggerates and vivifies. The amusing enhancement of trivialities lends the chapter the imitative likeness of a newspaper. The style of 'Eumaeus' aims at corresponding scintillating embellishment. The 'Aeolus' headline bridges times and cultures: it projects Sparta and Ithaka of a mythical past on the attitudes of the present, and this in incongruous conflation: Greek names were not shortened; modern (American) usages are superimposed on ancient patterns. Emphasis here is on intratextual crosscurrents even between passages that are as closely related as a distended headline and a not very long text.

With all those pens, real and imaginary, in mind, we turn to a stage appearance in 'Circe':

Mrs Dignam... in her weeds, her bonnet awry, rouging and powdering her cheeks, lips and nose, a pen... (U15.3837)

If we stopped here, what would we do with that pen? Perhaps, though unlikely, Dignam's widow turns up with something to write, one might also think of 'pen' as an enclosure for Circean swine; in reading we tacitly screen out such errant meanings, are in fact hardly aware of them, but a stodgy computer would signal uncertainty. The momentarily non-assimilable 'pen' transforms itself, true Circean fashion, into an animal, '...a pen chivvying her brood of cygnets.' This pen is a female swan, a mother swan with her young (brood). The clarifying word 'cygnets' (derived from Greek *kyknos* for swan) is fitting for 'Circe'. Ovid in his *Metamorphoses* lists three different persons named Cycnus, who were all transformed into swans (*Metamorphoses* 2:367f.; 7:371; 12:72, 150, 171). Mrs Dignam as a mother swan is one of the book's internal echoes, transposed from an earlier occurrence in Stephen's evocation of Shakespeare's passing the 'swanmews along the riverbank'. The poet does not stay

to feed the pen chivying her game of cygnets towards the rushes. (U 9.160)

This may be an instance of everybody inevitably running into oneself, for Shakespeare is called 'the swan of Avon' in the same line. He used the words Stephen is playing with:

> So doth the swan her downy cygnets save,
> Keeping them prisoner underneath her winge.
> (I *Henry VI* , V.iii.55)

In Stephen's presentation the words unmistakably refer to the birds, but even so, in a chapter devoted to writing, the proximity of 'pen' and 'cygnet' may be potentially distractive: Shakespeare also used the homophone 'signet'. When later on Bloom wants to engage in literary talk, he refers to 'the pen of our national poet' (*U* 16.840); with genial optimism he then provides encouragement to Stephen Dedalus: 'You have every bit as much right to live by your pen in pursuit of your philosophy as the peasant has' (*U* 16.1157). The pen of (not, strictly speaking, in Ireland) 'our' national poet, and also Philip Beaufoy's lucrative pen in *Titbits*, inspire an ambition:

suppose he were to pen something out of the common groove. (*U* 16.1229)

According to how some of us read 'Eumaeus', in a hypothetical way this has happened. The episode can be read as an imaginary product of what Bloom might have written if he were able to pen something out of the common groove.

What interests here in the context of retroactive semantics is a coincidental echo. Day-dreaming Bloom might 'pen something'—as though calling up, hours and pages before: 'What was the name of that priestylooking chap... Pen something... Pen... ?' '*Pen* [remembered fraction of a name] *something* [placeholder for the forgotten rest]' and 'Suppose he were to *pen* [active, creative verb] *something* [object]' have absolutely nothing in common except a certain similarity of sound and printed appearance. And yet they can be brought together by the reader's memory, perhaps aided by word lists. The shapes are linked. But in hardly any novel prior to *Ulysses* would one be likely to waste thoughts on such chance configurations. The problem, or non-problem, may be stated differently. Reading fiction has to do, as Aristotle knew already and Homer had practised long before him, with recognition. The shrivelled old beggar turns out to be stately Odysseus, the king, but no-one, save a dog and his old nurse, recognized him. Before the revelation takes place, and the showdown with it, it was important to keep one's identity secret and to find out who the others were. The second half of the *Odyssey* is full of disguises, pseudonyms, cover stories. Appearances are not to be trusted. Joyce takes this over and makes it infiltrate language itself. Readers are hard put to scrutinize the treacherous shapes of words and match them with what they know. A 'Simon Dedalus' in the reminiscences of a less than trustworthy storyteller and sailor (*U* 16.378ff) seems to be unconnected with the bearer of that name that readers have become familiar with. Several 'Antonios' confusingly compete for attention. Stephen refers to the 'soul' as a 'simple substance'; Bloom echoes that 'you do know across a simple soul once in a blue moon'—similar verbal embodiments, different entities (*U* 16.756, 765). So many words, or groups of words, have to be examined for cognitive meaning. In this process 'pen something' is manifestly not the reincarnation of an earlier 'Pen something', except in its typographical body. The semblance is a non-identity, but potentially significant within the context of abortive attempts at identification.

The vagaries of the graphic appearance PEN here serve to illustrate how later occurrences engage in serious or playful relationships with

earlier ones. It is quite possible to demonstrate vital Ulyssean contrasts by means of, on the one hand, a phrase that represents in psychological verisimilitude an attempt to reconstruct a real name, and,
on the other, the ambition of a fictional character to imitate his own
creator in what we might term self-reflective regression. The pen of
an author can do almost anything, irrespective of reality or probability. The cross- referential linking of the various pens do not add vital
meanings, but they show how meanings may vary at each stage of the
explorative processes of re-reading.

Ghost meanings are abroad, and parts of words play parts. Bloom
'got a bit of a start but it turned out to be only something about somebody named H. du Boyes' (*U* 16.1238). Bloom steps into Stephen's
territory and ventures into Shakespearean authorship, 'who precisely
wrote' the plays, '… like *Hamlet* and Bacon' (*U* 16.783). The emergent culinary overtones help to characterize Bloom. Though there is
neither ham nor bacon in his lines, the hovering infelicities are on a
par with associations towards the beginning of the episode, when
Stephen 'thought to think of' literature (Ibsen), yet Bloom inhaled
'the smell of James Rourke's city bakery' (*U* 16.52). Literature belongs
to Stephen, food to Bloom, as was already borne out by Bloom's concern with eating in 'Lestrygonians', where his own literary theory is
alimentary: 'I wouldn't be surprised if it was that kind of food you
see produces the like waves of the brain the poetical' (*U* 8.544),
while Stephen Dedalus ruminates on Shakespearean lore in the
Library.

What can be carefully gleaned and commented in 'Eumaeus' will
become a textual reflex in *Finnegans Wake*, which bases itself largely
on spectral semantics that haunt its verbal approximations. From a
word of no previous legitimacy like 'backonham' (*FW* 318.21) we
have no qualms to extract ham and bacon as well as a Shakespearean
figure, Buckingham. There we can no longer make a semantic 'home-
lette' without 'Your hegg he must break himself' (*FW* 59.31). The procedure is prefigured in the parasemantic agitation of *Ulysses* and,
above all, 'Eumaeus'. The fumbles occlude meaning, and they act out
subsidiary meanings. The message is in the near misses and the
'messes of mottage' (*FW* 183.22)

* * *

We know, and have often quoted, that 'Sounds are impostures' (*U*
16.362), and so are names and nouns. The chapter gleefully acts this

out. There is nothing whatsoever in the above parading of lexical friction that any dictionary would not take for granted by simply listing various meanings. It was up to 'Eumaeus' above all other chapters of *Ulysses* to show just how much potential for verbal conflict resides in the most ordinary words. They often become 'words to that effect' (*U* 16.1667) with the emphasis on strikingly inept but cumbersomely unfolding effects.

June 1989/January 1993

NOTES

1   *A Dictionary of Slang and Unconventional English* (London: Routledge & Kegan Paul 1951), 25.

2   Leslie Fiedler, 'To Whom Does Joyce Belong?', in Heyward Ehrlich (ed.), *Light Rays: James Joyce and Modernism* (New York: New Horizon Press 1984), 37.

EUMAEAN TITBITS—
AS SOMEONE SOMEWHERE SINGS

'Eumaeus' is more elusive than perhaps every other chapter in *Ulysses*. We cannot even describe it adequately. In this respect too, it seems not to fulfill some of our expectations. Positioned in the plot's unfolding just where the two protagonists are finally brought together without external disturbances, it might promise something climactic. What we find is Bloom's endeavour to reach across, a perseverance to get some response from Stephen Dedalus, poet and professor—it is a mainly one-sided endeavour, of little avail. Stephen is willing, or passive, enough to be led around and talked to; there is a lot of walking and more conversation, but communication is haphazard and sporadic. Disappointed in some legitimate and habitual expectations, we may well overlook the chapter's great returns. It is Bloom's expectations that are not fulfilled in the first place. He still remains neglected, but he goes on nevertheless, like an epic hero in charge. In one sense the chapter is also a literary feat in which Bloom as an oblique co-author can be made out. Subjectively there are a few triumphs. Chances are that in times to come the meeting and the conversation will be remembered and passed on with some pride. For once, Bloom is not continually interrupted; he can hold the limelight even if Stephen is not motivated by rapt attention, but by indifference and fatigue. Bloom even manages to bring the new acquaintance into his house as a visitor, further social relations in the future are not entirely excluded, though somewhat unlikely. All the successes, however, are not commensurate with the efforts undertaken or, in particular, with the excess verbiage so well in evidence.

A plot-minded reader, especially if bent on positive developments, may feel thwarted on a first exposure and, with no patience for the episode's humour and stylistic delicacies, may well remain so. At first there is much disorientation. Language seems hardly able to get to the point, any point—though, conversely, there may be fatuous points in overplus: 'observing that the point was the least conspicuous point about it' (U 16.819). Proliferation and circumlocutory tropes get in the way of any direct line of thought. (Odysseus wisely preferred not go straight home to his palace.) 'Eumaeus' is full of tropes, is what Homer called *polytropos* (*Od*.1.1) in the sense given to it by a classical critic, who applied it to the way Odysseus had of adapting the tropes or figures of speech in each predicament.[1] Unfortunately, the tropes are usually distractive or wrong turnings that do not lead to the goal at hand. Perhaps significantly, we are detained for a fleeting moment, early on, by a vacuous 'first turning on the right' that is not taken (U 16.54) and is at best confusing. Wrong turns of identification are frequent. The chapter is devoted, all along, to such epistemological concerns as recognition, ignorance, speculation, and tentative groping. Nowhere else are there so many rumours, pretenses, distortions, questionable origins and dubious identifications. The syntax takes part in all of these efforts; they often take the form of belletristic ambitions. High aspirations result in rhetorical fumbles. Stylistically, 'Eumaeus' is a pretense or an imposture, written—and very much *written*—in a literary manner, the sort of thing to which Bloom would like to rise, circumstances permitting. If—'a big *if*, however' (U 16.955)—he were to pen such an episode himself, the outcome might be similar. The supposed precedent of writers may be in his mind, such as the gentleman-author Philip Beaufoy of '*Matcham's Masterstroke*' fame, who even receives substantial payment for his labours, or of such literary persons as Stephen Dedalus, whom he would like to impress. Bloom as the elegant master of words also includes an Odyssean role, a disguise, but an inverted one: Odysseus, returning king, took on the humble appearance of a shabby beggar; Bloom, in contrast, comes on *more* majestic, a verbose *homme de lettres* and man of the world and, throughout, 'of many counsels'—*polymetis*.[2]

artificial respiration (U 16.293)

As though with a will of its own, the chapter strains towards Literature, in abortive imitation of the sustained perfomance of 'Scylla and

Charybdis'. As Bloom attempts to reach Stephen's supposed artistic level of speech, so 'Eumaeus' emulates the culture of the Library chapter, wants to be 'something out of the common groove' (*U* 16.1229), but becomes less of a Stephenesque *tour de force* than a forced accumulation of preformulated grooves[3] all too common. Both chapters sport borrowed plumes and elegant variation. Both are also inflated by newspaper usages as championed in 'Aeolus': 'Eumaeus' is characterized by rhetorical second wind, late at night; many of Bloom's figures of speech, tropes, are journalistic.

Ingenuity is exerted on such traits as *inquit* formulas. The narrative parts of *Ulysses* generally confine themselves to a simple 'said' (of which there are more than 1200), but the speakers of 'Scylla and Charybdis', in pointed variation, 'repeat... retort... muse... respond... exclaim... challenge... observe... cap... suspire... antiphone... affirm ... moan... keen... chant... whisper...', often in pliant response to the themes brought up in conversation or in meditation. The practice is prefigured in 'Aeolus', but patently echoed on almost every page of 'Eumaeus', which features 'concurred... affirmed... rejoined... pursued... confided... replied' (the samples are taken from about fifty lines, *U* 16.365–417). The diction is elevated in a visible effort and, naturally, the result is a much watered-down version. Journalism is often former literature diluted, with overblown flowers of speech.

Bloom was a peripheral figure in the National Library, no more than 'A patient silhouette' (*U* 9.597), chaperoned by an obliging librarian, the instant butt of Mulligan's jokes, aspersions, and warnings. Mulligan uses Bloom to display his own verbal brilliance and his conceits. Now, later at night, in the cabmen's shelter, it is Bloom's turn to be brilliant. He is in charge of the action, at least its logistics. He shepherds Stephen around and now reciprocally warns him against Dr Mulligan. It is his mind that gives shape to the story and many of its phrasings.

The *prima facie* inappropriateness of the Eumaean style needs no further comments. Paradoxically, the gaucheness and the incongruities are in part the consequences of an endeavour to get things right, against the biases and twists of the psyche and the chancy distortions of all communication. The stylistic mismanagement entails an awareness of its own ineptitude at each step. The additive wordiness (in itself also a feature of *Ulysses* as accretion in progress) indicates discomfort and resilience. At nearly every turn Bloom senses that his formulations (in so far as they *are* his formulations) fall short, and so he shifts ground and scrambles ahead in a new effort.[4]

He is hardly ever on target, but he knows he isn't. His corrective urge
is responsible for the chapter's lengthy qualifications, demurrers,
renewed attempts—signals, often clumsy ones, of the inadequacies of
linguistic strategies. The unedited language shows the traces of serial
hindsight emendation.

Bloom's effort towards improvement was the first thing we learned
about him when we found him in his kitchen, moving about, 'righting her breakfast things' (*U* 4.7): a matter of preparation, of arranging
plate and cup on an imperfect surface, a domestic dispositive quest
that is Bloomian as well as Odyssean. 'Eumaeus' begins similarly:

Preparatory to

and we might pause to wonder for a moment how such a gesture is to
be continued. The continuation is, bathetically, the least specific of
all possible items: '...anything else'. But the initial word confirms
Bloom as being in preparation once more; the impulse is the same,
the goal has changed from Molly's to Stephen's comfort, and the
kindly aspiration is magnified in the rhetorically memorable adver-
bial phrase, 'in orthodox Samaritan fashion'.

orthodox preliminary canter (*U* 16.1564)

Any fashion that is 'orthodox Samaritan' is *out* of the common
groove. The derivation of its two elements shows the Eumaean
incongruity: 'ortho-dox' means 'of the right opinion', or 'faith';
'*orthos*' denotes 'right, upright, true', and our semantic conscience
may be roused all the more when the word is misapplied. The parable of the Good Samaritan shows that a member of the 'wrong' faith
may well act with more propriety than the *orthodox* (Jews) did (Luke
10:30–7). The constellation 'in orthodox Samaritan fashion' is scrip-
turally askew, trying to have it both ways, but perversely right in
characterizing the Eumaean style, one of metaphorical inconsonance.
The Samaritan of the parable after all also modified a conception of
rightness. 'Orthodox' may serve as an etymological reminder of the
problem of getting things, also opinions, right. Out of a total of seven-
teen occurrences of 'opinion(s)' in *Ulysses*, six figure in 'Eumaeus', a
disproportionate amount (the chapter takes up about one fifteenth of
the whole book). It is one of the most opinionated of all chapters.

Among the few opinions that Bloom does *not* immediately question is his own ignorant assumption of Stephen as 'orthodox' (*U*
16.1126); there the word is used in its theological sense, and erroneously. The term can also be debased to mean hardly more than a

routine event: 'with the orthodox preliminary canter of compliment-playing and walking out' (*U* 16.1564). The only non-Eumaean use of the word is at the beginning of 'Ithaca', where Bloom's view of Stephen is rectified: both characters profess their 'disbelief in many orthodox religious... doctrines' (*U* 17.24).

'Eumaeus' is graven in the language of supposition and probabil-ity, with a preponderance of terms like 'evident(ly), seemingly, possi-bly, apparently, obviously, manifestly, etc.', all of which occur *only* in this chapter or else with relative frequency.[5] There is a pervading caution throughout, a basic distrust, even—and *especially*—in the stereotypes and in the hackneyed language: Stephen's mind was 'not exactly what you would call wandering' (*U* 16.4), we read; and stu-dents are being warned against that kind of haziness. But minds *are* called 'wandering', and it is not exact to call them so, and thus the phrase already heralds a hesitant wariness. 'Eumaeus' is a chapter in which a narrative mind does seem to wander; in *this* respect the expression is appropriate. Appropriate also in continuing the previ-ous chapter where minds were straying far afield. Joyce called the 'technic' of 'Circe' 'Hallucination'; Latin *(h)allucinari*[6] is rendered 'to wander in mind'—this is an old, classical metaphor, which 'Eumaeus' passes on and challenges.

The wandering and rambling essay which follows will concentrate on a few minute Eumaean exfoliations that might easily be over-looked and written off as a merely decorative feature of the chapter, sometimes with the dismissive label 'cliché' attached to it as though such a characterization, however suitable, could ever be the last word. But it is typical that many of the chapter's echoes could be eas-ily located in standard works of quotation, in storehouses of prefabri-cated literary set pieces. The specific origin of such familiar echoes may well be irrelevant: often it is pointedly incongruous. Many say-ings, once of noble descent, have deteriorated, like Corley, rumoured to be connected to the Talbots, but now a comedown, much of the previous lustre gone. (Corley is connected with coins, things of princely imprint, but now in common usage, often worn, debased.) There is something late-in-the-day-ish about almost everything; it includes what Joyce called 'Narrative old' in his schematic descrip-tion: 'Eumaeus' draws on locutions of long standing that are now generally available, ready at hand, but that have also, in the handing down, changed their application. Joyce was one of the first writers no longer to overlook the attrition involved and to exploit it: 'clichés' may function as shorthand for an extended development: a once 'memorable phase of the mind itself' may have become a 'vulgarity of speech' (*SH* 211). In 'Eumaeus' the mind's propensity to reach for the ornamental stereotype is exaggerated, but is also given an additional twist—perhaps a choice, unsuitable adjective: 'in *orthodox* Samaritan fashion'. This is an attempt to go one better, not to be satisfied—and a failure. In one sense the tiredness often alleged for the chapter is also justified; there is a manifest lack of selective control. Habit sometimes determines usage; one word or phrase may linger on by sheer inertia: 'Mr Bloom... *hit upon* an expedient... where they might *hit upon* some drinkables' (*U* 16.7ff). The chapter's hit or miss procedure seems to be impersonated in the awkward reiteration.

it is said (*U* 16.59)
An early allusive flourish exemplifies stereotyped usage with a turn towards twisted pertinence. Bloom and Stephen pass Baird's, the stonecutter's, and Rourke's city bakery. Their minds take different, characteristic, turns. Stephen, by way of memories already registered in *A Portrait*, where a city walk is transformed into a literary landscape (*P* 176). By contrast, the smell of the bakery reminds Bloom

of our daily bread... Bread, the staff of life, earn your bread, O tell me where is fancy bread, at Rourke's the baker's it is said. (*U* 16.57)

This looks like an afterglow of the accustomed 'stream of consciousness' presentation, like the immediate contents, without syntactical adaptation, of what passes through Bloom's mind. The technique in its strict form has been abandoned, or at least submerged, somewhere along the way. The short list may simply contain associations for 'bread'; we can imagine Bloom inwardly turning over suitable things to say (or an advertiser ransacking his brain for a slogan). The cluster would not be out of place in one of Joyce's notebook jottings for possible later use—out of such jottings, after all, the chapter grew and expanded, out of timehonoured phrases, often shopsoiled ones. The jumble brings to mind biblical echoes ('he broke the whole staff of bread', Ps. 105.16); the Lord's Prayer; a Swiftian recall of the Bible ('"Bread," says he, "dear brother, is the staff of life"').[7] It culminates in what has all the appearance of a facetious saying, most likely frequently used in Dublin, a deflection of Shakespeare's 'Tell me where is fancy bred/Or in the heart or in the head' (*Merchant of Venice*, III, ii, 63). The dislodged quotation may well be triggered off by the choice between plain and fancy bread offered by Dublin bakers.[8] 'Eumaeus' displays a contrast between plain everyday occurrences and literary fancies as well: baker's bread can be stylized into a Shakespearean tag. Bloom, normally factual and given to plain words and speech, becomes imaginative; his fancy and phantasies blossom into literary ornamentation. In a reversal of roles, it is Bloom who momentarily transmutes the bread of daily experience and nocturnal inhalation into something shortlived, as though in parody of Stephen's dreamy artistic programme of long ago—there it was 'into the radiant body of everlasting life' (*P* 221). By now Bloom has replaced Mulligan of the first chapter as an usurper of Stephen's antecedent roles and as the presiding genius of the stylistics at hand. Conversely Stephen, whose thoughts are otherwise abstruse and recondite, resorts to atypically plain internal phrasing, as if regressing to an earlier stage.[9]

If *we* want to work in *our* associations, we might align Stephen's response to a *stone*-cutter and Bloom's to *bread* into a Biblical contrast that implies paternity ('if his son ask bread, will he give him a stone?' Mat. 7:9) in further mental processing. Our example also unobtrusively calls up a low-key dominant authority, that of respected prearticulation: 'it is said.' The chapter draws on literary precedents.

there was the rub (*U* 16.11)

The following random notes try to uncover intertextual tensions that do not seem to have pointed out before, though they easily could have been. The procedure is based on the familiar tip-of-the-iceberg principle, which simply means there may be more to a passage than is visible to the disdainful eye, with the added hypothesis that what is submerged may contribute to the context. Icebergs are not just metaphors, but real dangers for sailors, and they obligingly turn up as navigational obstacles in the tales of adventure: 'I seen icebergs plenty, growlers', says Murphy; and 'collisions with icebergs' become a topic of conversation (*U* 16.461, 901).

Into the surface, Shakespeare, inevitably, is woven a lot. Bloom brings up the 'question of our national poet'; when he ventures into Shakespeare scholarship, this 'stickler for solid food' (*U* 16.811) combines '*Hamlet* and Bacon' and then immediately reverts to coffee and bun (*U* 16.783). The practical side in him comes up in a warning against 'marauders ready to decamp with whatever boodle they could in one fell swoop at a moment's notice' (*U* 16.124). Such a fell swoop felled Macduff's wife and children (*Macbeth* IV, iii, 219). In orthodox Eumaean fashion there is a slanted redundancy; it is in the nature of fell swoops to be 'at a moment's notice'. A common phrase, 'a man who had actually brandished a knife, cold steel' (*U* 16.1058), ultimately depends on 'brave Macbeth... with brandished steel' from the same play (I, ii, 17). In adventure stories 'steel' mates with 'cold' by sheer habit.[10] Such Shakespearean appropriations help to turn 'Eumaeus' into a popularized version of the thickly-layered Library episode. The echoes are signalled by an early, trivialized, 'But how to get there was the rub' (*U* 16.11), varied later in the chapter: 'That was the rub' (*U* 16.530). The tag is the first overt inroad into high literature. That it is taken from the best-known of all monologues, the one Stephen Dedalus had devalued as 'improbable, insignificant and undramatic' (*U* 9.77), brings out the two chapters' lopsided affinity and how much out of touch Bloom is with Stephen's mind. The transference of the stately 'rub' from a potential journey into non-existence in the play to a trite question of city locomotion, is in obvious rhetorical excess. A 'rub' once was an obstacle, an impediment to motion, a roughness or unevenness. Rubs are stylistic features of 'Eumaeus': syntactical movements are impeded. If we characterize its language as 'trite', we are using a similar metaphor for a slightly different observation.

echo answers

During a lull in the conversation, some unexciting news is read out aloud from a paper, and a response from the audience is rendered indirectly: 'To which absorbing piece of intelligence echo answered why' (*U* 16.1667). It was Lord Byron who authored the pattern in a context, originally, of emotional impact. A father is told about the death of his daughter:

> Hark! to the hurried question of Despair:
> 'Where is my child?'—an Echo answers—'Where?'
> (*The Bride of Abydos*, II, xxvii)

Bloom's maxim, 'Everyone according to his needs or everyone according to his deeds' (*U* 16.247), is multiply derivative. Its Marxian content ('From each according to his ability, to each according to his needs') has been better noticed than the Christian one: 'distribution was made unto every man according as he had need' (Acts 4:35), and 'God, Who will render to every man according to his deeds' (Rom. 2:6). Bloom would not know the separate ingredients, but the mixture expresses his vaguely socialist creed quite well; 'and the first socialist he said He was', Molly reports (*U* 18.178).

When Bloom imagines possible home-comings as predictable disap-
pointments he conjures up a scene in his mind: 'The face at the window!' (*U* 16.430). This coincides with the title of a melodramatic, but
anachronistic, novel which appeared in 1914.[11] A more timely source
is a poem in Longfellow's *The Seaside and the Fireside* (1850), with
a view of a fisherman's cottage near the rough sea:

> And a little face at the window
> Peers out into the night.
> ('Twilight')

Longfellow's poems were still very popular by 1904, as a brief mention of 'The Wreck of the *Hesperus*' may indicate (*U* 16.845). Bloom's
memory of a 'superannuated old salt' staring at the sea may be tinged
by a similar background: 'Possibly he tried to find out the secret for
himself' (*U* 16.634). 'The Secret of the Sea', a poem from the same
collection, evokes the ocean's romantic, legendary, and haunting,
attraction. Bloom is more matter of fact: 'There was really no secret
about it at all... Nevertheless the sea was there in all its glory...' Both
'fireside' and 'seaside' are to be found in 'Eumaeus' and may help to
bring to mind—distantly—Longfellow's maritime cycle of poems.
But none of the passages quoted depend on Longfellow's precedent—
a 'face at the window' could be left as a merely situational set phrase.
An oblique 'squint at that literature' (*U* 16.1669) remains one of the
reader's hazards.

a certain analogy there somehow was (*U* 16.1579)

The foregoing echoes appear predominantly ornamental, some even
pointedly fatuous; others may have devious reverberations. Murphy
tells about his adventures in the Black Sea: 'under Captain Dalton the
best bloody man that ever scuttled a ship' (*U* 16.462). Byron used the
phrase differently, and its deflection into the chapter looks like one
more sample of seemingly random irrelevancy. Byron characterizes a
husband returning from a sea voyage who finds a revelry going on in
his home. Cautious and controlled, he does not fly into a passion, as
one might well understand, but remains calm:

> You're wrong.—He was the mildest manner'd man
> That ever scuttled ship or cut a throat,
> With such true breeding of a gentleman,
> You never could divine his real thought;
> No courtier could, and scarcely woman can
> Gird more deceit within a petticoat
> (*Don Juan*, canto III, xli)

Being wrong, being deceitful, and guessing anyone's real thoughts,
all this enters essentially into 'Eumaeus' as well as into the *Nostos*
part of the *Odyssey*. Murphy has been relating exploits, real or
invented, that involve a knifing and a Greek named Antonio
(Odysseus returning and making up biographical fictions repeatedly
tells that he himself killed a man and therefore had to flee to Ithaka).
Byron's long-drawn episode from canto III of the poem that rings a
variant on the *Don Giovanni* motif includes some very Eumaean concerns:

> He did not know (alas! how men will lie!)
> That a report (especially the Greeks)
> Avouch'd his death (such people never die),
> And put his house in mourning several weeks, —
> But now their eyes and lips also were dry;
> The bloom, too, had return'd to Haidée's cheeks.
> Her tears, too, being return'd into their fount.
> She now keeps house upon her own account.
> (canto III, xxxviii)

This might be wholly accidental (and the 'returning bloom' simply
a spurious echo), mere selective gleanings from the enlarged context
of 'that ever scuttled ship'. If so, it would be one reader's strategic
application of what Walter W. Skeat, Joyce's etymologist in residence, took to be the original meaning of 'scuttle': 'to cut a thing so
as to make it fit...'—a common interpretative tendency. We are all
scuttlers of texts. The same episode, canto III of *Don Juan*, frankly
makes use of the Homeric prototype:

> An honest gentleman at his return
> May not have the good fortune of Ulysses;
> Not all lone matrons for their husbands mourn,
> or show the same dislike to suitors' kisses;
> The odds are that he finds a handsome urn
> To his memory—and two or three young misses
> Born to some friend, who holds his wife and riches; —
> And that *his* Argus bites him by—his breeches.
> (canto III, xxiii)

It happens that the attitudes expressed in the stanza are refracted
in Bloom's musings; he 'could easily picture his advent on the scene,
the homecoming to the mariner's roadside shieling... Judge of his
astonishment when he finally did breast the tape and the awful truth
dawned upon him anent his better half... Her brand-new arrival is on
her knee, *postmortem* child...' (*U* 16.422ff). Bloom even has a varia-

tion on '*his* Argus'—'Still as regards return. You were a lucky dog if they didn't set the terrier at you directly you got back' (*U* 16.1339).

Bloom might actually remember some of Byron's lines. We have it from Molly that at one time he tried to look like Byron. Leopold Bloom shares his poetic preference with an earlier would-be writer, Little Chandler of 'A Little Cloud'. Hermione de Almeida has shown that Byron's *Don Juan* is in part based on the *Odyssey*.[12] Many more minute correspondences may yet come to light. Byron's reservation,

> The approach of home to husband and to sires,
> After long travelling by land and water,
> Most naturally some small doubt inspires—
>
> (canto III, xxii)

stands midway between the distrust of the swineherd Eumaios in the *Odyssey* and the doubts nourished by Bloom about yarns, motives, faithfulness, or returns in general.

In his protective role Bloom can become sententious. Stephen, he admonishes, had better not trust—or rather not 'repose much trust in'—'Dr Mulligan, as a guide, philosopher and friend' (*U* 16.279). He uses a line by Alexander Pope:

> Shall then this verse no future age pretend
> Thou wert a guide, philosopher, and friend?
> (*Essay on Man*, IV, 389–90)

This is pretentious exaggeration, but even so these are all roles that Mulligan prominently affects, as we read in the first chapter, and as Bloom may have vaguely sensed during the evening. The circumlocutory 'repose much trust' reads like an echo from Pope's poem, which runs '... in dust repose', just two lines before (387). In any case both Bloom and Pope are exhortative, and it is tempting to examine the concluding sequence in the poem for possible indirect relevance:

> That, urged by thee, I turn'd the tuneful art
> From sounds to things, from fancy to the heart;
> (391–2)

To turn from sounds, acknowledged 'impostures' (*U* 16.362), to things becomes the discerning task of anyone who listens to doubtful tales or words spoken in a foreign language the sense of which is difficult to determine. A twisted Shakespearean quotation connected 'fancy' to 'heart' in a passage already discussed. Pope too knew how to twist Shakespeare's lines and to redirect them to his own uses.

The famous mirror held up to nature (which the hidden magic of 'Circe' actually stages after *U* 15.3820) is elaborated in the next line:

> For Wit's false mirror held up Nature's light; (393)

'Wit's false mirror'—like a characterization of Eumaean periphrastic habits. Of course we can make platitudinous remarks on the chapter without seeing them first mirrored in the *Essay on Man*. Bloom, in *his* sententiousness, would most likely give assent to Pope's peroration:

> That true self-love and social are the same;
> That virtue only makes our bliss below;
> And all our knowledge is,—Ourselves to know.
>
> (396–8)

Ulysses includes all of that in its broad human comprehension, but it also seems to caution us against precisely this kind of complacent moralizing.

à propos *of the incident* (*U* 16.44)

Bloom's admonitions are not, on the whole, well received, but he persists nevertheless. When he reports on the adventure with the citizen, we find him turning 'a long you are wrong gaze on Stephen of timorous dark pride at the soft impeachment' (*U* 16.1088). In the last scene of (Irish) Richard Brinsley Sheridan's play *The Rivals,* a character reveals a mystery and some petty deceit and admits: 'I own the soft impeachment' (V, iii). Here the implied significance may be the speaker, Mrs Malaprop, famous for the oratorical overreaching that makes her a patron saint of 'Eumaeus', which, on its surface, is manifestly *mal à propos.* The dandy French borrowing *à propos* (with a variant *apropos*) appears five times in 'Eumaeus'—and *only* there.

Homage should be paid to Mrs Malaprop and her creator as forerunners of the technique of misquotation. Sheridan in his play aims at comic effect. Joyce was to develop the art in polytropic variety, dislocutions that may be due to ignorance, subjective assimilation, psychological disturbances, or ingenious semantic redirection; it naturally escalated in *Finnegans Wake*. In a brief sustained flight Mrs Malaprop quotes from *Hamlet*:

Hesperian curls	Hyperion's curls
the front of Job himself!	... of Jove
an eye, like March	... like Mars
to threaten at command	to threaten and command
a station like Harry Mercury, new	a station like the herald Mercury

something about kissing on a hill	New-lighted on a heaven-kissing hill
(*The Rivals*, IV,ii)	(*Hamlet*, III, iv, 55–9)

Words approximating, but not reaching, their goal (Gerty MacDowell's 'for riches for poor, in sickness in health, till death us two part', *U* 13.216) meddle with identities and create different characters; the tendon of Achilles may turn to 'tender Achilles' (*U* 16.1006, 1640, 1716).[13] March and Harry Mercury are ancestors of M'Intosh, Miss Ferguson, and a part of the cast of *Finnegans Wake*.

Malaproperly, Bloom is a little off track when he reflects that 'In the nature of single blessedness' Stephen Dedalus would 'take unto himself a wife when Miss Right came on the scene' (*U* 16.1556), and he even thinks of Miss Ferguson as a candidate (who owes her origin to defective hearing and premature conclusion: Fergus, Celtic god in a Yeats poem, engendered her). The borrowed tag does not fit. In its proper context the questionable blessedness of staying *single* is pointed out. It is Hermia who does not comply with her father's wishes about a husband for her and may be sent to a convent. So she is warned:

> But earthlier happy is the rose distill'd,
> Than that which withering on the virgin thorn
> Grows, lives, and dies, in single blessedness.
> *Midsummer Night's Dream*, I, i,76–8

Bloom may construe the phrase highlighted as something like 'singular blessedness'. He is more to the point when he ponders 'the cause of many *liaisons* between still attractive married women getting on for fair and forty and younger men' (*U* 16.1550; notice the awkward possible liaison between 'younger men' and what married women are 'getting on for'). Dublin-born John O'Keeffe (1747–1833) seems to have introduced the phrase, 'Fat, fair and forty were all the toasts of the young men' (*Irish Minnie*, II, ii); Sir Walter Scott made it 'Fair, fat, and forty' in the Prince Regent's description of what a wife should be' (*St Ronan's Well*, VII). In either case, the submerged adjective makes it circumstantially evident that Bloom, as so often, has his own Irish Molly at the back of his mind. She, it is true, still has six years to go. On the other hand, she who is acknowledged to be a 'large sized lady' (*U* 16.1428), reciprocally thinks of 'men... at his age especially getting on to forty he is now' (*U* 18.51).

a deeper depth
Weldon Thornton has already noted the 'best-known source' of the

phrase 'in every deep, so to put it, a deeper depth' (*U* 16.223) in Milton's,

> Which way I fly is Hell;
> And in the lowest deep a lower deep
> Still threat'ning to devour me open wide,
> To which the Hell I suffer seems a Heav'n.
> (*Paradise Lost*, IV, 76–8)[14]

One of William Cowper's hymns may have contributed something:

> Mine is an unchanging love,
> Higher than the heights above,
> Deeper than the depths beneath,
> Free, faithful, strong as death
> ('Lovest Thou Me?')

and perhaps Dante Gabriel Rossetti's 'Blessed Damozel':

> Her eyes were deeper than the depth
> of waters stilled at even...

All in all, a conglomerate of disparate sources, as though the phrase wanted to make its own implicit statement about the uncertainty of genealogies and of authorship. Quotational conglomerates abound, and we can never be sure to have traced them all, or whether those we have noted are pertinently there: 'Guesswork it reduced itself to eventually' (*U* 16.1293).

Conglomerates may be in another language. While Stephen speaks in New Testament Latin ('*Ex quibus*', *U* 16.1091), Bloom can rise to classical depth with: 'Ubi patria', as we learned a smattering of in our classical days in '*Alma Mater, vita bene*' (*U* 16.1138), where 'patria' jostles uneasily with '*Mater*' (such transitions of gender were common in 'Circe'). The conflation includes '*Ubi bene ibi patria*' and '*Patria est ubicumque est bene*';[15] the remaining word may be accounted for by Maecena's '*Vita dum superest, bene est*' ('All is well, if my life remains', a survival formula in *Fragments*, 1); and by '*Vita nec bonum nec malum est; boni ac mali locus est*', one of Seneca's congenial aphorisms (*Epistula ad Lucilium*, Epist. xcix, 12). In its imperfect approximation of several prototypes, the language comes close to that in *Finnegans Wake*.

rather muddled

One of Stephen's tangential retorts—tangential because it does not relate to whether Kitty O'Shea 'was Spanish too', the question at hand—must be puzzling to Bloom as well as to most readers:

—The king of Spain's daughter, Stephen answered, adding something or other rather muddled about farewell and adieu to you Spanish onions and the first land called the Deadman and from Ramhead to Scilly was so and so many. (*U* 16.1414)

This is one of Stephen's longest speeches in the episode, and some of its ingredients have been traced: a nursery rhyme about 'the King of Spain's daughter came to visit me', and an old capstan chanty, 'Farewell and adieu to you, Spanish ladies', whose lines 'From Ushant to Scilly is thirty-five leagues' (stanza 2), and 'the first land we made, it is called the Deadman,/Next Ram Head, off Plymouth...' (stanza 4),[16] have been rearranged. The places named, headlands on the Cornish coast, bring to mind the proverbial 'When Dudman and Ramehead meet'—an impossibility, a way of saying 'Never.' Somehow that is what Bloom takes up in his next speech: 'I never heard that.' Stephen's aside has a bearing on the two persons' meeting and the unbridgeable distance between; the two places, navigational landmarks, are 'well-nigh twenty miles asunder'.[17]

It is not clear why Stephen, apart from being typically non-communicative, should say 'onions' in place of 'ladies'—if in fact he does (if not, the question is why *Bloom* should *hear* 'onions'). Twice during the day Bloom had been thinking of 'Spanish onion[s]'; memories easily get in the way of reports, as the chapter insists. Through whatever substitution, Spanish ladies have become edible, and so it is only in tune that 'the king of Spain's daughter' may be potable, this by way of an account of an Elizabethan chronicler of Dublin, who wrote about Winetavern street:

... the Irish never returne home till they have drunke the price in Spanish wine (which they call the King of Spaine's daughter).[18]

This historical reminiscence recalls a habitual *nostos*, as it is still re-enacted, with a few bibulous adaptations, in the nightly chapters of *Ulysses*. Whether the trope survived in Joyce's time as a local saying or not, it provides, at any rate, another link between Ireland and Spain, the topic at hand.

All of this does not determine what Stephen has in mind. He associates a cluster of names, all latently misleading. What Bloom for a moment must take to be a rumour about Katherine O'Shea's descent turns out to be some vague nursery-rhyme character on a different level of identification, or even a beverage. Something muddled which sounds like 'dead man' can, in various spellings, be an evil-boding promontory or, perplexingly, an empty bottle (this in the song 'Down among the Dead Men' briefly struck up in 'Sirens'). Two places seem to be confused, Deadman's Point (about three miles north of Rame Head), and Dudman (or else Dodman) Point, SW of St Anstell, at the distance from Rame Head already mentioned. (Intriguingly, the pseudonyms of two composers, Ivan St Austell and Hilton St Just, who occur later in the chapter [U 16.1851], are also Cornish coastal places.) Literary, personal, and topographical identities are treacherous to navigate for all but the best informed of readers. The whole, moreover, sounds like a tour of the Cornish coast (matching Bloom's plans), or as though Stephen were giving British variants of Odyssean types of sea adventures and strange-sounding places. 'Scilly' may, unconnectedly, remind us of Skylla (which, according to Victor Bérard, as recirculated by Stuart Gilbert,[19] was also a promontory). Towards the end of the chapter there will be a song about shipwrecks and sirens.

only a surface knowledge? (U 16.1754)

'Eumaeus' contains a number of yarns, and some may be more entangled than we might suspect if we disregard the stylistic features as interchangeable décor. Even the clichés, the flashy mannerisms and the rhetorical gestures emulate—in their ambition, not the achievement—the sustained pretensions of 'Scylla and Charybdis', and perhaps also the sequential exploitation of English prose styles as they are flaunted in 'Oxen of the Sun', in whose compendium of historical models 'Eumaeus' is proleptically represented (U 14.1174–97).

It would be hard to find a more clichéd expression than 'filthy lucre' within a choice metaphorical muddle: 'Not... that for the sake of filthy lucre he need necessarily embrace the lyric platform as a walk in life' (U 16.1841). Not that, for the sake of interpretation, we need necessarily embrace the ancestry of the two words so often paired, and yet their descent may lead to revealing entanglements. St Paul (implicitly acknowledged at least in 'that first epistle to the Hebrews', U 16.1268) used 'filthy lucre' four times; the version closest to our text is in his Epistle to Titus (Titus was the new bishop of Crete). The context is Eumaean enough—speech, truth, and falsehood:

For there are many unruly and vain talkers and deceivers... Whose mouths must be stopped, who subvert whole houses, teaching things which they ought not, for filthy lucre's sake. One of themselves, even a prophet of their own, said, The Cretans are always liars, evil beasts, slow bellies. This witness is true. (Tit. 1:10–3)

Deceits, lies, vain talk, testimony, witnesses—all of this has to be sorted out and investigated in the episode whose Homeric counter-

parts are the strategic fictions Odysseus makes up in his own Ithaca
—to Pallas Athene, to Eumaios, to Penelope, and others. In three of
those (*Od.* 13.256ff, 14.199ff, 19.172ff) he pretends that he comes
from Crete, famous in all antiquity for the untruthfulness of its
inhabitants. The connection was noticed early; William Cowper,
whose translation Joyce owned, adds a footnote to 'spacious Crete':

Homer dates all the fictions of Ulysses from Crete, as if he meant to pass a similar cen-
sure on the Cretans to that quoted by St Paul—*Kretes aei pseusai.*[20]

In our perspective, Homeric and apostolic usage may be linked. St
Paul calls up a tradition of Greek wiliness that is to be superseded by
Christian adherence to truth.

'Filthy lucre' seems to deserve little attention by itself except as an
example of the cliché.[21] It takes us back, via Latin *'turpis lucri gratia'*
in the Vulgate, to St Paul's *'aischrou kerdous charin'*. The key word
kerdos means gain, profit, advantage, with very bad connotations in
spiritual Christianity; but Homer had used the term with approval,
sometimes neutrally, at times ambiguously. Odysseus is out for his
own *kerdos*; he is frequently praised for his *'kerdosyne'*; when
attacked by fierce dogs, he 'in his wariness [*kerdosyne*] sat him
down' (*Od.* 14.31).[22] A 'wariness of mind' characterizes Bloom as
well (*U* 14.253).[23] When Odysseus makes up his first yarn to Athene,
he 'wrested words into guile, for he had a gainful and nimble wit
[*noon polykerdea*] within his breast' (*Od.* 13.254).[24] Immediately after
his tale, the goddess admires him: 'Crafty must he be, and knavish,
who would outdo thee in all manner of guile'; the word for 'crafty' is
another derivation of *kerdos*.[25] The term includes the cunning
resourcefulness of Odysseus, but also the more material concerns
about his treasures and possessions. Something of all of this is in
Bloom's mind when he craftily considers a projected singing career
for Stephen. The passage is full of potential benefits and monetary
gain: 'bargain... command its own price... ten a penny... financial
magnates... large way of business... could be utilised... the pecu-
niary emolument... tuition fees... for the sake of filthy lucre... to be
handed a cheque... a capital opening... command a stiff figure' (*U*
16.1832ff)—all of this is 'both monetarily and mentally' (*U* 16.1844).

The phrase *aischron kerdos* must have been a stereotype already
in Greek, when the two elements were fused into compounds (*ais-
chrokerd-*). For us it entwines strands of Greek and Jewish roots (St
Paul also exhorts: 'Not giving heed to Jewish fables', Tit. 1:14), of
Homer and Christianity, of imposition and verbal cunning, survival

and greed. At one point in the New Testament, '*aischrokerdeis*' is linked with '*dilogous* ' ('doubletongued', 1 Tim. 3:8); sounds are often contrived impostures. It is quite in tune that biblical scholars have doubted St Paul's authorship of the *Epistle to Titus*: the warning against liars and false prophets may have a forged signature, may be as unreliable as a postcard addressed to A. Boudin, and perhaps one of those 'genuine forgeries' that Bloom remarks upon, 'all of them put in by monks most probably'. It's the big question 'who precisely wrote them' (*U* 16.783).[26]

Homer was more tolerant of our striving for personal advantage than the Christians would be. Odysseus never neglected his own benefit or his earthly possessions. Gain and some other motive do not exlude each other; a farewell meal, for example, can be both[27] 'honour and glory and gain withal' (Od. 15.78). The word for 'honour' is '*kydos*' (or '*kudos*': splendour, renown, glory). Similarly, it would be an honour for Bloom as well as to Stephen's advantage if he accepted food and hospitality. Bloom suggests 'literary labour not merely for the kudos of the thing'; the same word in the common English transliteration reappears later: 'having gone into it more for the kudos of the thing than anything else' (*U* 16.1153, 1519). University slang put a word into circulation that appears to be lifted straight out of the *Odyssey*, but isn't.

as someone somewhere sings

Many quotations are not genuine, their exact paternity impossible to determine; often we would find a regress into an unrecorded past. Ultimate uncertainty is fitting for a chapter of doubtful genealogies and questionable origins. 'Eumaeus' contains many set phrases of uncertain ancestry. Occasionally authorship is vaguely acknowledged. The old salt Bloom remembers staring at the sea and perhaps trying to find out its secret was seen 'dreaming of fresh woods and pastures new as someone somewhere sings' (*U* 16.632). The words are not recognized as (approximately) the closing line of *Lycidas*, but as *some* quotation. The vague reference to irrelevant authorship in itself has been sung before, and it was, once more, Lord Byron:

> Oh! darkly, deeply, beautifully blue,
> As someone somewhere sings about the sky
> (*Don Juan*, Iv, cx)

A principle is acknowledged in a mirroring regression, Bloom quoting Byron quoting some predecessor and commenting on poetic automatisms that provide a tinge for 'sky'. Most epithets for sky are drawn from a common thesaurus. Byron goes on to associate the colour with feminine clothing: 'Blue as the garters...' ('violet' provokes the same association in Bloom). Byron's rhyme for 'sky', which the stanza demands, is,

> ... (Heaven knows why).

It is interesting that Bloom very soon after thinks similarly and ends on the identical word: 'And it left him wondering why.' This may leave us wondering if, who knows, he, who once gave Molly 'the present of lord Byron's poems', so that she thought: 'he was a poet like Byron', and who was even 'trying to look like lord Byron', has contributed an alternative line to the stanza which seems to be hovering in his mind.[28] The poem, *Don Juan*, is a Byronic alternative to the opera which occupied Molly Bloom part of the afternoon and evening. There is also a link with Stephen Dedalus who, years ago, tried to compose a poem in the manner of Lord Byron whom he later publicly acclaimed to be the greatest poet in English (*P* 70, 81).

The utopian plans flashing through Bloom's busy brain include,

> education (the genuine article), literature, journalism, prize titbits, up to date billing, concert tours in English watering resorts packed with hydros and seaside theatres. (*U* 16.1653)

Some of these are ingredients of the chapter in which they are listed. Centuries of education made 'Eumaeus' possible; there is literature watered down ('watering resorts packed with hydros'), Aeolian touches abound, journalism and advertising. Some of the paternities unfolded may be lectoral fictions, as dubious as the yarns spun by returning adventurers or pretenders. In one perspective, all the chapter's second-rate glitter is just ornamentation laid on without too much specific purpose. Yet even the stereotypes have changeful histories, perhaps outside of our pinpointing reach, but still worth looking into. With a little scratching, the text can be energized and analogies may be uncovered, some valid, some spurious—'by design or accidentally', but often 'quite within the bounds of possibility' (*U* 16.562, 827).

The near-quotations are not just static *débris* strewn over the text. At the very least, they function in Protean fashion 'like those crabs' in Stephen's memory: he could hear—as we might experience—'all kinds of words changing colour like those crabs about Ringsend in the morning burrowing quickly into all colours of different sorts of the same sand where they had a home somewhere beneath or seemed to' (*U* 16.1143). The home of the clichés somewhere beneath, to which they never can return, are often poetic sayings that changed their colour and their effect, 'one world burrowing on another', as the *Wake* puts it (*FW* 275.5).

But then, we are warned, 'life was full of a host of things and coincidences' (*U* 16.824), and reading is full of selective, biased extrapolation. It would be tricky to decide, for instance, which of the putative affiliations dredged up in the foregoing observations ought to become a fixed part of some *Notes* or *Allusions*. It is *Ulysses*, however, that activates us to look for such matchings, in the spirit of the game, to interconnect stray echoes with pertinent themes. We structure, chart, or shape the hidden parts of the icebergs we choose to collide with, and we forge the identities that we find rewarding and pleasurable.

NOTES

1 W.B. Stanford summarizes the argument of Antisthenes (see *U* 7.1035, etc.) the sophist: '*polytropos*... denotes Odysseus' skill in adapting his figures of speech ('tropes')... at any particular time'; *The* Ulysses *Theme* (Ann Arbor: University of Michigan Press 1968), 99.

2 One of the standard epithets of Odysseus (*Od.* 2.173, etc.), it is translated as 'wise—of many counsels—resourceful' etc.

3 In the Library chapter Mulligan mocks Bloom, voyeur of statues: his eyes 'were upon her mesial groove' (*U* 9.615). The technical word *mesial* merely denotes something in the middle (Greek *mesos*).

4 Even this could be construed as an Odyssean effort in reverse. In the first of the Eumaean books, Odysseus asks his way from a passing native (who is Pallas Athene in disguise) and is very careful in what he gives away. In a unique line that follows the standard formula of an answer, Odysseus catches himself '... *palin*... *lazeto mython*' (*Od.* 13.254) 'he took back his words, he checked them before they were uttered', he literally 'again (*palin*) seized (*lazeto*) his speech' (*mython*) and altered his words. In 'Eumaeus' words once uttered, or recorded, cannot be taken back, but the speech is altered—*afterwards*, by laborious rephrasings and alterations.

5 *The Handlist to James Joyce's* Ulysses: *A Complete Alphabetical Index to the Critical Reading Text*, prepared by Wolfhard Steppe with Hans Walter Gabler (New York & London: Garland publishing Inc. 1985), makes the verification of such claims easy.

6 *Hallucinari* or *allucinari* is said to be related to Greek *aluein* (or *alyein*), and this in turn is a cognate of *alaomai*, to wander, err, to be unsteady—and is sometimes applied to Odysseus (*Od.* 14.120, etc.). No, Joyce himself need never have made this remote connection, though Skeat's *Etymological Dictionary* would have guided him. But it is odd that the wanderings, errings, of the words or the metaphor signalled *in* the text might—very potentially—link the wandering prose of the chapter back to the changeful course of Odysseus.

7 *Tale of a Tub*, IV.

8 *Thom's Official Directory*, for example, listed 'Johnston, Mooney, and O'Brien (limited), plain and fancy bread and biscuit bakers...'

9   A. Walton Litz has traced the paragraph at *U* 16.270ff to some early manuscript pages, preceding *Ulysses*. See 'Early Vestiges of *Ulysses*' in *The Art of James Joyce* (London: OUP 1961), 133–4.

10   Stephen had already conjoined the two words in 'The cold steel pen' (*U* 1.153). See also *U* 16.589.

11   Don Gifford and Robert J. Seidman, *Notes for Joyce: An Annotation of James Joyce's* Ulysses (New York: Dutton & Co 1974), 442.

12   Hermione de Almeida, *Byron and Joyce Through Homer:* Don Juan *and* Ulysses (New York: Columbia University Press 1981). The study is concerned with broader outlines than the details served up here.

13   'Tender Achilles' expresses Bloom's own feelings; in the *Odyssey* the warlike, wrathful, reckless hero of the *Iliad* has become softened among the dead, less proud, and concerned about his son—more tender (Od. 11.487ff).

14   Weldon Thornton, *Allusions in* Ulysses (Chapel Hill: University of North Carolina Press 1968), 431.

15   Thornton, *Allusions*, 447.

16   Ibid.

17   *The Oxford Dictionary of English Proverbs* (Oxford: Clarendon Press 1957), 161.

18   J.T. Gilbert, *A History of the City of Dublin* (Dublin 1854), I, 219.

19   Stuart Gilbert, *James Joyce's* Ulysses (London: Faber & Faber 1952), 219.

20   *The Odyssey of Homer*, William Cowper (trans.) (London: J.M. Dent 1910), 197.

21   Karl Beckson and Arthur Ganz in their *Reader's Guide to Literary Terms* single it out in their sample sentence to illustrate 'cliché': 'Beckson and Ganz, *busy as bees*, are *working like dogs* to obtain *filthy lucre*' (London: Thames & Hudson 1961), 35.

22   The translations given of the *Odyssey* are by Butcher and Lang.

23   Bloom is in a very Odyssean role: 'A wariness of mind he would answer as fitted all and, laying hand to jaw, he said dissembling, as his wont was...' (*U* 14.253). In the *Nostos* books Odysseus continually dissembles.

24   This line (*U* 14.255) follows immediately the one commented on above, n.4 (a prime instance of Odysseus dissembling). The verb used, '*nomon*', means move about, handle; or revolve, turn over, in the mind—and might well do duty for the kind of thinking that Bloom does in the Eumaean passages, 'weighing the pros and cons' (*U* 16.1603).

25   (*Od.* 13.291). Right after, Pallas Athene compares herself to him: she wins renown among the gods for her 'wiles'—'*kerdesin*' (13.299).

26   Five out of seven occurrences of 'genuine' are in 'Eumaeus', as though to reinforce the inherent question of the *genus*—breed, kin, descent. They seem to match Mulligan's mocking 'the genuine christine' in the opening scene of *Ulysses* (*U* 1.21: pre-Gabler texts read 'Christine'); there 'genuine' is ironically paired with something Christian or Eucharistine.

27   Od. 15.78. Homer uses '*amphoteron*' for 'both', 'honour *and* glory'. The serial amphoteron looks like one of the words one is tempted to use, time and again, in commenting on *Ulysses*. All the comments in this essay are to be understood like that, as choices among others.

28   Byron in 'Penelope' is at *U* 18.185, 209, 1325. In 'Circe' Bloom is trying to look like Byron, he '*contracts his face so as to resemble... Lord Byron*' (*U* 15.1844).

IN CLASSICAL IDIOM:
ANTHOLOGIA INTERTEXTUALIS

as we learned a smattering of in our classical days (*U* 16.1138)

On the whole, we have not done our conventional homework very thoroughly. Much of Greek and Roman literature that almost by educational reflex went into Joyce's works has not been researched, or even labelled. Perhaps no one wants to do the tritely obvious, unexciting as it looks, but one reason may lie in our cultural background. Joyceans may no longer be well versed in the ancients. Nor am I, for that matter; in fact my Greek and Latin are poor and largely self-taught. But some initiative toward supplementation is overdue.

The multifarious samples that follow are fragmentary, random, arbitrary, a garner of probabilities. No claim is made that the relationships suggested are necessarily conscious adaptations, nor even that they exist. They are merely constructible by intertextual synergism or coactive readers' assiduity. One subsidiary question to bear in mind is whether any of the offerings should be condensed into tutorial Notes or Allusions, Lists or Glosses, and how it might be done so that the resulting entries would remain pertinent and useful. One implication is that Joyce eludes systematic annotation.

The 'intertextuality' invoked is not meant to be a bow to current phraseology, but rather to truisms that may be as old as literature. Perhaps the proper term would be 'interdynamisms'. One aim is to discern, provisionally, the diversified modulations in which older texts, techniques, or insights are transposed.

answer from the river

While crossing the Liffey Bloom notices a floating advertisement on the water: 'His eyes sought answer from the river and saw a rowboat rock at anchor on the treacly swells...' Take this in for a moment: a rowboat rock(ing) at anchor?; but no, we continue: 'rock at anchor on the treacly swells lazily its plastered board' (*U* 8.88–9). The verb that looked intransitive has, we now learn, a postponed object; 'rock' is not what it seemed at first. Maybe Bloom's glance noticed the boat before his glance moved to the board. He then reads the advertise-ment (for trousers) and, being in the profession, wonders if the com-pany 'pays rent to the corporation'. But, 'How can you own water really? It's always flowing in a stream, never the same, which in the stream of life we trace. Because life is a stream' (*U* 8.93–5). Running water and ownership do not quite go together, but the point is not just a legal one; Bloom's 'really' is a metaphysical speculation. The contrast between being fixed, like property, and being in motion is an old one. No doubt Bloom has in mind some echo from Greek thinkers, mainly Herakleitos, who is reported to have said that you cannot enter the same river twice.

This clearly applies to Joyce's works; it is a relation that has also become a cliché, that we can overemphasize. But the works *are*, as it were, in motion, do not stay put, and they change with us, just as we, having absorbed them once, reapproach them different and differ-ently. They are not, though many of our books treat them like this, stable things to be critically owned, but goings on. 'Flux' was attached to them as a characterization very soon; 'stream of con-sciousness' looked a fitting metaphor. Everything moves; nothing is. Therefore verbs may do Joyce's works more justice than identifica-tory labels like nouns or adjectives.

As it happens, the advertisement for trousers is of a real British firm and a Dublin branch office, named 'Kino's'. *Kino*—if it were Greek, which it is not—would mean 'I move'. Running water cannot be owned. Notice that the sentence introducing Kino's trousers moved too: a rowboat in an apparent self-contained rocking turned out to be rocking a board. Ever after, rereading this, we will know-ingly construe 'rock' as transitive: we will not, in Herakleitean metaphor, re-enter the same error twice.

Interestingly enough, the familiar quotation is to be found in at least two different versions, different only in the grammar and the order of the words:

(1) *dis es ton auton potamon ouk an embaies* (twice in the same river you do not
     step) (Plato, *Kratylos*, 402A)
(2) *potamo ouk esti dis to auto embenai* (river not is twice the same stepping [in])[1]

Herakleitos' sentence has not remained the same in the various
recordings and transmissions. The sense remains more or less the
same, but the wording and the order change. Version 2 acts out what
it says: it begins with '(into the) river' and follows later with 'the
same', and by being delayed it is not the same; sameness is taken
syntactically apart. This is a type of sentence Joyce revived. We saw
that our understanding of a rowboat rocking on the river also changes
as we move along its word order.

A little bit of investigation will also show that the most famous
formula of Herakleitos, '*Panta rhei*', appears relatively late and is
commonly attributed to Aristotle.[2] Plato's summary is '*panta chorei
kai ouden menei*' (*Kratylos*, 402A). What all of this means, which
delving in sources would further complicate, is that appropriately
the sayings of Herakleitos did not remain constant; the unreliable
words prove the principle. No wonder that 'Pantharhea' occurs in
Finnegans Wake along with 'Oropos Roxy' as pantomime characters
(*FW* 513.21–2). The first word of *Finnegans Wake*, 'riverrun', looks
like such a river that we step in, and which on rereading (the first
syllable is an Italian *ri-*) will have become notably different. Joyce
readers cannot step into the same text twice.

We often do not remember the same quotation twice. In 'Lotuseaters' Bloom meditates. The weather is unstable: 'Won't last.
Always passing, the stream of life, which in the stream of life we
trace is dearer thaaan them all' (*U* 5.563–4). We know that he mentally changed a flow of words from a ballad:

> Some thoughts none other can replace,
> Remembrance will recall;
> Which in the flight of years we trace,
> Is dearer than them all.

The 'flight of years' has given way to 'the stream of life'. Fittingly the
Herakleitean interference occurred in connection with 'remem-
brance' and 'recall': memory is particularly changeable; every recall
tends to be a different call. Joyce also presented memory as a flux or
aptly 'stream of consciousness'. The ballad from which Bloom mis-
quotes is 'In Happy Moments Day by Day'.[3]

Some of the metaphysical hyperboles displayed by our day-by-day
new theories often come fairly close to old insights of Herakleitos,

who was called 'Skoteinos', the Dark One. He was fond of semantic ambiguity. He deserves more study. The above is only a first tracing, a tentative dip into a pervasive riverrun.

more turnings

That we cannot step into the same river twice is brought home to us readers when we come back to favourite passages: it is precisely those that we (think we) know best that seem to change most often. Joycean passages are *pass*ages indeed, with a 'passencore' drive of rearrival (*FW* 3.04). If there is one topic that I thought I had pretty well exhausted it is the polytropic force that *Ulysses* shares with the *Odyssey*, where the quality is named as the foremost attribute of Odysseus: '*polytropo[s]*' (*Od.* 1:1,10:330). The epithet, including in its semantic sweep the notions of much-travelled, much-wandering, turning many ways, versatile, shifty, wily, etc., seems to provide manifold leverage.[4]

Though casting about fairly widely, I had overlooked that the Bible uses the same metaphor, once only, and as an adverb. The Epistle to the Hebrews begins on a high note: 'God, who at sundry times and in divers manners spake in time past unto the fathers by the prophets... has now spoken through His Son' (Heb. 1:1). The original Greek sets off in emphatic, poetic parallelism: '*Polymeros kai polytropos palai ho Theos.*' The flourish of 'much/many' at the beginning may bring to mind a similar, fourfold cluster of muchness in the first lines of the *Odyssey*: '*poly, polla, pollon, polla*'. The Latin version substitutes '*multi*': '*Multifariam multisque modis olim Deus loquens*'.

What it took me twenty pages to articulate and document, St Paul said succinctly in a few words. It looks as though Joyce (who may never have considered this opening at all) had deflected verbal energies from the Gospel to his own concerns. *Ulysses* does in fact speak 'at sundry times' (*polymeros*, literally 'in many portions') and 'in divers manners' (*polytropos*). We are still learning the diversities. The prophets, one implication is, spoke differently in different periods. We notice that St Paul, addressing the Hebrews, links to his God the Greek survivor who was never at a loss, but also, at sundry times, known to be shifty and deceitful, in Christian eras no longer a model to imitate.

A Catholic in Dublin would have heard the Latin words at the Mass on Christ's Nativity, as any missal will tell you. If anything, *Ulysses* is '*multis modis*', of many modes or moods. The other adverb, 'multifariam' (from *fari*: to speak), makes the point a philological one. *Ulysses* begins with a versatile character who is wordily multifarious, of diverse manners, and he speaks first in a mocking mode about God. *Ulysses* offers its own translation: 'in various manners' (*U* 17.1251), but this phrase proves as little as does 'multifarious' (*U* 14.1289): *Ulysses* does not depend on particular echoes; it prefers to perform multifariously and to speak in many ways. That is even more pragmatically true of *Finnegans Wake* where the Latin adverb may interfere with a local name in 'the battle of Multaferry' (*FW* 580.12). There was a battle at Multafarry; there is an Irish place named Multifarnham; the Latin approximation 'Multaferry' may suggest that much is brought or carried.

St Paul's Letter to the Hebrews surfaces in both works, as it ought to. Stephen's strange question, '—Is that first epistle to the Hebrews ... in?' (*U* 16.1268–9), puzzles Bloom; it is strange because there is only *one* such Epistle. What makes the reference fitting is that the author of the letter was in all textual probability not St Paul;[5] the letter may be a 'genuine forgery' in this respect. St Paul was an Israelite (according to Rom. 11:1) writing in Greek to Greeks or Hebrews, a 'jewgreek' combination.

The opening sentence majestically heralds God and His Son; its first chapter, *Ulysses*-like, recalls many passages from the Old Testament and adapts them to its own purposes. Perhaps 'the brightness of its glory' (1:3, echoing as it does Ezekiel 1:28), got twisted into 'the glory of the brightness' of Bloom-Elijah's ascent (*U* 12.1912). The same verse (1:3) says that God's Son 'sat down on the right hand of the Majesty', which is parodied, through other sources, in 'Cyclops': 'sitteth on his beamend' (*U* 12.1358), and inverted in 'Eumaeus', where paternal Bloom chooses to sit and walk on Stephen's right.

The *multis modis* of *Ulysses* are open for coincidences too. In an attempt to connect the intrusive 'l' in Martha Clifford's 'world' with the omission of the same letter in the *Telegraph's* report on the funeral, 'L. Boom', I once followed up Stephen's lead and turned to the Epistle to the Hebrews. The second verse of its first chapter says that by his Son God 'made the worlds', but in the Catholic Douay version this same passage reads 'made the word'. This looked as though a mistake in a typewritten letter were somehow linked to disparities of Biblical translations. On inquiry it turned out that the Catholic rendering was a misprint in my particular edition (which the publisher said they would correct).[6]

In the *Wake* the Epistle to the Hebrews becomes a weapon or a broadside. The author-exile Glugg would 'for othersites of Jorden...

fire off... his farced epistol to the hibruws' (*FW* 228.31–4). This takes in both *Ulysses* and *Finnegans Wake*, stuffed, spiced, and seasoned, as well as 'farcical, forced', perhaps even 'forged', as may be St Paul's authorship. There is some redundancy in 'othersites of Jorden', for the word 'Hebrew' has been explained to mean 'from the other side' (of Jordan). (I always wondered whether 'Thersites' is functionally in 'othersites'.)

The *Wake* speaks in even more multiple modes and manners; sometimes 'the melos yields the mode and the mode the manners' (*FW* 57.2–3), 'millions of moods used up slanguage' (*FW* 421.17). Conceivably a phrase from Hebrews 1:8, 'Thy throne, O God, is for ever and ever', in its Greek version, *'eis ton aiona tou aionos'*, is sounded in a passage dense with religious overtones in several languages: 'our aeone tone aeones' (*FW* 552.8). The form comes also close to a plural variant, *'eis tous aionas ton aionon'* (as in Gal. 1:5 and I Tim. 1:17), the equivalent of *'in saecula saeculorum'*.

All of this, in my little circuit, started with the epithet *'polytropos'* in the *Odyssey*. So it was gratifying to find, in a postcard that Joyce had written to his French translator Auguste Morel, the following variations of shrewdness (Morel had obviously married without telling anyone): 'Mais quel homme rusé, quel fils de Minerve, quel disciple d'Ignace, que vous êtes *polytropos*.'' This combination of the beginning of the *Odyssey* and the Jesuit strain takes us back to the first chapter of *Ulysses*, whose multiple turnings, with Homeric and Biblical echoes and all, Morel had to render into French.

crackling raillery

Grandfather Virag's performance on the Circean stage entails some of the densest, still most cryptic, passages in all of *Ulysses*. A few of Virag's roles have been put on record; a further, transient one is proposed here. Virag's utterances are shrewd, unpleasant, often disgusting, as are his features and gestures, unsightly in one stage direction after another. A number of his sayings appear unrelated to the rest of the book; many words occur only in his speeches.

The vilest of all the Greeks fighting against Troy, but also a very perceptive one, was Thersites, 'wagging his unbridled tongue', 'a railer', 'in scandal busy'; he is called the ugliest man (*Il.* 2:212 ff). In one scene, a description of old Virag, *'head askew, arches his back and hunched wingshoulders'* (*U* 15.2460), may in part derive from Thersites, 'with his two shoulders rounded and hunched over his chest' (*Il.* 2:217). The words are those of Samuel Butler in his translation, *The Iliad of Homer*. A briefer version, 'whose shoulders were hunched over his chest', had been given when Butler was trying to prove that a line in the *Odyssey* was borrowed from Homer's characterization of Thersites in the *Iliad*. Joyce might have come across the phrases in Samuel Butler's *The Authoress of the Odyssey* (1897).[8] A standard Victorian translation of the *Iliad* (which Samuel Butler wanted to replace) may have contributed a tiny touch: 'and his two shoulders rounded, *arched* down upon his chest.'[9]

In a general manner, some of Pope's version of the *Iliad* 2:213–16, might apply to Viragian features:

> Loquacious, loud, and turbulent of tongue:
> Awed by no shame, by no respect controll'd,
> In scandal busy, in reproaches bold:
> With witty malice studious to defame,
> Scorn all his joy, and laughter all his aim.

(Note that similar pronouncements were made about *Ulysses* when it came out.) The description of Thersites in the *Iliad* is characterized by *hapax legomena*, words that occur only there.

in medias res

In the last stage of proof and revision, Joyce added something to the last speech of 'Eumaeus', which ran: 'My wife, he intimated... would have the greatest of pleasure in making your acquaintance as she is passionately attached to music of any kind' (*U* 16.1800–2). On the page proofs, after 'My wife, he intimated' Joyce inserted: 'plunging *in medias res*' (*JJA* 27:134). Before it, he added a faltering 'What's this I was saying? Ah, yes!'[10] which is manifestly *not* plunging *in medias res*. The additions cause some problems. We might construe the participial clause wrongly, with 'the wife' as its antecedent, but this would be erroneous, even though Mrs Marion Bloom has done some independent plunging. The insertion amplifies Eumaean diction. Joyce put something—which by its nature and by proverbial use properly refers to a beginning—close to the end. It occurs, moreover, in the last of Bloom's speeches, the last one rendered in his own words. The addition was made late, practically in the last week (the proofs are dated 25.1.22): *in medias res*, when the *res* are nearly over!

Since Bloom at long last introduces a topic, that his wife would have 'the greatest of pleasure in making [Stephen's] acquaintance', the epical *in medias res* might potentially initiate another story, a story, incidentally, that William Empson once completed.[11]

The formula that, *as* a cliché, fits the surface texture so well, is of course Horace's, in the familiar characterization of Homer's craftsmanship. Homer does not start the tale from the beginning (*ab ovo*, another classical tag), but *'semper ad eventum festinat et in medias res/non secus ac notas auditorem rapit.'* This is from Horace's aesthetic theory, a letter now known as the *Ars Poetica* (148–9). Homer, says Horace, always hastens to the issue and hurries his hearers into the midst of things, as if they knew it before. Now Bloom is finally hastening his companion to the issue at hand, though Stephen can hardly be said to be captivated or rapt (*rapit*). In fact 'Eumaeus' is everything but a hastening to any issues; it is in ironic contrast to the model epic manner that follows in the *Ars Poetica*: *'et quae/desperat tractata nitescere posse, relinquit'* (150) (And what Homer fears he cannot make attractive [shining] with his touch, he leaves out); there is nothing too much. In Horatian terms, and by common consent, 'Eumaeus' is about as unhomeric as one might imagine. On the other hand, it is also, in its striving for epic description, perhaps the most Homeric episode of them all. Horace's summary would certainly apply to that chapter: *'atque ita mentitur, sic veris falsa remiscet,/ primo ne medium, medio ne discrepet imum'* (151–5) (He lies [or invents] so well, and mixes facts and fiction, that the middle is not discordant [discrepant] with the beginning, nor the middle with the end). 'Eumaeus' with its multiple discrepancies is a prime blend of truth and falsehood, a true continuation of the Odyssean tactics to make 'the many falsehoods of his tale seem like truth' (*'iske pseudea polla legon etymoisin homoia'*, *Od.* 19:203). The Latin treatise proved a middle link. In Horace's own words, after all, the middle is not inconsistent with either beginning or end. In fact Homer's beginning *is* a middle (*'in medias'*). Joyce takes him at his words and places a traditional beginning, called middle, near the end.

Finnegans Wake combines Horace's formula with Ovidian touches of King Midas: 'The siss of the whisp of the sigh of the softzing at the stir of the ver grose O arundo of a long one in midias reeds' (*FW* 158.6–7). 'In midias reeds' takes us into the middle of the reeds that betrayed the secret of King Midas, who was somewhat obtuse; for his bad taste in music his ears were turned into those of an ass for punishment; a servant cutting his hair saw it and buried the secret in the ground. But the reeds growing there gave it away. Ovid may have provided the images and some words:

> creber harundinibus tremulis ibi surgere lucus
> *coepit, et, ut primum pleno maturuit anno,*

prodidit agricolam: leni nam motus ab austro
obruta verba refert dominique coarguit aures.
(*Metamorphoses* XI:191–4)

(There a grove with quivering reeds [*harundinibus*] began to rise; as soon as it came to maturity, after a complete year, it betrayed its planter. For, stirred by the gentle south wind, it repeated the covered-up words and disclosed the ears of his master.)

The contrast may be between burying a secret and the full proclamation in a standard epic. Whispering reeds[12] have become proverbial. The Latin for reed is taken over: 'arundo'; the form without the 'h' enables the text to stay close to 'The Green Grass Grew All Around.' Ovid's '*motus*' can be rendered as 'stir', which rhymes with the Latin *ver* (spring). The ears, of course, were long ('the long one').

Ovid may have set a bit of a precedent by echoes and ambiguities and metamorphoses of sound and meaning. He uses *(h)arundo* both for the reeds and for the pipe that Pan plays upon in his contest with Apollo: '*cerata... harundine*' (XI:154). Both meanings were disastrous for the stupid king. Midas championed Pan's rude notes on the rustic pipe over Apollo's lyre; for this he received his ass's ears: *aures* (as in line 194, the conclusion of the episode). But the barber, who had seen what kinds of ears they were ('*domini quales adspexerit aures*', 186), was eager to make it known, to spread the news 'in the air': '*efferre sub auras*' (183): '*refert... aures*' may echoingly transform this. And of course Midas, in his first affliction, had been troubled by the gold to which everything he touched was changed: gold is *aurum*—similar looking words, differentiated only by their endings. So Ovid the precursor may deserve honorable adaptation in Joyce's Metamorphoses of the Night.

Another *in medias res* seems to echo the ass: Shem, the implication is, would 'begin his beogrefright in muddyass ribalds' (*FW* 423.17–18). A biography, something frightful, full of ogres, dirty, unrespectable, might begin right in the disgusting midst of things. The final 'ribalds', apart from the ribaldry, also sounds like bad Latin, as though someone had construed the phrase not with the accusative *res*, but with a wrong ablative plural, *rebus*. There is an epical touch about 'all repeating ourselves, in medios loquos' (*FW* 398.8), where *res* has been replaced by Latin speech or Greek word (*logos*); but 'medius loco' can occur in a chance collocation: '*loco medius rerum*', where Sol, the Sun, sits at the beginning of the second book of Ovid's *Metamorphoses* (II:31).

ulixes dolosus

Horace, like most Roman poets, could be critical and contemptuous of Ulixes (the hybrid 'Ulysses' had not been formed yet). In the fifth item of the Second Book of *Sermones* (now termed *Satires*), Ulixes belabors the seer Tiresias in the underworld about the recovery of his worldly belongings. This is Odysseus out for material gain, the whole a simoniac travesty of the *Nekuyia* (*Od.* 11).

Ulixes fears poverty ('*pauperiem horres*', line 9). So does Bloom who imagines detailed 'reverses of fortune' (*U* 17.1933ff). Ulixes of many wiles (Horace says '*dolosus*') is given advice in a text heavy with allusions. Tiresias reveals 'by what means to acquire wealth' ('*qua ratione queas ditescere*', 10); schemes to get rich flash through Bloom's mind before he returns to bed, 'means to opulence' (*U* 17.1672).

The main advice is to sneak into someone's good graces so as to be considered in the person's will. This, according to Molly, is what Bloom tried to do with Mrs Riordan in the City Arms Hotel. We know he was kind to her, 'a widow of independent means', and had performed 'special corporal work[s] of mercy' for her (*U* 17.479, 487). The narrator in Barney Kiernan's reports the same story from a different angle: 'and Bloom trying to get the soft side of her doing the mollycoddle playing bézique to come in for a bit of the wampum in her will' (*U* 12.506–7); the story includes her nephew and a shady event in which Bloom's motives appear suspect. Horace's garrulous Tiresias could have given the instructions.

None of this need come through Horace's satire; anything might. Horace reprocessed the well-known epic; so did Joyce, and he may well have reprocessed some of Horace. The mockery includes one particularly intriguing bit of advice. If the target is an old dotard (*senem delirum*) who has to be won, and if he should be a fornicator, one might resort to compliance: '*ultro/Penelopam facilis potiori trade*' (76–7) (Obligingly hand over Penelope to your better). Bloom, of course, practically does it, and does it with stagy exaggeration in 'Circe'. His reasons for doing so, without putting up a macho fight, is one of the concerns of *Ulysses*. Homer's original Tiresias made no such flippant remarks, but Joyce hardly limited himself to any one script.

finished example

Horace also set up Odysseus as an instructive pattern and model; this in one of his *Epistles*. I have, says the poet, been reading the story of

the Trojan war again, with a stress on *rereading* (*'relegi'*, *Ep.* I.2.2).
The epic, for which the Latin term is *fabula*, is of the love of Paris
and a foolish war arising from it, with the common people suffering
for the folly of the kings. But then the poet turns to *exemplar Ulixen*,
a paradigm for the power of *virtus* and wisdom. Then the opening of
the *Odyssey* is paraphrasingly translated:

> *qui domitor Troiae multorum providus urbes*
> *et mores hominum inspexit latumque per aequor,*
> *dum sibi, dum sociis reditum parat, aspera multa*
> *pertulit, adversis rerum immersabilis undis . . .*
>
> (*Ep.* I:2, 19–22)

(The tamer of Troy looked closely on cities and the manners of many men, and suffered many hardships across the broad seas, while he strove for his own and his comrades' return, but he could never be drowned by the waves of adversities.)

He was *'providus'*, someone who looks ahead, who is prudent.[13]
He not only 'sees' many cities (as the *Odyssey* neutrally has it, 1.3),
but 'inspects' them; similarly Bloom is one who scrutinizes his city
and the behaviour of its inhabitants. This 'finished example of the
new womanly man' (*U* 15.1798–9), when we get to know him, is
preparing a breakfast; 'Eumaeus' introduces his 'Preparatory' action.
    The summary goes on with highlights of seduction: '*Sirenum
voces et Circae pocula nosti*' (23) (You know, or have heard, of the
Siren voices and Circe's cups). And now the poet tells us, for our
enlightenment, what might have happened ('If Pyrrhus... or Caesar
had not been knifed to death. They are not to be thought away... infinite possibilities', *U* 2.48). Horace specifies a probability, a turn that
might have been taken, an alternative. It is in the subjunctive mood
throughout, as are many of the later *Ulysses* episodes ('Circe',
'Eumaeus', 'Oxen' all have a strong element of 'what if'): '*quae si cum
sociis stultus cupidusque bibisset*' (24) (if he had drunk with the others, foolish and greedy, with cupidity); compare 'Bella... with anger
and cupidity' (*U* 15.4275), then, '*sub domina meretrice fuisset turpis
et excors*' (25) (he would have been *turpis*: deformed, and *excors*:
without heart, stupid, brutish; he would have been under Circe, the
domina). In Joyce's 'Circe' Bella *is* dominant; Bloom 'enormously'
desiderates her 'domination' (*U* 15.2777). On the floor, 'His eyes
grow dull... his nose thickens... Empress!' (*U* 15.2830–1, 2837); he
calls her: 'Master! Mistress! Mantamer!' (*U* 15.3062). Above all, however, the Horatian road not taken makes Circe a *meretrix* or whore.
Joyce chooses the whole Circean site in accordance with this variant,

one current in antiquity. And as in Joyce's Nighttown chapter, Ulixes would have '*vixisset canis immundus vel amica luto sus*' (26) (lived like a dog *immundus* [unclean], and like a swine that loves the mire). Joyce features both animals prominently. Horace even anticipated a change of sex: male dog (*immundus*) and female swine (*amica*). Bloom is made to love mud; he is 'coated with stiffening mud... Mud head to foot,' or 'a poor old stick in the mud'; he becomes a 'Dungdevourer' (*U* 15.271–2, 274, 330, 2843).

Joyce's longest chapter suggests the alternative that Homer's and Horace's exemplars prudently avoided. To do this Joyce did not need the intermediate variant, but it is interesting to know that such prototypes were available and commonly accessible, mainly in reference works like Roscher's *Ausführliches Lexikon der griechischen und römischen Mythologie*.[14] Chances are that Joyce, once he knew he was going to use the *Odyssey* as a shaping pattern, would have inspected traditional variants to be used in his book of many variants. Horace would have been a well-known intermediate processor of the myths.

the art of telling

Ulixes, wrote Ovid in his *Art of Loving*, was not beautiful, but he talked well: '*Non formosus erat, sed erat facundus Ulixes*' (*AA* II.123) (not fair of face was Ulixes, but of speech), and yet he tormented two seagoddesses with love: '*Et tamen aequoreas torsit amore deas*' (124). This so much so that Calypso kept saying that the waters of the sea were not fit for rowing home. She also would ask him again and again about the fall of Troy, which he told so vividly. Once they were standing on the beach, and the goddess wanted to hear the bloody fate of King Rhesus (his killing is told in Book 10 of the *Iliad*). And so, '*Ille levi virga—virgam non forte tenebat—Quod rogat, in spisso litore pingit opus*' (131–2) (with a slender rod—which he kept by chance—of what she asked, he drew [painted] a work in the dense shore). *Levi* (light, slender) is not in contrast to strong; *forte* means 'as it happened'. You cannot trust words and yet the specious antithesis is effective, or would be if this were *Finnegans Wake*. A map drawn of the setting of a bloody deed is mentioned in 'Aeolus'; this is Gallaher's model exploit. But of course we have Bloom, alone on Sandymount strand, taking a stick that was there by chance and writing in the sand. In 'Nausicaa' Joyce's art is painting ('like the paintings that man used to do on the pavement... leaving them there to be all blotted out', *U* 13.406–8). This is what Ulixes says, and does: '"*Haec*" inquit "*Troia est*," *muros in litore fecit:*/"*Hic tibi sit Simois, haec mea castra puta"'* (133–4). Ovid instructively distinguishes the signifiers (the walls he made) from the signified (Troia); the scratchings in the sand are not identical with the city, but there is a serviceable connection, one also of *pars* (walls) *pro toto*. Ulixes goes on, in detailed words and picturings: '*Campus erat, "campumque facit" quem caede Dolonis/Sparsimus'* (135–6) (this was the plain that we strewed with the blood of Dolon). 'This was the plain', and he made the plain. Ovid did not know that his instance of artful recreation echoes divine creation in Genesis. The whole Trojan episode need not concern us here, but it is interesting that Ulixes would also point out himself: '*Hac ego sum captis nocte revectus equis'* (137) (here I am, come back at night, with the captured horses). Bloom writes: 'I.' and 'AM. A.' (*ego, U* 13.1258, 1264). The instruction goes on, Ovid continues: '*Pluraque pingebat, subitus cum Pergama fluctus/Abstulit et Rhesi cum duce castra suo'* (139–40) (more he painted [would have painted], but an upcoming and sudden flood, wave, took, washed away, Troy and the tents of Rhesus, with its leader and the whole lot). Things written in sand will not last: 'Some flatfoot tramp on it in the morning... Washed away. Tide comes here' (*U* 13.1259–60). So Mr Bloom effaces the letters.

Calypso shrewdly uses the occasion to prove that he cannot trust in such waves for sailing, for they '*Perdiderint undae nomina quanta, vides?'* (142) (see, the waves have destroyed so many names). And once more words, names, their pictorial representations, and the referents are knowingly brought together. But now, after Calypso, Ovid turns the event to his advantage: '*Ergo age, fallaci timide confide figurae'* (143) (do not trust looks and deceptive shapes: only timidly [with fear] trust a deceptive figure [beauty]), and the next line translates, 'whoever you are, have something more than body' (144). Names (in the poets' words) have remained; figures disappeared (*figurae*), both those sketched into the sand and our physical shapes. So Ovid has returned to his point of origin.

In this version Ulixes tells part of the *Odyssey*, not for the first time, but it is a different section, a new variant and perspective of something the listener knows already.

There may be, then, a few situational correspondences: Ulixes drawing a map, Gallaher passing on information about a crime, Bloom idly writing in the sand perhaps. What seems more dynamically relevant, however, is the manner of the telling, as Ovid exemplifies it. Calypso wanted to hear the stories all over: '*Haec Troiae casus iterumque iterumque rogabat'* (127) (she would ask him again and again the fall of Troy). *Iterumque iterumque* is the motto of

Finnegans Wake: again and again, the same anew. The next line looks like a narrative program for *Ulysses*, for all of Joyce perhaps: '*Ille referre aliter saepe solebat idem*' (128) (he used to relate the same differently [otherwise]). Translations may say, 'She made him find fresh words for the same old tale', and illustrate the point, the 'how' of the telling changes. Joyce's works are pivoting around *idem* and *aliter*, sameness and difference. The *Wake* may (coincidentally) almost pick up the terms: 'olderwise since primal made alter in garden of Idem' (*FW* 263.19–21); 'alter' is akin to *aliter* and 'olderwise' means *aliter* plus aging. *Ulysses* and *Finnegans Wake* are characterized by aliterity. Otherwiseness of the same infuses Ovid's art (he told the invention of Daedalus' flight once in *Ars Amatoria* and again in *Metamorphoses*) and Joyce's, so this is nothing new, but by Joyce it is done much more consciously: 'the same identical... the identical same' can be paired in 'Eumaeus' (*U* 16.1079, 1331), where Bloom exemplifies it, pointedly and laboriously.

But now notice that Ovid also *does* it, alters his way of presentation. Ulixes gives several illustrations, all different. First, as told before, he says: '"*Haec*" inquit "*Troia est*," *muros in litore fecit*' (This is Troy, and he made walls in the beach). Then he uses a conjunctive of imagination: '*Hic tibi sit Simois*' (Here this *be* Simois for *you*); then there is an imperative: '*haec mea castra puta*' (This is *supposed* to be my camp!; *call* this my camp!). Finally he says simply: '*Campus erat*' (There was a plain). Perspectives, moods, and tenses are varied. These are alternatives of verbalizing pictorial representation.[15] Ovid implicitly gives a lesson in rhetoric: Do not repeat yourself in the modes of telling.

Let us not forget, this is also advice to a prospective lover. Ovid had promised, in his opening lines, that the reader of his poem (and he says this twice, in variation) would become skilled in love: '*Hoc legat, et lecto carmine doctus amet*' (*AA* I.2). One might also learn how to relate, how to tell a story, how not to be a bore, how to be *facundus*.

deceitful men (*U* 18.1236)

At times we consciously refer to the classics, but we may also use the poets' words without knowing that we do. Molly thinks of her journey with Boylan to Belfast. Things might get complicated if Bloom came along too, with whom she then would have to share a room, Boylan perhaps occupying the one next door: 'hed never believe the next day we didnt do something its all very well a husband but you cant fool a lover' (*U* 18.354–5). This does not sound like the voice of experience but has all the air of a popular saying, something handed on. The source, or one source, is Virgil. Aeneas has to obey a divine command and to leave Carthage; he considers ways to break the news tactfully to queen Dido; she however sees through his manœuvres. Virgil puts a general sentence in parentheses, which has become proverbial: '(*quis fallere possit amantem?*)' (*Aen.* IV.296) (who can deceive a lover?).[16] This is ancient wisdom surfacing in Molly Bloom. But the situations are different: Virgil's male hero wants to break away from a loving woman. As so often, a quotation has become independent of its original anchorage and has acquired general applicability. In Molly's thoughts this is no longer conscious, or even a quotation. Such echoes deserve a passing mention. On the one hand, a connection is established, in fits and starts, with the *Aeneid*, in many ways a Roman transformation of the *Odyssey* and an alternative epic grid for *Ulysses* whose vestiges we yet have to trace. Minimally we may claim nothing more than that all archetypal situations have once been put into words, sometimes memorable ones, and—that is one thing Joyce could have taught us—we cannot help repeating them. There is a strandentwining cable of all phrases.[17]

saturation

As Bloom is walking among the graves of Glasnevin cemetery his associations are, almost unavoidably, down to earth: 'It's the blood sinking in the earth gives new life... Well preserved fat corpse, gentleman, epicure, invaluable for fruit garden... I daresay the soil would be quite fat with corpsemanure, bones, flesh, nails' (*U* 6.771–7). We note how the well-preserved fat corpse gentleman easily blends into the soil in metamorphic recycling. The analogy between teeming soil and a text permeated with literary phantoms calls up some classical precedents.

Because of the familiar Homeric disposition of the book, blood in the earth can be related to Odysseus who, on the fringe of Hades, digs a pit and lets the blood of a sheep flow in as nourishment for the pale shades that flock around him. In this context, Bloom's 'Then begin to get black, black treacle oozing out of them' (*U* 6.779) would correspond to 'the dark blood flowed forth' (*Od.* 11:36, Butcher and Lang). Shakespeare, who is acknowledged a few lines later (*U* 6.792), used variations of this. The first part of *Henry IV* has an instance of it: 'No more the thirsty entrance of this soil/Shall daub her lips with her own children's blood' (I, i.4–5). In *II Henry IV* there is a related constellation: 'Most subject is the fattest soil to weeds/... The blood weeps from my heart' (IV, iv.58, 60). The topos dates back to antiquity; it was connected with the site of Troy. These are Ovid's words *'iam seges est, ubi Troia fuit, resecandaque falce/luxuriat Phrygio sanguine pinguis humus'* (now there are fields of corn where Troy was, and the soil ready for the sickle and fat with Phrygian blood brings forth abundantly). This is Penelope writing to her absent husband, in the first of the *Heroides* (*Epistulae Heroidum I: Penelope Ulixi*, 53–4). The letter continues: *'semisepulta virum curvis feriuntur aratris/ossa'* (*Ep. Her.* I.55–6) (half-buried bones of heroes are dug up by curved ploughs). The vision Bloom conjures up, similarly gruesome, occurs within schemes for more sensible sepulchral techniques: 'More room if they buried them standing... Standing? His head might come up some day above ground in a landslip with his hand pointing' (*U* 6.764–6). Conceivably, Tertullian's famous *'Semen est sanguis Christianorum'*, traditionally rendered as 'The blood of the martyrs is the seed of the Church,' has a similar origin. Compare Bloom's 'God wants blood victim. Birth, hymen, martyr, war, foundation of a building, sacrifice' (*U* 8.11–12).

Of course it may be as futile to sort out specific literary infusions as it is to trace the origin of soil components. The verbal abundance of *Finnegans Wake* is fertilized by decayed corpses of former writing. The idea of a blood-soaked field is expressed in 'bluddle filth' (*FW* 10.8–9), or 'being humus the same roturns' (*FW* 18.5); within the context it seems admissible to read 'same' as the German for seed *Same*. A large portion of our reading of *Finnegans Wake* amounts to the exhumation of decomposed previous texts: 'on the bunk of our breadwinning lies the cropse of our seedfather' (*FW* 55.7–8). One composite may be 'the seed of the father' as preserved by the daughters of Lot (*Gen.* 19:32, 34). The passage follows an Iliadic echo: 'The house of Atreox is fallen indeedust (Ilyam, Ilyum!)... but deeds bounds going arise again' (*FW* 55.3–5). The 'deeds bounds' translate into 'dead bones', and bones, ruins, even dust can potentially be identified; the nineteenth century perfected scientific techniques for it. The 'cropse of our seedfather', however, 'lies'—and so caution is necessary. The 'bunk of our breadwinning' is suspiciously close to 'bunkum'.

We do well to remember that literary disinterment is not an exact science.

till then—but now

In 'Nausicaa' we stay with a group of girls and children for a long time and watch some of their doings; we also share Gerty MacDowell's thoughts, aspirations, perceptions, her environment and social background. A gentleman in black appears to be within sight; toilette formalities have to be hidden from him; he may be able to tell the time. He comes in handy retrieving a ball for the twins. But the ball rolls to Gerty who misses it with her foot; she becomes self-conscious and blushes. We thereby learn something we have not been told: 'Till then they had only exchanged glances of the most casual but now under the brim of her new hat she ventured a look at him' (*U* 13.367–8). There was no mention of glances, however casual, and this in part because no report on anyone's mental processes could be remotely complete. Storytelling needs opportunities to fill us in on tangential events or facts. Such incidental looks might simply be too unimportant to register consciously, or else so unsettling that their exclusion is intentional. We now realize, naturally, that the stranger had been on Gerty's mind for a while: the casualness was highly conscious. A different angle of observation has been added; the set-up changes. We now understand Gerty's recent embarrassment much better. She was being noticed all along, and she knew it. The elisions are a psychological giveaway. Something else has been going on for some time, at the same time. This emphasis on a narrative excision makes it much easier for us to guess at the identity of the gentleman opposite.

Bloom himself has used deliberate repression all along, especially when questions about Boylan and Molly came up. The previous episode mentioned a Cyclopean variant: 'the Nelson policy, putting your blind eye to the telescope' (*U* 12.1193–4). What is omitted on purpose becomes retroactively underscored. Gnomonic absences are efficacious.

Homer handled them skillfully, sometimes explicitly. After her dream the princess Nausikaa gives her father a number of plausible reasons for granting her the use of wagon and mules for the laundrying excursion, all except the main one that Pallas Athene in the dream had pointedly insinuated. Homer comments on what Nausikaa left out: '*aideto gar thaleron gamon exonomenai*' (*Od.* 6:66) (She was ashamed [*aideto*] to speak of her marriage [*gamon*]). Similar shame motivates Gerty MacDowell at times. Much of what moves her is not mentioned (*exonomenai*). Pope freely elaborates on the Odyssean line with a gratuitous 'but blushes ill-restrained betray/Her thoughts intensive on the bridal day.' The translation also illustrates the father's simple understanding (*noei*): 'The conscious Sire the dawning blush survey'd.'[18] Gerty MacDowell displays many tell-tale flushes; they betray thoughts, and so do omissions. The reader understands as well as Nausikaa's father does, though not perhaps everything (*panta noei*). Structured elisions or disclosive blushes are ways of conveying what words do not say.

The unexpected 'Till then', out of temporal sequence, changes the key and the mood. We are no longer quite alone with the group of girls. Previous events have to be reviewed. The dark foreigner who watches Gerty rises from casual presence to a stylized role in a fictional convention; he is in fact 'strangely drawn' as the continuation says of his face. The text is true to the new pattern: 'His eyes burned into her' (*U* 13.412); we are on a new track whose origin we may trace in what preceded, and we are on the way to the predestined climax.

The casual observations offered here are mainly concerned with perception, with narrative revelation, and with the handling of time, an instance of dissimulation. 'Dissimulation'[19] here means that what happens simultaneously (Gerty does things and knows she is being watched with fascination; we are aware of two actors) is treated in separate ways, taken apart, *dis-simul*. Once we are aware of an exchange of glances, we read the sequence differently, giving attention also to the gentleman. Gerty is also dissimulating in the ordinary sense of dissembling.

So was Nausikaa dissembling. The Homeric flutter is not one of a parallel occurrence, nor of an influence (Joyce need not have derived Gerty's blushes from Pope's embroidering). An epic technique has been reused, the potency of absence, interdynamically.

NOTES

1 The form given in Liddell and Scott's *Greek-English Lexicon*. One may also find the sentence transposed: '*potamo gar ouk estin embenai dis to auto*', where the language seems to act out the fact that, once you come to the final '*auto*', it is indeed no longer what '*potamo*' was at the beginning.

2 The *Oxford English Dictionary of Quotations* (1959) has: '*Panta rhei, ouden menei.*' All is flux, nothing is stationary. Alluded to by Aristotle in *De Caelo*, 3.i.18 and elsewhere', 242. A German monograph says, in substance, 'The lapidary shape of the thought of the famous *Panta rhei* is based on wordings by Aristotle, where, however, it is not to be found in this form' (Wilhelm Capelle, *Die Vorsokratiker* [Stuttgart: Alfred Kröner Verlag n.d.], 132). The wording of the last part, '*wo es aber so wörtlich auch nicht steht*' (where it does not stand), is a beautiful exemplification of the principle that nothing remains stationary.

3 See Weldon Thornton, *Allusions in 'Ulysses'* (New York: Simon and Schuster 1973), 87–8.

4   Fritz Senn, 'Book of Many Turns', in *Joyce's Dislocutions: Essays on Reading as Translation*, John Paul Riquelme (ed.) (Baltimore: Johns Hopkins University Press 1984), 121–37.

5   The earliest witness is Eusebius in his *History of the Church*, III, 3.

6   See *JJQ*, 7 (Spring 1970), 216–7, n. 8.

7   Greek characters in the original.

8   The quotation is to be found in a 1967 reprint by the University of Chicago Press, 235.

9   Andrew Lang, Walter Leaf, and Ernest Myers, *The Iliad of Homer Done Into English Prose* (London: Macmillan 1891), 28.

10 Actually it is not easy to determine what Bloom *was* saying last.

11 William Empson, 'The Theme of *Ulysses*', in *A James Joyce Miscellany*, Third Series, Marvin Magalaner (ed.) (Carbondale: Southern Illinois University Press 1962), 127–54. In this version it would be Stephen Dedalus who plunges into something new and decisive.

    Bloom is right in his formula of courtesy, 'the greatest of pleasure': Molly in her imagination anticipates an involvement with Stephen as something gratifying and pleasant. Molly also uses 'plunging' in connection with fine young men: 'naked like a God or something and then plunging into the sea' (*U* 18.1347–8).

12 In 'Alone' Joyce used the myth: 'The sly reeds whisper to the night/A name—her name.' The classical background makes the whispering more mysterious and perhaps a trifle less than complimentary.

13 A newer translation revives the etymological potential of *providus* and says 'a man of vision' (*Horace: Satires and Epistles*, Niall Rudd [trans.] [Harmondsworth: Penguin Books 1973], 133).

14 Wilhelm Heinrich Roscher, *Ausführliches Lexikon der griechischen und römischen Mythologie*, 6 vols and 2 supp. vols (Leipzig: B.G. Teubner 1884–1937). This important source was discovered by Phillip F. Herring.

15 Similarly Rhesus is referred to as 'Odrysian leader', then as 'Sithonian', and again by the name (lines 130–40)—*aliter idem*.

16 The translation is by Davidson, *The Works of Virgil* (New York: Harper's Classical Library 1871), 184; Dryden's version is 'What arts can blind a jealous woman's eyes?'; William Morris translates: 'But who may hoodwink loving eyes?'

17 As Aeneas ponders his possible excuses, he realizes that it will be hard to use subterfuge: '*heu quid agat, quo nunc reginam ambire furentem*' (IV.283) (ah! what can he do? in what terms can he dare to approach the queen?). The verb used, 'ambire', literally means 'go around'. This is interesting in view of Molly's own tactics: 'I knew I could always get round him' (*U* 18.1579–80), but most likely a coincidence.

18 Book VI.79–81, in Alexander Pope, *The Odyssey of Homer*, Maynard Mack (ed.) (London: Methuen 1967), 208–9.

19 See Fritz Senn, 'The Narrative Dissimulation of Time', In *Myriadminded Man: Jottings on Joyce*, Rosa Maria Bosinelli, Paola Pugliatti and Romana Zacchi (eds) (Bologna: Cooperativa Libraria Universitaria 1986), 145ff.

BEYOND THE LEXICOGRAPHER'S REACH:
LITERARY OVERDETERMINATION

In implying a special status for 'literary' translation—as against some hypothetical 'ordinary', middle of the road, kind—the term would have to be defined, or at least given a more precise air than is possible. 'Literary' tends to imply a value judgement, inclusion in some canon which, again, would be hard to delimit. For practical and strategic purposes literature is characterized by seeming to be communication without 'noise', without anything that would ever be negligible, not significant. Everything is functional ('every*thing*' is already wrong, it is not a matter of things, but relations, movements, dynamisms). The 'message' is inseparable from its wording. Sound, word order, repetition, grammatical structure—they all contribute to the sense. Literature is what cannot be paraphrased: 'Being or not being, this ain't the problem' won't quite do. Translation, however, is paraphrase; the words in which the supposedly same thing is being said are others, foreign ones. Translation is in fact more 'para' than anything within the same culture.

That nothing is negligible, as was just claimed, is not a principle that could possibly survive in translation. Priorities must be set. They include above all the constraints of the real world which have to be obeyed. 'Correctness' normally dominates against, say, the sound or the length of a word, so that 'pass' may very well translate as '*Annäherungsversuch*' in certain circumstances. If the heavyfootedness of the German non-equivalent is part of the selective consideration, we are already using something like literary discernment.

'*Annäherungsversuch*' fails to suggest the passing nature of many passes, we could never even consider the ponderosity for Dorothy Parker's pithy 'Men seldom make passes/At girls who wear glasses.'

In the remarks that follow a few characteristic insolubilities will be highlighted in close-ups, literary intricacies taken from the prose of James Joyce, a prose that brings the all too familiar dilemmas into clearer focus. Even ideal lexicographical tools might be of no great assistance. But lexical entries may well help to spell out the problems. Literary translation cannot afford to ignore—though in point of fact it frequently has to—all the information that precedes the head entry of a word: oddities of spelling or pronunciation, usage labels, notes on origin, social variety, etc. The case in point is English *ptarmigan,* a kind of grouse (genus *Lagopus*). Its meaning would normally present no difficulty: equivalents would be *Schneehuhn* or *pernice bianca*, and so on, and these would generally do (in ornithological works a translator might want more detailed refinement, and, with a bit of educated rummaging, would find it). In a work of literature, however, the mere fact that some dictionaries do not carry the word at all may be relevant. The *Collins Cobuild English Language Dictionary*, for instance, according to its ground rules, does not list the word. Such an absence in a certain type of reference work may become part of the meaning. In James Joyce's *Ulysses* a character, at lunch, is thinking about strange foods and eating customs, he imagines genteel, upper-class, aristocratic dinners with 'evening dress, halfnaked ladies' who partake of delicacies like lobster, and you might overhear table talk of this kind:

Do ptake some ptarmigan (*U* 8.887)

That would be an easy dish to translate except for that wayward obtrusive and powerful initial 'p', which makes all the difference. The erratic letter in *ptake*, in a way, calls attention to all the dictionary entries that are usually bypassed. Such an entry would tell us, in its own chosen code, that the first letter in *ptarmigan* is silent (and might suggest a reason for the erratic spelling, perhaps some pseudo-Greek analogy). Such a word points out the difference of language as a sequence of sounds or as a chancy system of written signs, a difference that is of course particularly marked in English. The mere fact that some people would not know what the word stands for, or how to pronounce it, bestows a special aura and standing upon it (high-society diners would probably be familiar with the rare bird and its lettering). How to manage *ptarmigan*, in other words, is a social issue that is built into Joyce's phrase. That a few dictionaries need not acknowledge the word shows it to be unusual, puts it out of proletarian reach. One may go through life without ever knowing what *ptarmigan* is; but even someone wholly uninformed would at least deduce from German *Schneehuhn* that it is a kind of *Huhn*, therefore an edible bird. So a rendering like '*Nehmen Sie doch etwas Schneehuhn*' (Goyert 199–200) is paraphrastically accurate, once the silent correction is accepted, but falls short of its aim. *Schneehuhn* is prosaic and unexciting, without any flutter among the signifiers; the original sentence is above all a comment *on* a strange type of signifier. A *Schneehuhn* is not worthy of a remarkable phrase. The original hinges on the nonsense of *ptake* and not on *Lagopus albus* or *alpinus*. The bird in question is irrelevant *as* bird, but noteworthy as a lexical absurdity. '*Nehmen Sie doch etwas Schneehuhn*' translates everything but the reason for its being there. *Schneehuhn* and *ptarmigan* are not words of a feather.

With some patience and assiduity one might list requirements for an adequate translation: something edible, possibly fowl, limited to high society, with an odd lexical appearance and some educational obstacles. No dictionary is geared to needs of that kind. It becomes possible to imagine a viable translation in which the specific bird would give way to one with a similar de luxe spelling or pronunciation; even a change of the bill of fare from fowl to flesh, or strange-sounding fish, might be appropriate, as long as it allows of the same kind of jocular analogous transformation. In which case every translator would be afraid of the inevitable critic to point to his ornithological or culinary ignorance.

An existing Spanish translation—'*Psírvase un ptrozo de pchocha*' (Subirat 210)—uses an edible bird, *chocha*, and submits it and the environment to an invasion of 'p', which may well appear pointless to Spanish readers. The French version '*Ptrenez un pteu de ptarmigan, croyez-moi*' (Morel 172) makes quite a show of the intrusive and consistent 'pt' cluster in *ptarmigan* which, however, is not a French word but a foreign import mirrored in the surrounding idiom. The Italian translation follows this pattern: '*Ptrendete un ptò di ptarmigan*' (de Angelis 238): an alien word seems to affect the native ones by phonemic sympathy. Entirely within the German language, in contrast, is '*Bitte schnehmen Sie noch etwas Schneehuhn*' (Wollschäger 246), where, this time, the identical *Schneehuhn* modifies the active verb in a corresponding, imitative, technique: *schnehmen*. The modification is true to type, and yet of a different nature, not so much due to any peculiarity of the German vocabulary. The non-word might rather suggest a personal speech defect. In Hungarian the dish has been changed to cheese: 'Egy pppici ppparmezánit' (Miklós 214), with a visibly exaggerated labial which, again, looks more like the idiosyncracy of a speaker, maybe a stutter, than something radiating from the Hungarian word for parmesan. What is common to all these solutions is the attempt to recreate the event of phonetic encroachment.

Ironically though, all the translations offered that retain the fowl in question or the English *word* for it, also change the 'content'—reverberations, that is, which include complex cultural, societal, and linguistic constellations. The prime *raison d'être* for '*Do ptake some ptarmigan*' is its initial verbal absurdity. A Czech version opts for sound repetition in '*Treba nebo netreba jeste porci tetreva?*' (Skoumal 165), where the bird is a related one (something like a wood grouse) that can echo an idiomatic phrase that need not be phonetically violated.

We have no theoretical ground rules for translating absurd signifiers but still have to rely on inspiration or serendipity. What also gets naturally short shrift is the prior use of passages, the fact that many of them are handed down, all the way from direct quotation to faint echoes. Take some associations of someone on the beach, looking out on the ocean:

Children always want to throw things in the sea. Trust? Bread cast on the waters. (*U* 13.1250)

The problem at first sight might boil down to a contrast between an ordinary 'throw' and a more refined 'cast', and a marked change of diction, which is not attempted in:

Kinder wollen immer was ins Meer werfen. Glauben? Brot ins Wasser geworfen. (Go 430)

Here *werfen* is repeated, bread is thrown *into* water; the impression is of repetition and of waste—'*Brot ins Wasser geworfen.*' We remain on the beach, here and now; no tradition is at hand, a tradition that English readers might either vaguely sense or bring to mind directly: 'Cast thy bread upon the waters: for thou shalt find it after many days' (*Ecclesiastes* 11:1). By way of this biblical source nothing has in fact been thrown away, the point is in the finding again, therefore 'Trust?' (which is also somehow echoed in 'cast', a minor fringe benefit that in translation naturally has to be sacrificed as peripheral). In German the essential evocation of the biblical proverb has to be based on Luther's version, so Hans Wollschläger's informed rendering is:

Kinder wolln immerzu Sachen ins Meer schmeißen. Vertrauen? Laß dein Brot übers Wasser fahren. (Wo 532)

This preserves the tension between children's habits and a venerable citation. The wording from *Ecclesiastes* is unavoidable, even though in German it has never become a household phrase. '*Laß dein Brot übers Wasser fahren*' has a biblical ring but does not ring a bell. Because a common heritage has gone different ways, a German reader is less likely to have any trust in the bread's ultimate return. Associations alter cases. The sentence in German also emerges far less naturally from the preceding observation; Luther's composite *fahren lassen* does not easily lend itself to a passive form, the imperative, unabbreviated ('*dein*' can hardly be left out), had to be kept. It would be easy to spell out more minor shortcomings in what seems to be an optimal achievement.

Joyce's next and last work, *Finnegans Wake*, twists the biblical phrase into more accretive meaning and may therefore serve as an extreme of literary overdetermination without any wastage. The selection begins:

how his breadcost...

We can still make out the proverbial 'bread cast'; only one vowel has been changed and the two words run together. Now the cost of bread becomes part of the associative network. But an entirely new overtone also rises which is developed

how his breadcost on the voters would be a comeback... (*FW* 510.27)

The biblical bread cast on the waters so as to come back has been overlaid with a political broadcast to the voters (votes, too, can be cast). Such election addresses may well concern the cost of bread and may be considered, by the candidates, good returns for a comeback. Joyce's phrase, based on a recognizable biblical matrix, works out in several areas, it joins daily needs to religious and political hopes or promises. It is full of semantic comebacks. The phrase contains nothing—bread cast on the waters, cost of bread, broadcast to the voters, etc.—that in itself would defy translation, but the point, obviously, is not a serial stock-taking, but the economic conciseness, the multiple duty of all elements, the contextual shifts. The sentence does what it pretends to say: it allows nothing to be cast away, wasted, for good: every element is being recycled. We can see the deprivation in a translation of the above into French, a version that has been completely streamlined and pushed in one particular direction:

sur le dos de ceux qui l'avaient élu pour lui donner la réplique (Lavergne 533)

The literary translator's first step is often the laborious hunt for quotations in the target language. Often they exist and if they do, they do not always help (like *'fahren lassen'*). Few passages by Sappho, Dante, Rabelais, Milton, Cervantes are memorable in translation. On another level, the words of many popular songs have never been put into other languages, songs like Thomas Moore's *Irish Melodies*. They once were commonplace and familiar in Ireland, but hardly outside. One of them, entitled 'The Meeting of the Waters', celebrates the beautiful vale of Avoca where two rivers flow together. The poet's statue was put up in Dublin, still to be seen, and in *Ulysses* it leads to the following remarks: 'They did right to put him up over a urinal: meeting of the waters' (*U* 8.415). The urinary confluence can be salvaged without effort: *'Treffpunkt der Wasser—incontro di correnti—Conjonction des Eaux'*, etc. But few German, Italian, French readers are put in a position to hear a song title, or to be aware of the poetic counterpoint. Another Thomas Moore song is about the glorious Irish past and begins with an evocation of a national emblem and the ancient capital: 'The harp that once in Tara's hall/The soul of Music shed,/Now hangs as mute on Tara's walls/As if that soul had fled.' Such an opening line can give rise to a jocular variation like: 'The harp that once did starve us all' (*U* 8.606), which might be considered just surface mockery, or else a social comment on retrospective patriotism, or even a recall of another Irish historical event, the Famine of the 1840s. In translation hardly more is possible than to *signal* some quotation: *'"Die Harf", die einst uns hungern ließ'* (Wollschläger 235), but no specific resonance can come alive. Nor can a bathetic drop to 'The harp that once or twice...' be transferred into another culture when no prototype is there to be called up.

Such frustrations are well known to every translator of modified quotations. It is the most specific items that, intriguingly, have to be sacrificed. Occasionally the translator is lucky, as when Joyce incorporates the words of an opera, Flotow's *Martha*, which were originally German, *'Martha, Martha, du entschwandest'*. For once there seems to be the original to fall back on when this aria is being sung:

—When first I saw that form endearing...
— *...* Sorrow from me seemed to depart. (*U* 11.665)

The German is '*Ach! so fromm, ach so traut, hat mein Auge sie erschaut!*', and it would normally be used with impunity. However, the words of the song are reflected and transformed by the audience, who feel 'that flow endearing flow over skin limbs human heart soul spine.' Music affects them physically; 'form endearing' instantly becomes a 'flow endearing'. The song also easily blends into memories of early courtship: 'First night when first I saw her...' Later associations are made possible, from 'second I saw' (in the sense 'at the moment, second') to the implied numeral 'first I saw'. The words are then transferred to an incongruous context: 'A frowzy whore' comes along and provokes an echo: 'When first he saw that form endearing' (*U* 11.1253).

It stands to reason that the correct rendering of the aria, '*Ach! so fromm, ach so traut*' with its homely overtones would never correspond to the associative network; '*fromm*' would be particularly out of place. If the aria had been performed in German, it would have generated wholly different associations; if, consequently, '*Ach so fromm*' were to serve as the basic text for a translation, whole passages would have to be altered accordingly, ultimately *Ulysses* would have to be retextured. So that, in this case, synthetic lines had to be confected out of the surrounding passages: '*Als meinem Blick zum ersten Mal ihr süsses Bild erschien*' (Goyert 307), or '*Als ich ihr lockend Bild zum erstenmal erblickte*' (Wollschläger 379). With the effect that the melody is thrown away, that the connoisseur of the popular opera does not hear the tune from the words on the page. The German retranslation of an English translation has replaced the original words of *Martha*. Such a paradoxical necessity is in part also due to the liberties generally taken with opera texts; libretto translations owe their first duty to the sound and rhythm of the music, or rhyme, and not the exact content. In *Ulysses* the signifiers of the lines have become independent starting points for echoes and correspondences.

What translates least is translation itself, the process of change (like 'form' ➤ 'flow'), or the deviation from a norm. 'Ptake' or 'the harp that once did starve us all' are meaningful deviations. Seen differently, they are mistakes. Modernist writers knew with Freud, though not necessarily from him, that mistakes have their own causation, are not to be dismissed as meaningless interferences. For writers, mistakes, errors, are also economic devices, semantic loaves and fishes. The *Finnegans Wake* sentence quoted above consists of nothing but fumbles: 'breadcost' has no lexical existence, is deficient, but its deficiency resolves itself into exuberance: biblical bread cast on waters, a broadcast, the cost of bread, and all the interrelationships we may bring to bear on the ingredients. When a stage orator is carried away and babbles of the idle rich 'shooting peasants or phartridges' (*U* 15.1396), the nonsense indicates, at the very least, the speaker's agitation and blundering. We mentally supply the intended meaning: shooting pheasants and partridges (again birds with spelling problems attached to them), an exaggerated carnage ('shooting peasants') and possibly a rude noise ('phart') are thrown in for free, material for speculation and interpretation. No doubt the dynamism went unnoticed when Georg Goyert in 1930 seriously translated '*Bauern und Rebhühner schiessen*' (Goyert 521). The expressive blunder was accommodated, up to a point, in the French version: '*qu'ils tirent les paisants et les ferdrix*' (Morel 457).

Joyce had used such economy already in *Dubliners* where an elderly woman is reminiscing about her dead brother, a priest:

If we could only get one of them new-fangled carriages that makes no noise that Father O'Rourke told him about – them with the rheumatic wheels. (*D* 14)

Something went wrong with them 'rheumatic wheels'. It is interesting to see how translations deal with this oddity. We find officious interference, tacit correction, normative emendations; the wheels in question are, of course, *pneumatic*, and an unfractured reality is given in: '*di quelle con le ruote gommate*' (Cancogni 17). There may be an explicative paraphrase that sets things right: '*de ces voitures à roues pour rhumatisants*' (Reynaud 12), or '*die so leise und leicht fahren, dass der Rheumatismuskranke nichts davon merkt*' (Goyert, *Dublin* 16). Since the erudite adjectives *pneumatic* and *rheumatic* are equally available in most European languages, it would be simple to reproduce the malapropism literally. A few translations mark the deviation typographically (which Joyce never did): '*quelle con le ruote* reumatiche' (Balboni 20). Most, however, just translate—what otherwise might be mere inattention—word by word: '*quelli con le ruote reumatiche*' (Papi 8); '*die mit den rheumatischen Rädern*' (Zimmer 15). A new French translation substitutes a mistake of a different construction: '*vous savez, celles qui ont des roues à pneumoniques*' (Aubert 41).

For once the 'literal' (perhaps even unreflected) rendering is the most adequate. Phrases like '*mit rheumatischen Rädern*' reproduce the right wrongness, retain also the social situation, the lack of educational possibilities. A new invention put air in rubber tires and called them, scientifically, *pneumatic*. Someone not educated might well put a similar kind of word, one all too familiar, *rheumatic,* in its stead. The substitution is psychologically and sociologically right, an expression moreover of the state of women of the period. The shift has thematic reverberations: the whole story, 'The Sisters', is about illness and corruption; spiritual values are being debased. A term like *pneuma* (which is not in the text, 'present' only as a ghost) in New Testament Greek happens to denote the holy spirit, *hagion pneuma*. That a disease has supplanted such a sacred concept is quite in tune with what the story is about. The verbal slip on this level microscopically mirrors what we find elsewhere. It is, in other words, functional or overdetermined. Translation is possible simply because both Greek derivates are part of many vocabularies, a highly exceptional state of affairs.

Literary texts are overdetermined. Ideally, they carry no wastage, no noise, their fittingness is all-round. One result is that many diverse, partial, translations become possible, different according to preferences. It does not seem that translatology has made too many efforts as yet even to tabulate all the various aspects to be considered. At a certain stage it will have to devote itself to the problem of translating movement, change, distortion, deviation—in other words, how to translate translation itself.

BIBLIOGRAPHY

Collins Cobuild English Language Dictionary, J. Sinclair et al. (London & Glasgow: Collins 1987).

Joyce, James (1922), *Ulysses*: the Corrected Text edited by Hans Walter Gabler (Harmondsworth: Penguin Books). [*U*]

—— (1914), *Dubliners* (London: Granada Publishing Ltd 1984).

—— (1926), *Gens de Dublin*, Yva Fernandez, Hélène du Pasquier & Jacques Paul Reynaud (trans.) (Paris: Plon). [Reynaud]

—— (1939), *Finnegans Wake* (London: Faber & Faber). [*FW*]

—— (1945), *Ulises*, traducción por J. Salas Subirat (Buenos Aires: Santiago Rueda 1959). [Subirat]

—— (1964), *Gente di Dublino*, traduzione di Franca Cancogni (Torino: Einaudi). [Cancogni]

—— (1968), *Ulisse*, unica traduzione integrale autorizzata di Giulio de Angelis (Milano: Arnoldo Mondadori). [de Angelis]

—— (1970), *Gente di Dublino*, traduzione Maria Pia Balboni (Milano: Fratelli Fabbri Editore). [Balboni]

—— (1974), *Dublin*, Deutsch von Georg Goyert (Basel: Rhein-Verlag). [Goyert, Dublin]

—— (1974), *Dubliner*, Deutsch von Dieter E. Zimmer (Frankfurt: Suhrkamp). [Zimmer]

—— (1974), *Gens de Dublin*, traduit par Jacques Aubert (Paris: Gallimard). [Aubert]

—— (1974), *Ulysses*, fordította Szentkuthy Miklós (Budapest: Europa Könyvkiadó). [Miklós]

—— (1976), *Gente di Dublino*, a cura di Marco Papi (Milano: Aldo Garzanti). [Papi]

—— 1976), *Odysseus*, prelozil Aloys Skoumal (Praha: Odeon). [Skoumal]

—— (1982), *Finnegans Wake*, traduit et présenté par Philippe Lavergne (Paris: Gallimard). [Lavergne]

—— (1948), *Ulysse*, traduction intégrale par Auguste Morel, assisté de Stuart Gilbert, entièrement revue par Valery Larbaud et l'auteur (Paris: Gallimard). [Morel]

—— (1956), *Ulysses*, vom Verfasser autorisierte Übersetzung von Georg Goyert (Zürich: Rhein Verlag). [Goyert]

—— (1976), *Ulysses*, übersetzt von Hans Wollschläger (Frankfurt: Suhrkamp Verlag). [Wollschläger]

LINGUISTIC DISSATISFACTION AT THE *WAKE*

In the extended sighs of mine to be unfolded in these observations, I am sorry to say—and those who know of my skeptical bias will appreciate this—that I can speak, for the first and presumably only time in my career, with full authority.[1] For once I know more than anyone else about the subject. Because I am the subject: my own responses to, well, our *Finnegans Wake* scholarship. That limits its validity. But I also assume I am not alone in my uneasiness. My reluctant Defeatist's Creed, as conversations reveal, is silently shared by at least a few—and it is fortunately not contagious for the competent majority.

When, some three decades ago, I began to occupy myself seriously with *Finnegans Wake*, we did not understand much of it; and there was much to do. ('Understand' is meant in the most trite sense of the word.) Now, after some thirty years, much research has been done about it; publications have increased perhaps a hundredfold. And we do not understand much of *Finnegans Wake*. 'Understand' is meant in the most trite sense of the word: in the way we would understand a phrase in another language. In other words, we have—collectively—not done our most basic homework, the sort of perhaps pedestrian semantic rummaging that would make all the further, superior, exertions that depend upon it remotely possible. I find this collective failure sad. And I wonder why I seem to be almost alone to find it so. The response is one of *dissense* in the original meaning of a different *sensus*, a different feel, emotion, perhaps an irrational one. It is a *dis*intuition.

When I set out in characteristic youthful Wakean elation, I imagined that, by a pooling of resources and small-scale discoveries, we might arrive at the sort of minimal, provisional grasp that after a period—a necessary, inevitable, initial, period—of groping in the dark would enable *Wake* scholarship to become honest. I no longer imagine so. We obviously can proceed without even the semblance of a workable basis, but with self-complacency.

There are, in broad simplification, several ways of dealing with *Finnegans Wake*. It can be approached abstractly, theoretically, and we all do so up to a point. No present-day theory, moreover, would be acceptable if it did not take the extreme, the superlative, case of the *Wake* into account. For the *Wake* is superlative in whichever perspective. Whatever *Finnegans Wake* is, it is *most*. For all its decenteredness, the *Wake* also centralizes all traditional peripheries. But whatever we think of theories, those currently fashionable or any other, we will hardly offend their adherents by implying that their ambition would ever be to help us understand the *Wake*. ('Understand' in the most trite sense of the word.) It is neither their aspiration nor their function. It is wholly legitimate for critics or scholars to think about the largest possible issues, literature as metaphysics. It is legitimate for thinkers to include *Finnegans Wake* in their broad spectrum even if they never bother to unravel any of its verbiage. One might ask, perhaps, whether at any one given instant of time there may not be more theories produced, or circulated, than can be consumed by any honest reader, but that is beside the point. I am therefore not addressing those with a theoretical concern. The theories, in my view, have not failed; there is no way in which they could. My remarks merely suggest that at least some of the theories, no matter how sublime and cavalier their intentions, are also dependent, to a small but nevertheless ultimate degree, on preliminary, humble, philological, spade work and low-level curiosity.

the trite, hypolectic sense of 'understanding'

What is that 'understanding' that I put so much stress on against the grain, as it seems, of Wakean behaviour? It is here meant in the most elementary sense of philological support. If in,

Sir Tristram... had passencore rearrived (*FW* 3.4)

we cannot detect French *pas encore*, or at least a non-syntactic approximation to 'passenger', then we are at a loss. Once we have got so far as to enlist a French meaning, there remains still a lot of understanding to be done on whatever higher plane we choose, but that sort of inexhaustible interpretation out there—and up there—is very much facilitated by primary semantic translations of the *pas encore* sort. Nothing more exciting is meant by elementary understanding.

I will name this simple, basic, limited, ground-floor, understanding. It is interesting to note that the metaphor *under-stand* in Latin and Greek has different, powerful, meanings: *sub-stance*, and *hypo-stasis* have become meaningful in the History of the Church as well as in Joyce's works. I make use of this transferential link in supposing that a very elementary grasp of what words and phrases and even sentences might mean—in the schoolboy glossing sense—is a kind of *sub*-stance for whatever construction—or structure—we will erect upon it. When I say 'understand' in the following I will limit myself to such elementary translations of a Wakean surface, let us call them *Wake insignifiers*, into something *prima facie* comprehensible and assimilable to our views of the world. It has to do with words, with speaking, Latin *legere*, Greek *legein*, *lexis* and all that, so the underlying job is called 'hypo-lexis'. Once we have hypolected, say, 'thuartpeatrick' into: *tu es Petrus*/'thou art Peter', and, perhaps, 'thwart', 'pea', 'trick' (*FW* 3.10), and all the rest, there is still a lot to do about all the emergent meaningful substances. But the ground (a most shaky ground, to be sure) is at least laid for a more valuable understanding—'overstanding' may be what such secondary and later interpretations could be called. *Wake* readers seem to engage in a little bit too much of premature overstanding.

My contention now is simply that we do not have enough hypolectic substance to proceed in a scholarly way. I take this back, speaking only for myself: that *I* do not have it. This is not a contention so much as a 'feeling'. A sense of tremendous passage to passage frustration. This ignorance still looms very large against intermittent insights. In order to get a predictable misconception out of the way from the start, my assumptions—though it may appear like that—are *not* that the basic and intrinsic obscurity of the *Wake* could ever be glossingly transformed into daylight lucidity and reason, either on a hypolectic or any superior level. No ultimate clarity is aimed at, no neat solution, decisive formula. There will always be, and should, enough semantic turbulence and contextual options. There is no danger of our ever understanding too much. I am merely arguing for a subsistence minimum of comprehension.

before and after

I am addressing only a straggling handful of anachronistic attentive readers who go on searching and hoping to find something like hypolectic meaning. For only they can have a part in the failure that I am talking about. Among those who do pay attention to the text (whether there is something like a text or not), a basic distinction in approach and critical technique seems possible. It may have to do with temperamental differences, or the set-up of our minds.

When it comes to the late Joyce, the 'difficult' Joyce, two broad procedures may conveniently be separated. I call them 'pre-quoting' and 'post-quoting' (apologies for using a word beginning with 'post', but it is meant literally and accurately). The way quotations in critical work are handled is a good rule of thumb. There are those scholars who are proving some thesis, making some point, and to illustrate it they habitually end the point they are making with an appropriate quotation. The quote shows what has been submitted: QED, in terminal, clinching, evidence. This is often necessary. It supposes that the meaning of the quote is—more or less—obvious. Postquotation is an excellent traditional approach.

In *Finnegans Wake* meaning, however, micro-meaning, is not always obvious, though often approximately extractable. The 'pre-quoter' tends to regard a passage as something primarily cryptic, in need of commentary before anything constructive can be done with it; and so he or she tends to put the passage first in clear view, and THEN tries to figure out what its contents may be.

The classification is not one of values: obviously we need, for our multiple endeavours, both post- and prequoters. If all our criticism were of the postquoting type, it would assume that the *Wake* can be studied like most other literary works where we know, at least, what most of the words, sentences, stanzas, paragraphs, etc. mean or do within a determinable context. At times the simplifications of postquotative assumption are inevitable. But the *Wake* emphatically demands a certain kind of initiatory glossing. A good bit of preliminary exploration paves the way for all further sublimations. On the other hand, as we all know there is nothing more tedious than a pedantic, uninspired, prequoter and commentator.

It is the prequoters, that is readers like myself, that have failed in their aims. Perhaps fortunately, but also precariously, we somehow seem to manage the *Wake* without the usual prerequisites, the kind of supports we have, for example, for Dante's *Divina Commedia*: in order to read the work, a certain knowledge of Italian, of medieval data, of theology comes in very useful. We do not have, as yet, the analogous bases for *Finnegans Wake*. Though, surprisingly, nobody seems to care. Some of us go on regardless—I mean regard-less—with all the appearance of scientific procedure.

esthetic expectations

Of course *Finnegans Wake* does not exist, except as a collection of signs on paper; what it mainly is ('mainly' from the point of view adopted here) is a bundle of vague, maybe congenital, ingrained, expectations. My *Wake*, and what I expect from it, is different from other readers'.

As an example, of necessity concrete and textual, I take two *Wake* readers of very high standards of relevancy—both minimalist and impatient with free-for-all interpretation—who once joined issue over a trifling matter. Roland McHugh long ago drew up a list of Cornish words that roused the late Nathan Halper to vivid protest. Halper was ever impatient with word lists unless the context signalled—to *his* satisfaction—some pervasive authorial intention. McHugh's list included a Cornish word *pyth*, explained as 'a thing, an article, a substance', and he found it in a fish-and-bread passage:

you would quaffoff his fraudstuff and sink teeth through that pyth of a flowerwhite bodey (*FW* 7.13)[2]

Halper's objections were, (1) that *pyth* is merely an older form of *pith*, a historical spelling variant, and, more importantly, (2) that this 'scholarly addition', dragged—or 'forced'—into the passage, only 'dims its radiance. The meaning is diminished.' The 'quality' of the book is therefore 'debased'.[3]

There is no doubt that Halper was right: the radiance *is* dimmed, the quality debased—*for him*. I am convinced that for Roland McHugh the inclusion of a Cornish substance had some satisfaction of *equal* emotional validity. The point is simply that something like subjective satisfaction comes into play, some private esthetic requirement. Once the semantic presence of a Cornish *pyth* is at stake in a minor controversy, we may wonder how to go about discussing the problem.

True, there is no Cornish ambiance in the passage. Even so, a Joycean reflex—conditioned by Ulyssean trinitarian tossings—might at least combine the pith of bread with the dictionary rendering of 'substance'—a meaning gained from a *Cor*nish word. I am not sure our passage would gain essentially by such consubstantial linking;

the associations by themselves, however, seem equitable ('pyth = Cornish substance' is in McHugh 1980).

The difference of opinion might be phrased simply and representatively: one (type of) reader is content with 'p-y-th' as a spelling variant or older form; while others remain frustrated until the wayward 'y' in pyth is accounted for, the semantic blank removed. I belong to this category of philological agonizers, and am definitely *not* satisfied with the intrusive letter 'y' in the word. For this reason I groped around in dictionaries and toyed with a Greek verb *pytho* (to rot or decay), and naturally with *Pythia* and the oracle at Delphi (as others may have done). I do not believe that those meanings obtain at all; but I emphasize that for some of us the gap—the substantial deficiency—rankles. It remains an irritant, though a minor one (at least we can accommodate 'pyth' into the daily bread of our surface understanding). In itself it is insignificant, but it represents so many other similar irritants. It represents the norm in the *Wake*, not a rare, isolated, exception. It militates against comfort.

gishing

At the 1977 Symposium in Dublin there was a similar clash of *Wake* attitudes, a friendly and instructive one, when Mark Troy, discussing a passage:

And gish! how they gushed away, the pennyfares, a whole school for scamper, with their sashes flying sish behind them, all the little pirlypettes! (*FW* 80.33)

wondered aloud whether the word 'gish', that initiates a minuscule cluster of sound variation, might refer to a name Gish in some Egyptian source. It was at this point that Margot Norris interrupted with evident signs of impatience—an impatience that I am sure is shared by other readers—and proposed vehemently that we should, at long last, get away from pointless concern about single words and their meaning and—for *Wake*'s sake—rise to the larger issues, see and discuss the work as a whole, not a collection of minute puzzles. I always hoped there might be an occasion to convene the two contestants and to focus on the difference in our orientation, our tacit expectations. Naturally if we stopped at every word and worried at its philological justification (especially when 'gish' may be considered to earn its keep already by doing an onomatopoetic job), we could never even envisage such a thing as *Finnegans Wake*, much more than the sum of its mysterious parts; it would disperse into bits. But perhaps equally naturally, how can we do something like understand a whole complex if we cannot come to terms with its individual intricacies? Two different, complementary and necessary attitudes.

I can share the impatience of the panoramic *Wake* scholar. But I also empathize with the uneasiness of the thwarted mini-glosser. And in exaggeration I might state that I cannot dare to take a scholarly pose in view of a work in which there is not one little wayward 'pyth' once in a while, but which seems to abound in unexplained 'pyths' and 'gishes', to say nothing of entire phrases, of syntax, whole paragraphs, chapters, most overall contexts—and this *still*, after my own thirty years of once very devoted and at times laborious and *vain* application. In the old pioneering days we could take semantic gaps in our optimistic stride, but perhaps less so now, with our shelves bristling with *Wake* studies.

In my intestinal response, *Finnegans Wake* is still disproportionally full of the elementary cruxes we bypass. Of course we can disregard every single one of them; we have to. The stress is on proportion. For reading to be profitable, a certain amount of insight may provide us with a working basis so we can face the surrounding obscurities a bit better. A small test was made at a conference in Leeds (13–17 July 1987) by showing a few lines, the beginning of I, 4 (*FW* 48.1–4), to the resident experts, and none of us could come up with anything pertinent. What surprises me is how scholars blissfully manage to overlook such dark patches in their disheartening plenitude. Of course we can all, on demand, brilliantly display a selected passage that we unfold beautifully; if we were honest, we would have to admit that most passages do not unfold in this way at all. *Finnegans Wake*, in other words, still has too much *terra incognita*, white spots on the map.

Compare for a quiet moment how much hermeneutic energy has been lavished, and rightly so, on a single obscure phrase in the short story 'Eveline': *'Derevaun seraun!'* (*D* 40). Though we can easily ascribe it to the confused, garbled state of a mind that lost its reasoning, it does not leave us in peace and becomes almost automatically one of the most intriguing parts of the whole story. Don't we all wish we knew who 'Madeline the mare' is in Proteus, from what poem she originated? And yet we are at least fairly sure she is some horse, commemorated or purely fictional. Now imagine the same sort of conscience applied to the *Wake*. It would not get us very far. In spite of that, we have got pretty far, but in the process also lost part of our con-science, the urge for preliminary, fundamental, knowing. So maybe I am arguing, obsessively, for an ingredient of linguistic *Agenbite of Inwit.*

I am arguing for a subsistence minimum of comprehension. Characteristic of our Wakean insights is their uneven distribution. Those passages which we seem to understand best become richer and richer as we go on; more and more dynamic signipotence seems to emerge. I myself recirculate the same old favourite samples and they seem to acquire more relevant and intriguing meaning each time. Other passages, alas, remain inert, almost wholly impenetrable. It is the proportion that frustrates me, the disenchanting balance of a few euphoric gains against many depressive losses.

There are, in concrete terms, too many blanks in *Annotations* (McHugh 1980) where we can hardly afford so many. Since I used to be a silent collaborator in those *Annotations*, since my own spare notes have gone into it, I am not of course complaining about the compiler, but am selfishly worried about *my* ignorance that does not seem to have decreased very substantially in all those years. The *Wake Newslitter* was launched precisely and predominantly to assemble helpful hypolectic glosses, and at its best it made quite a few of them commonly available. It has also, inevitably, spread a large clutter of not very valuable guesses, annotative dust, lacklustre encumbrances, the kind of explications that we may hold in abeyance against a rainy hour, but that do not really do much to enliven the text—'enliven' may be an operative concept.

How do we 'evaluate' a hypolectic gloss? As many arguments in print and at meetings have shown, we cannot reach a scholarly agreement. What we produce are possibilities and declarative circularities. (In the long run, sure enough, there may be something like an agreed canon of information to be thought worthy of perpetuation and repetition.) But we will hardly arrive at a consensus. Nor of course should we.

Most Joyceans have the experience of *Wake* Reading Groups. Participants very soon tend to go in two directions. On the one hand the free-for-all, encyclopaedic, sweepers, on the other the selective purists. The two camps do not usually convince each other. Things are not fundamentally different in, well, scholarship, where we perpetually waver between the Charybdis of the associative shotgun approach and the Skylla of constrictive pertinence, or even—Joyce help us—authorial intention or reductive Notebook evidence. And in between we have all those readings that had best been kept in a referential limbo or cold storage, meanings that may be corroborated by

further orders, and often are. We have been trying to generate theories of relevance, or rules, or guide-lines, but the dilemma is clearly
not to be solved that way.

emotivation

There is one kind of evidence that we have not yet accepted within
our critical scope, and it is not at all intellectual. It is the emotive
response which is often a physiological reaction. As far as I know,
only Georgia Herlt[4] has ventured into this area, paying attention to
facial expressions, laughs, gasps, signs of surprise, stupor—what a
videocamera might pick up, and, for all I know, physiological
responses, heartbeat, perspiration, blood pressure. We might imagine
an anoded *Wake* reader in a laboratory. The facts would be worth
knowing, the affective power of *Wake* texts. I am referring to the cognitive joy most readers are familiar with, which is released among
novices when, for example, in a well-known passage the two words
'atoms and ifs' (*FW* 455.17) translate into our first parents, and our
adepts begin to rearrange the atoms of understanding into new and
appropriate molecular combinations, satisfactory constellations that
are immediately valid.

Something in us often responds with approbation (or conversely
with a sort of disgust, a noticeable resentment at an inappropriate
reading). What I refer to from reading groups—in fact what makes
these activities so uniquely rewarding—are the tell-tale inarticulate
symptoms: the titterative response, the chuckulative release, the
hypolectic exultation (*exult*—'leap out' of a neutral frame). We have
no reason to dismiss somewhat high-handedly this 'lots of fun' part
of *Finnegans Wake*, its potential getting-a-kick-out-of-ability. So the
'rapture test' is a useful indication. It is the glory of *Wake* reading
that it provides that thrill of recognition, the semiogenetic orgasm. I
am talking of the ineluctable modality of the Aha-effect.

This may be the point to mention *Hart's Law*. Clive Hart—on the
level of hypolectic *Wake* glossing—on occasion said succinctly something like: 'If you think you're right, you're wrong. If you are right,
you *know* you are right!' He meant the intellectual and emotive burst
of 'Aha!', the inner certainty of recognition. So far, so thrilling —and
so subjective. For of course *Wake* readers are heterorgasmic. My 'aha'
may be your yawn. Many published raptures are wholly private
ecstases, not communicable. But the inevitable subjectivity of the
effect does not of course deny its existence and the emotive force of
Wakean recognition. And so it is precisely that the triumphs of

Finnegans Wake are the main reason for its frustrations, the necessary reverse. Spoiled and conditioned by the unique *Wake* Aha-experiences, the semantic rapture, we come to expect very much—too much perhaps, and are then all the more discontent when let down. We become the victims of our interpretative successes and scores. I tend to think that most passages are potentially capable of epiphanic ahas, if only we could get at them, if we but knew. So Wakean emotivation raises expectations that then are but rarely fulfilled. The defeats, at least in my emotional economy, predominate.

Most of our hypolectic glosses are in a somewhat sluggish limbo of possibility, or carried by some unexciting systematic compulsion. We have, collectively, produced a lot of commentary that does not set the Liffey on fire. And I do not blame us, for we are of course doing our obtuse best. We are up, in actual fact, against the semantic inertia of large blocks, an inertia which is our own collaborative bluntness. If this is inevitable, part of the ground rules, we might at least acknowledge it, not ignore the condition and pretend it no longer exists.

The author himself, who gave us valuable exemplary insights, could come up with strange commentaries. In explaining,

L'Arcs en His Cieling Flee Chinx on the Flur

(an earlier version of *FW* 104.13), Joyce pointed out that 'flur' 'suggests also Flut (flood) and Fluss (river)',[5] and thereby clearly opened the flood(Flut-)gates of concurrent fluvial wishy-washiness. I do hope the principle of adapting final consonants will not spread generally, for it might easily change any stray 'floor' into flood or even floss, and why not flot?, without contributing greatly to the valuable knowledge of meaning.

My remarks are not aimed at those scholars who—in wholly legitimate enterprises—compound Wakean obscurity with theoretical impenetrabilities, but at the diminishing group of those hankering after some basic philological illumination, those who want to transform parts of the overwhelming ignorance into a modicum of live knowledge—those, in other words, who cannot quite step outside the old humanist tradition. Those who want minimal contextual and semantic supports, to which discoveries and obscurities can be related, even if these supports will remain in dire need of modification or later replacement.

Shifting the ground a little, I wonder how many *Wake* scholars feel the same embarrassment when in group readings, within which they are, by definition, the expert, they have to admit that they do not really know even an overall, or approximate, meaning of a sentence, nor what its context may be.

Rather than deplore the lack of sufficient hypolectic subsistence, one may say Who cares anyway? Who, but a few old-fashioned philistines? Perhaps nothing is held more in contempt than the accumulation of useful philological meanings. It is indeed quite possible, no doubt, to say something relevant about *Finnegans Wake* without ever stooping to the actual 'curios of signs' (*FW* 18.17) on its 600 pages. Some of us would not be caught thus stooping, not to save their academic reputations. By now *Finnegans Wake* is known to the entire literary crowd by osmosis, by hearsay, by rumour—at several removes, enough to generalize from. In fact perhaps the most enlightening insights do come from those who never put their noses close to the text at all. And the myopia of prequotational close readers is not, needless to say, always a great advantage. Ultimately, however, *some* devoted close reading has to be done, if only to give the panoramic luminaries the ground to look down on.

No matter how abstract we are, how disdainful of prerequisite spade work, we still and in spite of the *Wake*'s 'nocturnal' concerns, tend to use metaphors of light and there is still a group of researchers who actually try, as the image has it, to 'throw light on' the obscurities rather than increase them by further abstraction.

Our shared but not acknowledged hypolectic deficiency imparts to most *Wake* scholarship (certainly including my own) an element of pretense. Pretense with a stress on *pre*: there is something premature about our activities, perhaps we do not as yet have an alternative. But pretense also in one of the original Latin senses: of offering or showing something deceptively, something for which we are not ready. Perhaps of course we'll never be and we simply cannot wait. Perhaps we simply have to be 'pretumbling forever' (*FW* 13.18), it is in the order of that preposterous book that begins with Fin and ends with nothing but an urge to begin. So I find it difficult to take most of our results very seriously—this is certainly true of the customary reprocessings of all the previous guesswork in print; quoting secondary works, that is quoting ourselves, is one way to bypass the issues. What mainly replaces customary understanding in *Finnegans Wake* is familiarity. Puzzles become less puzzling by repetition. Often we may not know what a phrase means, but we find out, with satisfaction, that it occurs elsewhere again, in modified form. Our commentaries often consist in transversal leaps, a system of cross-references. That is in the nature of the book, but frequently the leaping becomes self-sufficient, a concatenation of undigested *déjà-lus*.

Since, in the nature of the *Wake*, we may never have sufficient hypolectic supports, perhaps a certain amount of pretense is inevitable. We could not go on without *presumption*: we have to consume, or perform, before we are ready. Even so, a bit of critical *post*-sumption might be a sobering check, even though it will make our tasks more difficult and circumspect.

NOTES

1   This is a revised version of a talk at the '*Finnegans Wake* Contexts' Symposium, Leeds, 13–17 July 1987.

2   Roland McHugh, 'The Language of Tintangle', *A Wake Newslitter* VIII, 5 (October 1971), 76.

3   Nathan Halper, 'Pyth', *A Wake Newslitter* XIV, 1 (February 1977), 15–16.

4   Georgia Herlt, '*Finnegans Wake*—Ein Lese-Abenteuer: Versuch einer Aktivierung seines Sprachmaterials anhand der Jolleschen "Einfachen Formen"', unpublished doctoral dissertation.

5   Letter to Harriet Shaw Weaver, 26 July 1927, *Selected Letters of James Joyce*, Richard Ellmann (ed.) (London: Faber & Faber 1975), 326.

INDEX

The index contains names, terms and words/phrases that are commented on. There is no entry for *Ulysses*, since most essays deal with it anyway.

à propos 187
Achilles, Achilleus 120, 163, 188, 196
active/passive 18ff
Aeneas 211, 215
Aeneid 135, 211
'Aeolus' 40, 85, 89, 171, 178, 194, 208
Aeschylus 151, 154
'*Adonai*' 13
Agamemnon 123–4
aha-effect 234ff
Aigyptios 127–8
'Algy' 142, 153
'Alone' 215
ambiguity 123ff
Ambrose, St 143ff, 152
anagnosis 83–95
androgyny 26ff
annotation 31, 76–7, 93–5, 133–55, 197ff
Antiphos 127–8
Antisthenes 90, 170, 195
Antonio 173
'Araby' 38, 88
archemorph 60
Argos 162
Aristotle 83, 112, 137, 173, 199, 214
Arius 149
Arnold, L. 154
Ars Poetica 204ff

Athanasius 149
Athene, Pallas 116, 148, 192, 195, 196, 213
Atherton, James S. 34
Aubert, Jacques 223
Autolykos 10
'*Autontimoroumenos*' 21

'backward eye' 88
Balboni, Maria Pia (trans.) 223
Bannon, Alec 94
Barnacle, Nora (Joyce) 69
Beckson, Karl (and Arthur Ganz) 196
'belongs to' 166–7
Benstock, Bernard 34, 154
Benstock, Shari 34
Bérard, Victor 191
Berkeley, George 137
'Bildung', 'buildung' 67–8
'blind' 87
'Bloom' (name) 10, 36
Bloom, Leopold 13, 22–5, 42, 44, 52, 55, 66, 68, 70, 87, 92, 102, 116, 126, 131, 147, 176, 192, 195, 196, 201, 203, 206ff, 215
Bloom, Milly 94
Bloom, Marion 24, 38, 53, 69, 83, 84, 124, 161, 210–11

Blumenbach, Johann Friedrich 65ff
'Boarding House, The' 20, 116
Boehme, Jakob 137
Boisen, Mogens (trans.) 95
boots 159–60
Bosinelli, Rosa Maria 215
Boudin, A. 193
'*Bous Stephanoumenos*' 12, 21–2
Boylan, Hugh ('Blazes') 23, 71, 82–3, 88, 210
'bread' 160, 181–2
'Bride street' 142
Brown, Alan 146
Budgen, Frank 57, 60, 69, 73, 98, 109, 113
Bull, John 164
Butcher, S.H., and A. Lang (trans.) 110, 117, 123, 127, 196, 211
Butler, Samuel (trans.) 123, 202
Byron, Lord 183–6, 193–4, 196

Campbell, Foxy 141
Cancogni, Franca (trans.) 223
Capelle, Wilhelm 214
cat 162
Chamber Music 10, 120
Chandler, Malone ('Little') 5, 11, 186
Chaplin, Charlie 111
Chapman, George 120
characters 69ff
'Chrysostomos' 25
cinematographic presentation 97ff
'Circe' 23–4, 46–7, 84, 114, 158, 159, 164, 172, 180, 187, 189, 202, 206–7
Citizen 44, 52, 54
Clarke, Samuel 148, 154
cliché 180, 191, 195
Clifford, Martha 201
Cohen, Bella 207
Coleridge, S.T. 120
'*color*' 137
commas ('Eumaeus') 110
confession 29–33
'*contretemps*' 109
Corley, John 11, 92, 107, 180
'Counterparts' 38, 88
Cowper, William 154, 189, 192
Crete 192

'cunning' 149
'Cyclops' 13, 40, 43–4, 52, 68, 101, 116, 167
cycnus 172

Daedalus, Daidalos 21, 36, 54, 62, 113, 149
Daiches, David 154
Dante 55, 112, 137, 229
'Dante' (name) 12
Davidson (trans.) 215
Davitt, Michael 12, 93
de Almeida, Hermione 186, 196
de Angelis, Giulio (trans.) 109, 218
'Dead, The' 37, 55, 70
Deadman 190–1
deceit 117ff, 211
Dedalus, Simon 91, 139, 173
Dedalus, Stephen 21, 28, 52, 62, 67, 70–1, 73, 85–6, 99–100, 139–40, 157, 176, 194
deponents 18
devection, devective 52–4
Dignam, Mrs 172
Dignam, Patrick Aloysius 70
'dilapidate' 158, 165
Dillon, John 154
dissimulation 214, 215
dog 162
Don Juan 184–6
Doran, Bob 116
dream 29, 49
Dryden, John 215
Dubliners 11, 37, 38, 52, 112, 223
Dudman 190–1
Duffy, James 11

Earwicker, H.C. 14, 130
Ehrlich, Heyward 154
Eidothea 121–2, 148, 150
elegant variation 165, 178
Ellmann, Maud 131
Ellmann, Richard 34
Empson, William 203, 215
entelechy 62, 70, 165
epiphany 18, 101, 125, 127
errors 224
etymology 136, 165

Euclid 155
'Eumaeus' 17, 53, 64, 105–9, 176–196, 203, 207, 210
Eumaios 162, 163, 186, 192
Eusebius 215
'Eveline' 22, 38
exaggeration 40–56, 90, 101
excess, *see* provection
Exiles 56, 110
expectation 77
'eye' 136, 162

'face' 166
Farrington 11
Ferguson, Miss 188
Fiacre, St 142
fiction 13, 75, 130
Fiedler, Leslie 170, 175
'figure' 164
'filthy lucre' 191–2
Finnegans Wake 48ff, 63, 67, 95, 111–2, 119, 143, 169, 174, 208, 210, 212, 220–3, 227–38
Fitzgerald, Robert (trans.) 123, 128, 130
footsteps 161
'*Frauenzimmer*' 135, 142
Freud, Sigmund 222

Gabler, Hans Walter 18, 34, 109, 195
Gallaher, Ignatius 11
Garnett, Edward 37, 57
Genesis 27ff
'genuine' 193, 196
ghost meanings 174, 224
Gibraltar 161
Gifford, Don (and Robert J. Seidman) 94, 95, 138, 154, 196
Gilbert, J.T. 196
Gilbert, Stuart 53, 57, 96, 110, 191, 196
'girdle' 76
'gish' 230–2
Goff, master 138ff
Gold Cup 152, 157, 158
Goldberg, S.L. 36–7, 56–7
Goulding, Richard 90–1, 138ff
Goyert, Georg (trans.) 110, 154, 218–23
'*gnomon*' 8, 151
'Grace' 88–9

Griffith, Arthur 116
Groden, Michael 47, 57
Gumley 158–9

'Hades' 91
hallucination 180, 195
Halper, Nathan 230, 237
hamothen 119–21
hand 166
'handkerchief' 99–101
Hart, Clive 234
hat 158–9
headlines ('Aeolus') 89, 169
heart 161
Helen (of Troy) 90, 117–8, 142, 170–1
Herakleitos 198–200
Herlt, Georgia 234, 237
Hermes 116
Herring, Phillip F. 65, 73, 92–3, 96
Holmes, Sherlock 159
Holohan, Hoppy 11
Homer 24, 59, 111–132, 161, 173, 192–3, 204, 206, 213–4
Horace 23, 95, 150, 204–8
horse 107, 121, 156–8
Huston, John 70
Hyde, Douglas 86
hypertrophy 40
'hypolectic' 227ff

'I' 13
iceberg 182
identity; identification 160, 165, 173, 177, 191
idioplasm 62
Iliad 120ff, 163, 202–3, 212
'ineluctable' 135ff
inquit formulas 178
interior monologue 24
'Ithaca' 45, 53, 80, 83
Ithaka (island) 161, 170, 171
'Ivy Day in the Committee Room' 97–8

Jonson, Ben 103, 110
'Joyce' 7
'Joycean' 9
Jung, Carl Gustav 78
'Jungfraud's Messongebook' 48

Kalypso (Calypso) 114, 117, 121, 131, 147, 208–9
Kenner, Hugh 137
Kernan, Thomas 91
'Kino' 198
Kirke 48, 114, 117, 118, 130
'kudos' 193

Lang, Andrew, Walter Leaf and Ernest Myers (trans.) 215
Latin 77ff, 142ff, 189, 197ff
Lavergne, Philippe (trans.) 221
Lenehan 11, 92
'Lestrygonians' 71, 174
Liddell and Scott 214
Lily 11
Linati, Carlo 63, 73
literal and figurative use 156ff, 223
'literally' 159
'A Little Cloud' 88, 186
Litz, A. Walton 196
Longfellow, H.W. 184
'Lotuseaters' 199
Luther, Martin (trans.) 221
Lycidas 193

M'Coy, C.P. 13
M'Intosh 13, 188
MacDowell, Gerty 23, 25–6, 81–2, 84, 213–4
MacHugh, professor 171
Maddox, Brenda 73
Madeline the mare 231
Maecena 189
Malaprop, Mrs; malapropism 159, 187–8
Maria 11
Marivaux, Pierre 57
Martha (opera) 221–2
masturbation 25, 28
McHugh, Roland 230–1, 233, 237
medium, see Middle Voice
memory 78, 87, 169, 173
Menelaos 116–8, 122, 143, 148, 154
Menton, John Henry 159
Metamorphoses 44, 58, 171, 172, 205–6, 210
metaphor 157ff
'metempsychosis' 78, 90

Midas, King 204–5
Middle Voice (medium) 18–31ff, 39
Miklós, Szentkuthy (trans.) 219
Minotauros 54
mistakes 222
modernism 111, 222
Moore, Thomas 221
Morel, Auguste (trans.) 109, 154, 202, 218ff
Morris, William 215
'A Mother' 38, 88
'mouth' 160
Mulligan, Buck 23, 26, 30, 41ff, 47, 75ff, 95, 98ff, 117, 141, 147, 160, 178, 182, 186, 195, 196
Murphy 161, 184
Murray (trans.) 117, 131

'nacheinander' 98
names 8, 89, 124, 138, 141, 174, 209
'Nausicaa' 25–6, 44, 52, 61, 81, 114, 208, 213
Nausikaa (Odyssey) 124
'Nestor' 53, 158
'nisus formativus' 64–73
nomen 8
notebooks 59ff
notes, see annotation
Noon, Father William, SJ 144
Norris, Margot 231
noun 7, 8, 14ff

Ó Hehir, Brendan 154
Odysseus 10, 16, 36, 54, 59, 92, 109, 114ff, 147, 160, 162, 173, 177, 192–3, 195, 206ff
Odyssey 54–5, 58, 114–132, 146–50, 171, 185, 193, 207–9, 211
O'Keeffe, John 188
'oinopa ponton' 142
'omphalos' 142
'orthodox' 179–82
O'Shea, Kitty 8, 190
Outis 129
'Overture' ('Sirens') 84
Ovid 44, 74, 112, 150, 172, 204ff
'Oxen of the Sun' 30, 62, 64ff, 191, 207

'Painful Case, A' 38, 88, 97
Palmer (trans.) 120
'palpably' 165
Papi, Marco (trans.) 223
'Parable of the Plums' 89
'*paraesthesis*' 104ff
parallax 116ff, 169
'paralysis' 11, 52
Paris 142–3
Parker, Dorothy 216
Parnell, Charles Stewart 93, 159, 164, 165
Partridge, Eric 159
passive authorization 16
Passive Voice 18
'pen something' 167ff
Pendennis 168–9
'Penelope' 51, 80, 196, 211
Penelope (wife of Odysseus) 90, 116–7, 123–6, 170, 192, 206, 212
Penrose 168–9
perception 98ff
Plato 199
Plevna, battle of 92–3
pluperfect 104, 105
'point' 156, 163, 166, 177
Polyphemos, Polyphemus (Kyklops) 44, 119, 128–9
'*polytropos*' 200–2
Pope, Alexander 120, 128, 154, 186–7, 203, 213–14, 215
Porter 14
Portrait of the Artist As a Young Man, A 11, 35, 61ff, 93
Poseidon 116–7
'post-quoting' 229ff
Pound, Ezra 46
'pre-quoting' 229ff
'*prix de Paris*' 142ff
'Proteus' 85–6, 96, 123, 133–55
Proteus (god of the sea) 118, 121–3, 135, 150
provection 35–58, 169
'ptarmigan' 217ff
Pugliatti, Paola 215
'pyth' 230–2

'quandary' 166

Quintilian 57
quotation 30–1, 219ff

reading, reader 33, 56, 72, 75–96, 122, 127, 129, 133, 151–2, 165, 199, 206–7, 227
recognition 83ff, 151–2, 173, 177, 234
reflexive 18, 20, 24
repetition 53, 156
retroactive semantification 127
'retrospective arrangement' 91
Reynaud, Paul (trans.) 223
'rheumatic wheels' 223–4
rhythm 61ff
Rieu, E.V. (trans.) 128
Riordan, Mrs 206
Riquelme, John Paul 154, 215
'riverrun' 24, 32, 199
rocks 161
roles 165, 182
'Romeville' 142
Roscher, Wilhelm Heinrich 208, 215
Rossetti, Dante Gabriel 189
Rouse, W.H.D. (trans.) 122
Rudd, Niall (trans.) 215
'rum' 142

'salt' 160–1
scar (Odysseus) 124ff
schema (*Ulysses*) 60
Scott, Sir Walter 188
'Scylla and Charybdis' (the Library chapter) 71, 177–8, 183, 191
'sea' 161
self-reflexiveness 18, 119
Seneca 189
sequence 97ff, 120
Shakespeare 19, 23, 41, 71, 90, 138, 172, 174, 181, 182–3, 186, 210
'shape' 165
Shaun 14
Shaw, T.E. (trans.) 128–9
Shem 14, 205
Sheridan, Richard Brinsley 187
shoes 160
Sirens (*Odyssey*) 118, 207
'Sirens' 44, 46, 84, 105
'Sisters, The' 29, 88, 224

Skeat, Walter W. 8, 34, 73, 185, 195
Skoumal, Aloys (trans.) 219
Skylla 191
'snotgreen' 100–1
'soul' 173
'Spanish onions' 190
St Austell, Ivan 191
St Just, Hilton 191
St Paul 144ff, 191–2, 200–2
Stanford, D.B. 195
Stephen Hero 37
'Stephen Dedalus' (name) 11, 12, 14
Steppe, Wolfhard 195
Strick, Joseph 70, 74
Subirat, Salas (trans.) 219ff
subject 167
'substance' 228
Swift, Jonathan 140–1, 181
Swinburne, Algernon 136, 154
syntax 177

Tandy, Napper 138–40
Tandy, Shapland 138ff
Telemachos (*Odyssey*) 100, 116, 162
'Telemachus' 80
'tender Achilles' 1886, 196
Temple 141
Tertullian 212
'tether' 158
Thackeray 169
'*Thalatta! Thalatta!*' 30
Theory 1–5, 227, 234
Thersites 202–3
Thom's Dublin Directory 139, 195
Thornton, Weldon 73, 95, 154, 188, 196, 214
Throwaway 157

time 32, 77, 95, 109, 129, 134, 136, 153, 213
'tinily' 78
titles 88–90
translation 99–102, 106, 131, 141, 160, 210, 217–25
Troy, Mark 231
Tweedy, Brian 93, 96
'Two Gallants' 92

Ulixes, Odysseus 206ff
'Ulysses' 18, 30, 52, 89, 113
'Uncertainty principle' 152
'understand' 226ff
'ungirdled' 75–7
'untonsured' 76–7
'usurper' 34

Vandenbergh, John (trans.) 138
verbs 9, 14ff
villanelle 86
Vico, Giambattista 32
'vicus' 32
Virag 202
Virgil 39, 135–7, 150, 153, 211
'*voglio*' 17
Vreeswijk, Harry 154

'Wandering Rocks' 63, 78, 82–3, 105
Wilde, Oscar 104
Wollschläger, Hans (trans.) 100, 110, 220ff
word order 98ff

Zacchi, Romana 215
Zeus 117
Zimmer, Dieter E. (trans.) 223

PASSAGE INDEX

This list contains page and (except for *Dubliners*, *A Portrait* and *Stephen Hero*) line references of words or phrases that are commented on. Editions used and referred to:

Ulysses, Hans Walter Gabler (ed.) with Wolfhard Steppe and Claus Melchior (New York: Random House, Garland 1986). The edition with marginal line numbering is the most convenient one to use since there is a companion *Hand List, A Complete Alphabetical Index to the Critical Reading Text*, prepared by Wolfhard Steppe with Hans Walter Gabler (New York: Garland 1985).

At present (spring 1994) many editions of *Ulysses* are in circulation, with one more pending. Readers might consult *The 'Ulysses' Pagefinder*, compiled by Gunn and Alistair McCleery (Edinburgh: Split Pea Press 1988), to find the passages in most current editions.

All editions of *Finnegans Wake* (London: Faber & Faber 1939, or New York: Viking Press 1939 and following) have practically identical pagination.

Dubliners: Robert Scholes and A. Walton Litz (eds), The Viking Critical Library, New York, Viking Press, 1969.

A Portrait of the Artist As a Young Man, Chester G. Anderson (ed.), The Viking Critical Library (New York: Viking Press 1968).

Stephen Hero, John J. Slocum and Herbert Cahoon (eds) (New York: New Directions 1963).

ULYSSES	1.123 165	1.657 41	'Proteus'
	1.134 104	1.684 94	3.5–6 137
'Telemachus'	1.136 25	1.744 34	3.11 98
1.2 75	1.147 103		3.16 160
1.5 78	1.152 104	'Nestor'	3.18 142
1.13 22	1.153 196	2.49 149	3.30ff 142
1.21 196	1.213 42	2.48 207	3.33 141
1.70 34, 99, 147	1.276–7 79	2.51 59	3.36ff 142
1.73 100	1.366 93	2.238 80	3.51 41
1.78 42	1.446 160	2.257 141	3.52 149
1.80 30	1.508 77	2.301 158	3.56 170
1.100 22	1.555 42, 90	2.302 142	3.80 138–40

3.88 90
3.100 90
3.111 140
3.154 149
3.193 142
3.215 143
3.260 138
3.397–408 85
3.375ff 142
3.391 96
3.392 142
3.394 142
3.399 135, 152
3.440 145
3.462 145
3.464 147
3.466 143
3.469 145
3.483 142
3.486 145

'Calypso'
4.1 42
4.7 179
4.27 24
4.29 162
4.219 142
4.250 87
4.256 88
4.263 87
4.270 87
4.336 78, 90
4.343 161
4.365 136
4.472 30

'Lotuseaters'
5.370 160
5.534 83
5.541 127
5.352 142
5.563 199

'Hades'
6.30 94
6.52 91
6.56 139
6.146 91

6.202 71
6.333 94
6.361 160
6.764 212
6.771 211
6.779 211
6.792 211

'Aeolus'
7.34 170
7.61 170
7.177 63
7.485 40
7.522 85, 96, 155
7.630 170
7.811 119
7.843 145
7.910 136
7.922 27
7.930 27
7.985 160
7.1032 169
7.1034 89, 169
7.1038 90, 170
7.1053 137
7.1057 89
7.1070 89

'Lestrygonians'
8.8 33
8.11 212
8.51 102
8.62 103
8.88 198
8.93 198
8.95 135
8.176 168
8.196 142
8.373ff 146
8.415 221
8.544 71, 174
8.606 221
8.887 217
8.969 78
8.1112 168

'Scylla and
   Charybdis'
9.43 164
9.77 183
9.84 157
9.114 17, 20
9.160 172
9.205 165
9.212 13
9.350 163
9.462 71
9.493 26
9.519 72
9.597 178
9.615 195
9.763 72
9.794 17
9.1021 16, 22
9.1023 19
9.1041 20
9.1200 153

'Wandering Rocks'
10.125 78
10.302–36 71
10.322–3 82
10.470 139
10.486 88
10.557 83
10.783 91
10.791 91
10.1121 70
10.1205 82

'Sirens'
11.1–2 84
11.298 36
11.345–430 71
11.426 88
11.463 70
11.493 159
11.519 119
11.557 165
11.569 119
11.665 222
11.828 91
11.991 91
11.1027 167

11.1049 84
11.1056 167
11.1058 84
11.1061 84
11.1126 74
11.1148 91
11.1192 46
11.1252 158
11.1253 222

'Cyclops'
12.1 68
12.3 45
12.70 43
12.119 44
12.152 52
12.362 40
12.401 21
12.506 206
12.560 133
12.789 43
12.1193 213
12.1358 201
12.1434 101
12.1438 101
12.1467 167
12.1475 52
12.1550 87
12.1558 157
12.1574 92, 116
12.1649 77
12.1658 23
12.1901 44
12.1912 201
12.1915 13

'Nausicaa'
13.9 81
13.162 26
13.210 23
13.216 188
13.367 213
13.412 214
13.435 23
13.474–85 81
13.688 81
13.695 25
13.708–744 25

13.769 82
13.846 25
13.1122 26
13.1174 152
13.1258ff 209
13.1264 209

'Oxen of the Sun'
14.253 192, 196
14.994 54
14.1010–37 64
14.1097 157
14.1174–97 191
14.1236 65
14.1289 201

'Circe'
15.105 62
15.195 158
15.271 208
15.274 208
15.878 23
15.1347 47
15.1396 223
15.1777 48
15.1798 23, 48, 207
15.1824 24
15.1844 196
15.1953 48
15.2120 153
15.2460 202
15.2752 117
15.2777 207
15.2830 207
15.2843 208
15.3062 207
15.3820 187
15.3821ff 105
15.3837 172
15.4275 207

'Eumaeus'
16.1 179
16.3 179
16.4 180
16.7 181
16.9 127, 158
16.10 165

16.11 183
16.15 161
16.31 166
16.32 161
16.44 187
16.46 163
16.51 163
16.52 174
16.54 177
16.57 181
16.58 160
16.60 163
16.92 163
16.105 164
16.112 164
16.124 182
16.126 163
16.128 107, 164
16.155 161
16.195 163
16.204 160
16.214 159
16.215 162
16.218 156
16.220 158
16.223 189
16.230 162
16.247 183
16.269 162
16.274 162
16.279 186
16.281 160
16.282 160
16.293 177
16.337 165
16.362 174, 186
16.365ff 178
16.366 160
16.367 162
16.375 162
16.378 173
16.380 161
16.422 185
16.430 161, 184
16.461 182
16.462 184
16.468 160
16.479 165

16.492 159
16.502 161
16.507 161
16.539 161
16.562 194
16.570 165
16.607 156
16.614 163
16.622 161
16.630 161
16.632 193
16.634 184
16.639 161
16.653 165
16.665 164
16.675 164
16.686 163
16.704 158, 161
16.705 165
16.756 173
16.765 163, 173
16.770 157
16.774 163
16.777 163
16.783 174, 182,
   193
16.790 159
16.807 164
16.811 182
16.812 43
16.817 156
16.819 162, 177
16.823 159
16.824 195
16.827 194
16.831 159
16.840 172
16.845 184
16.858 165
16.877 163
16.901 182
16.906 161
16.922ff 105
16.930 165
16.939 106
16.940 157
16.952 158
16.955 177

16.988 161
16.1002 163
16.1006 188
16.1011 165
16.1012 165
16.1024 161
16.1034 162
16.1036 162
16.1040 163
16.1058 183
16.1068 163
16.1079 210
16.1081 59, 147
16.1088 187
16.1091 189
16.1100 165
16.1101 161
16.1109 160
16.1126 179
16.1138 189
16.1143 157, 195
16.1153 193
16.1157 172
16.1164 166
16.1172 166
16.1179 167
16.1192 157
16.1213 166
16.1223 161
16.1229 173, 178
16.1238 174
16.1243 157
16.1268 201
16.1269 160
16.1278 158
16.1293 189
16.1302 163
16.1326 164
16.1331 210
16.1335 163
16.1339 162, 186
16.1387 37
16.1414 190
16.1428 188
16.1444 161
16.1445 164
16.1457 161
16.1474 164

16.1486 162
16.1505 164, 165
16.1519 193
16.1520 165
16.1524 159
16.1550 188
16.1556 188
16.1564 179
16.1579 162, 184
16.1597 156
16.1603 196
16.1640 163, 188
16.1653 194
16.1667 175, 183
16.1716 163, 188
16.1739 159
16.1754 191
16.1769 164
16.1774 164
16.1783 157
16.1790 162
16.1796 162
16.1800 203
16.1832ff 192
16.1841 191
16.1844 192
16.1851 191
16.1854 164
16.1874 158
16.1877ff 108
16.1883 43
16.1886 164

'Ithaca'
17.24 180
17.160ff 125
17.306 83
17.479 206
17.487 206
17.1251 201

17.1350 25
17.1419 96
17.1672 206
17.1817 131
17.1864 91
17.1933 206
17.1974 45
17.2019 45
17.2133 168
17.2217 23
17.2241 45

'Penelope'
18.51 188
18.143 124
18.178 183
18.185 196
18.209 196
18.354 211
18.542 124
18.478 8
18.572 168
18.695 96
18.843 10
18.1114 84
18.1236 210
18.1308 74
18.1325 196
18.1347 215
18.1579 215

FINNEGANS
WAKE
3.1–10 29, 32,
    50–1, 228–9
7.13 230
13.17–8 236
13.28 169
16.24 122

18.5 212
29.14 28
31.2 130
48.1ff 232
55.3 212
55.7 212
57.2 202
59.31 174
79.2 28
80.33 231
104.1 24
104.13 235
122.36 48
156.8 28
158.6 204
183.22 174
187.2 19
196.22 130
215.17 71
223.28 154
228.31 202
261.F3 29
261.5 28
263.19 210
269.29 19
270.17 18
272.4 49
275.5 195
298.14 48
301.11 169
304.L3 28
318.21 174
353.25 29
375.17 154
398.8 205
421.17 202
423.18 205
455.17 234
460.20 48
513.21 199

523.10 14
523.7 19
531.2 29
552.8 202
580.12 201
594.1 57
597.8 49
597.21 54
613.33 28
619.30 55

DUBLINERS
14 223
40 232
114 97
118 98
149.10 38

A PORTRAIT
7.1ff 35
70 194
78 29
81 194
82 29
143 29
169 38, 54, 67
176 181
206 61
212 62
214 74
215 21
221 182

STEPHEN HERO
211 181
213 125

FRITZ SENN'S WRITINGS
SINCE 1985

This bibliography is an updating of the comprehensive listing of Fritz Senn's writings in Fritz Senn, *Joyce's Dislocutions: Essays on Reading as Translation*, John Paul Riquelme (ed.) (Baltimore and London: Johns Hopkins University Press 1984).

[1985]

'"Stately, plump", for example: Allusive Overlays and Widening Circles of Irrelevance', *James Joyce Quarterly*, 22, 4 (Summer 1985), 347–54.

'Book of Many Turns', *Critical Essays on James Joyce*, Bernard Benstock (ed.) (Boston, Mass.: G.K. Hall & Co. 1985).

James Joyce, Aubert, Jacques; Senn, Fritz (eds) (Paris: Editions de l'Herne 1985).

Joyces Dubliner, Klaus Reichert, Fritz Senn and Dieter E. Zimmer (eds) (Frankfurt a. M.: Suhrkamp 1985).

[1986]

'The Narrative Dissimulation of Time' and 'Mean Cosy Turns', *Myriadminded Man: Jottings on Joyce*, Rosa Maria Bosinelli, Paola Pugliatti and Romana Zacchi (eds) (Bologna: Cooperativa Libraria Universitaria Editrice 1986), 147–65, 263–7.

'"The Boarding House" Seen as a Tale of Misdirection', *James Joyce Quarterly*, 23, 4 (Summer 1986), 405–13.

'Parachronic Wakeing', *A* Finnegans Wake *Circular*, 1, 4 (Summer 1986), 69–78.

'*Ulysses* between Corruption and Correction', *Assessing the 1984* Ulysses, C.G. Sandulescu and Clive Hart (eds) (Gerrards Cross: Colin Smythe 1986), 188–206.

'"All the errears and erroriboose": Joyce's Misconducting Universe', *International Perspectives on James Joyce*, G. Gaiser (ed.) (Troy, New York: The Whitston Publishing Company 1986), 161–70.

'Piling Big Tedium on Little Sources', review of Eckley, *Children's Lore in* Finnegans Wake, *Irish Literary Supplement*, 5, 1 (Spring 1986), 29.

'Tasting the *Pléiade*', rev. of Aubert (ed.), James Joyce, *Œuvres I*, *James Joyce Broadsheet*, 18 (October 1985), 1.

[1987]

[Letter to the Editor] ('Poststructuralist Joyce'), *James Joyce Quarterly*, 24, 1 (Fall 1986), 115–6.

'Miswriting of our Tongue', *A Finnegans Wake Circular*, 2, 1 (Autumn 1986), 19–20.

'Literarische Übertragungen—empirisches Bedenken', *Übersetzungswissenschaft— eine Neuorientierung: Zur Integrierung von Theorie und Praxis*, Mary Snell-Hornby (ed.) (Tübingen: Francke Verlag 1986), 54–84.

'Carey Was His Name', *James Joyce Quarterly*, 24, 2 (Winter 1987), 214–6.

'Collisions', *A* Finnegans Wake *Circular*, 2, 2 (Winter 1986), 32

'*Ulysses*: Book of Dislocution', *Il Confronto Letterario*, IV, 7 (May 1987), 66–92.

'Naming in *Dubliners* (a first methermeneutic fumbling)', *James Joyce Quarterly*, 24, 4 (Summer 1987), 465–8.

[Letter to the Editor] (on Skeat), *James Joyce Quarterly*, 24, 4 (Summer 1987), 495.

'Eumaean Titibits: As Someone Somewhere Sings', *Lingua e Stile*, XXII, 3 (September 1987), 397–417.

'Joyce und Huston—Die Innenwelt und ihre Illustration', *Tages-Anzeiger*, 21 (October 1987), 11.

'Backprocessing', *A* Finnegans Wake *Circular*, 2, 3 (Spring 1987), 46–8.

'In Classical Idiom: *Anthologia intertextualis*', *James Joyce Quarterly*, 25, 1 (Fall 1987), 31–48.

[1988]

'*A Portrait*: Temporal Foreplay', *Etudes Irlandaises*, 12 (December 1987), 65–73.

'Distancing in "A Painful Case"', *James Joyce 1: 'Scribble' 1: genèse des textes*, Claude Jacquet (ed.) (Paris: Minard 1988), 25–38.

'Vorwort', *Joyce in Zürich*, Thomas Faerber and Markus Luchsinger (eds) (Zürich: Unionsverlag 1988), 7–9.

'Anagnostic Probes', *Dutch Quarterly Review*, 18 (1988/2), 117–43.

'The New Edition of *Ulysses*: An Assessment of Its Usefulness One Year Later', *New Alliances in Joyce Studies*, Bonnie Kime Scott (ed.) (Newark: University of Delaware Press 1988), 226–9 (summary).

'Joyce in Triest', *Neue Zürcher Zeitung*, 229 (1–2 October 1988), 72.

'*Ulysses* auf dem Prüfstand', *Tageszeitung* (Berlin) (1 October 1988), 17–20.

'Charles Peake: An Appreciation', *James Joyce Literary Supplement*, 2, 1 (June 1988), 11–12.

[1989]

'James Joyce mit seinem Anspruch'; Jürgen Schneider and Ralf Sotschek (eds), *Irland: Eine Bibliographie selbständiger deutschsprachiger Publikationen; 16. Jahrhundert bis 1989* (Darmstadt: Verlag der Georg Büchner Buchhandlung 1988), 71–6.

'Dublin, Zürich, James Joyce', 'Catalogue: Pat Liddy: Irish Perceptions of Dublin and Zürich' (Zürich 1989), 13–17, 41–5.

'Unbeholfen sagt's der Schweizer', *Weltwoche*, 3 (19 January 1989), 73.

'James Joyce, Briefsteller', *Kultur-Magazin* (February–March 1989), 22–5.

'James Joyce und Tzvetan Todorov, oder: Es ist immer auch anders', *Lettre Internationale*, Vol. 4/89A, 95.

'Joyce the Verb', Morris Beja and Shari Benstock (eds), *Coping with Joyce: Essays from the Copenhagen Symposium* (Columbus: Ohio State University Press 1989), 25–54.

'A rump and dozen', *Notes on Modern Irish Literature*, 1 (1989), 4–6.

'"There's a Medium in All Things": Joycean Readings', Susan Dick, Declan Kiberd, Dougald McMillan and Joseph Ronsley (eds), *Omnium Gatherum: Essays for Richard Ellmann* (Gerrards Cross: Colin Smythe 1989), 333–50, 466–8.

'Protean Inglossabilities: "To No End Gathered"', Christine van Boheemen (ed.), *Joyce, Modernity, and its Mediation*, European Joyce Studies, 1 (Amsterdam: Rodopi 1989), 151–76.

'Beyond the Lexicographer's Reach: Literary Overdetermination', Mary Snell-Hornby (ed.), *Translation and Lexicography: Papers read at the EURALEX Colloquium held at Innsbruck 2–5 July 1987*, A Paintbrush Monograph, XVI (August 1989), 79–87.

'Hankering, Insatiable and Indubitable—Editorial Procedures—The Notational Apparatus—Margins of Error', *'Ulysses*: The Text—The Debates of the Miami Joyce Conference', *James Joyce Literary Supplement*, 3 (Fall 1989), 10–11, 19.

'Cold Comfort', *James Joyce Quarterly*, 27, 1 (Fall 1989), 126–9.

'Bucolic Strands in "Aeolus"', *Ibid.*, 129–32.

'*Habent sua fata*', *Ibid.*, 132–4.

'Micro-Cycloptics', *Ibid.*, 134–6.

[REPRINTED]

'Nausicaa', Bernard Benstock (ed.), *Critical Essays on James Joyce's* Ulysses (Boston: G.K. Hall 1989), 186–214 (reprint from Hart and Hayman [eds]: *James Joyce's* Ulysses [1974]).

'Anagnostic Probes', Christine van Boheemen (ed.), *Joyce, Modernity, and its Mediation*, European Joyce Studies, 1 (Amsterdam: Rodopi 1989), 37–61 (reprint from *DQR* [1988]).

'Righting *Ulysses*', Harold Bloom (ed.), *Modern Critical Interpretations: James Joyce's* Ulysses (New York: Chelsea House Publishers 1987), 99–121 (reprint from James Joyce: *New Perspectives*, Colin MacCabe [ed.] [London: Harvester Press 1982]).

[EDITION]

James Joyce, *Finnegans Wake Deutsch*, Klaus Reichert and Fritz Senn (eds) (Frankfurt: Suhrkamp Verlag 1989), 340.

[1990]

'Sequential Close-Ups in Joyce's *Ulysses*', Reingold M. Nischik and Barbara Korte (eds), *Modes of Narrative: Approaches to American, Canadian and British Fiction; Presented to Helmut Bonheim* (Würzburg: Königshausen & Neumann 1990), 252–64.

'A Cerebration of the Fiftyfication of the Publication of *Finnegans Wake* at Berkeley', *James Joyce Quarterly*, 27, 2 (Winter 1990), 407–9.

'Denkmal des unbekannten Lektors', *Der Übersetzer*, 24, 1–2 (Jan.–Feb. 1990), 8.

'Intellectual Nodality of the Lisible: "*genus omne*"', Claude Jacquet and André Topia (eds), *James Joyce 2: 'Scribble' 2: Joyce et Flaubert* (Paris: Minard 1990), 173–88.

'In Quest of a *nisus formativus Joyceanus*', *Joyce Studies Annual*, Thomas F. Staley (ed.) (Austin: University of Texas Press 1990), 27–42.

'Inherent Delicacy: Eumaean Questions', *Studies in the Novel, A Special Issue on Editing* Ulysses, XXII, 2 (Summer 1990), 179–86.

'Critical Sensitivity: Or, Minding the Stones', *Ibid.*, 189–91.

'Ovidian Roots of Gigantism in Joyce's *Ulysses*', *Journal of Modern Literature*, XV, 4 (Spring 1990), 561–77.

'Vexations of Group Reading: "transluding from the otherman"', *European Joyce Studies*, 2 (Rodopi: Amsterdam 1990), 61–78.

[REVIEWS]

'Ulysses *Annotated: Notes for James Joyce's* Ulysses', Don Gifford with Robert J. Seidmann, *James Joyce Quarterly*, 27, 3 (Spring 1990), 653–62 (reprinted in *James Joyce Literary Supplement*, 4, 2 [Fall 1990], 5–6).

'Die kecke Frau des grossen Mannes', Brenda Maddox, *Nora: Das Leben der Nora Joyce*, *Sonntags-Zeitung* (Zürich: 16 September 1990), 43.

[1991]

'Gestaltung, Umgestaltung: zum 50. Todestag von James Joyce', *Neue Zürcher Zeitung* (12–13 January 1991).

'Disjected Comments on Transformative Circe', *De Joyce à Stoppard: Ecritures de la modernité*, Adolphe Haberer (ed.) (Lyon: Presses Universitaires de Lyon 1991), 133–45.

'*Ulysses* in neuer Färbung' (foreword), Hannes Vogel, *Die Farben im* Ulysses: *gespiegelt im Zufall* (Helmhaus Zürich 1991), 7–9.

'Rereading *The Books at the Wake*', Janet Egleson Dunleavy (ed.), *Re-Viewing the Classics of Joyce Criticism* (Urbana: University of Illinois Press 1991), 82–9.

'James Joyce: 50 Jahre nachher', 'Programm Junifestwochen Zürich, James Joyce John Cage' (June 1991), 7.

'Vom filmischen Joyce zum verfilmten: Zu einem Programm des Filmpodiums der Stadt Zürich', *Neue Zürcher Zeitung* (21 June 1991), 65.

'Joycean Provections', *Joycean Occasions: Essays from the Milwaukee James Joyce Conference*, Janet E. Dunleavy, Melvin J. Friedman and Michael Patrick Gillespie (eds) (Newark: University of Delaware Press 1991), 171–94.

'Satisfaction?' (Scholarly failure with *FW*), *The Abiko Quarterly Literary Rag*, 2, 4 (Winter 1990–1), 35–44.

'History As Text in Reverse', *James Joyce Quarterly*, 28, 4 (Summer 1991), 765–75.

[1992]

'James Joyce', Hades (ed.), *Einleitung, Anmerkungen, Erklärungen, excerpta classica*, IX (Mainz: Dieterich'sche Verlagsbuchhandlung 1992), 304.

'May I Trespass On Your Valuable Space?: Bruce Arnold, *The Scandal of Ulysses*, A Postscript', *James Joyce Literary Supplement*, 5, 2 (Fall 1991), 5.

'AnaCalypso', Daniel Ferrer, Claude Jacquet and André Topia (eds), Ulysses *à l'article: Joyce aux marges du roman* (Tusson, Charente: Du Lérot 1992), 83–108.

'Leituras de Estrangeiro', Arthur Nestrovski (ed.), '*riverrun': Ensaios sobre James Joyce*, Biblioteca Pierre Menaud (Rio de Janeiro: Imago Editore 1992), 239–63 (translation of 'Foreign Readings' [1982]).

'Wie finde ich meine Sprache', *Der Rabe: Magazin für jede Art von Literatur*, 32 (1992), 14–20 (reprint of 1988).

'On Not Finding Places', *James Joyce Quarterly*, 29, 2 (Winter 1992), 397–401.

'Ovid's Not-yet-icity', *Ibid.*, 401–3.

'Joyce i Trieste', *Joyce i Trieste*, Johannes Hedberg (ed.) (Lund: The James Joyce Society of Sweden and Finland 1992), 12–22 (Swedish translation of 'Joyce in Triest' 1988).

'Entering the lists: sampling early catalogues', Vincent J. Cheng and Timothy Martin (eds), *Joyce in Context* (Cambridge: University of Cambridge Press 1992), 241–58.

'"In the original": Buck Mulligan and Stephen Dedalus', *Arion, A Journal of Humanities and the Classics*, Third series, 2.1 (Winter 1992), 215–17.

'Linguistic Dissatisfaction in the *Wake*', R.M. Bollettieri Bosinelli, C. Marengo Vaglio and C. van Boheemen (eds), *The Languages of Joyce: Selected Papers from the 11th International James Joyce Symposium, Venice, 12–18 June 1988* (Philadelphia: John Benjamins Publishing Company 1992), 211–22.

[REPRINTED]

James Joyce, *Briefe an Nora*, Fritz Senn (ed.) (Frankfurt: Suhrkamp 1992), 172 (reprint of 1971 edition [suhrkamp taschenbuch 1931]).

'A Reading Exercise in *Finnegans Wake*', Patrick McCarthy (ed.), *Critical Essays on Finnegans Wake* (New York: G.K. Hall 1992), 48–58.

[1993]

(On the new Penguin *Ulysses*), 'Litters From Aloft', *James Joyce Literary Supplement*, 6, 2 (Fall 1992), 38, and *James Joyce Quarterly*, 30, 1 (Fall 1992), 146–9.

'Scrivendo il libro di se stesso', *Il Segno dell'Io: Romanza e Autobiographia nella Tradizione Moderna*, Elena Agazzi and Angelo Canavesi (eds) (Udine: Campanotto Editore 1992), 109–22 (translation by Canavesi of 'Writing the Book of Himself').

'Perspectives on the Symposium', *James Joyce Quarterly*, 30, 1 (Fall 1992), 15–17.

'Met Whom What?', *Ibid.*, 109–13.

'Transmedial Stereotypes in the 'Aeolus' Chapter of Joyce's *Ulysses*', *Word & Image Interactions: A Selection of Papers Given at the Second International Conference on Word and Image*, Martin Heusser (ed.) (Basel, Wiese Verlag 1993), 61–8.

'Wehg' zu Finnegan? Dieter Stündels Übertragung von "Finnegans Wake"', *Neue Zürcher Zeitung*, 157 (10–11 July 1993), 59–60.

[REPRINTED]

'Joyce's Misconducting Universe', Mary T. Reynolds (ed.), *James Joyce: A Collection of Critical Essays, New Century View* (Englewood Cliffs: Prentice Hall 1993), 48–55.

'From "The Boarding House" Seen as a Tale of Misdirection', Michael Meyer (ed.), *The Bedford Introduction to Literature* (Boston: St Martin's Press 1993), 359.